NEW ZEALAND TRAG[E]

Shipwrecks

& Ma[ritime] Disasters

A wave breaks over the bow of the *Pacific Charger* while salvage operations get underway at Baring Head, just a few kilometres from the entrance to Wellington Harbour – May 1981. *Evening Post*

NEW ZEALAND TRAGEDIES
Shipwrecks
& Maritime Disasters

Gavin McLean

for Captain John

Grantham House
New Zealand

By the same author

Spinning Yarns (1981)
Oamaru Harbour: Port in a Storm
(1982)
Otago Harbour: Currents of
Controversy (1985)
Moeraki: 150 Years of Net and
Ploughshare (1986)
Canterbury Coasters (1987)
Richardsons of Napier (1989)
Sam's Grief (1989)
Spirits (with David Hindley)
(1990)
Masters or Servants? (1990)
Ships of the Union Company
(1990)
Ships of the New Zealand Shipping
Company (1990)
New Zealand Coastal Passenger
Ships (1990)
The Southern Octopus (1990)
Local History: a Guide to
Researching and Writing Local
History (1991)

First Published 1991

GRANTHAM HOUSE
PUBLISHING
P.O. Box 17-256
Wellington 5
New Zealand

ISBN 1 86934 029 9

Edited by Anna Rogers
Typeset by Wordset Enterprises
Limited, Wellington
Designed by Bookprint Consultants
Limited, Wellington
Printed in Hong Kong through
Bookprint Consultants Limited,
Wellington

Acknowledgements

Writing this book has been pure pleasure, largely because of the help and support that I received from a variety of sources. First and foremost was the staff of the Wellington Maritime Museum and Gallery. Colin Watson, Ken Scadden and Emanuel Makarios all gave freely of their time and advice, were charming hosts and gave me complete access to the museum's superb photograph collection.

Equally unstinting were the staff of the photographic and newspaper rooms of the National Library. I would also like to thank the pleasant and helpful staff of National Archives, a 'user-friendly' institution if ever there was one.

Other photographs are acknowledged as they appear; thanks to the Hocken Library and Grant Ogle and the photographic staff of the newspapers credited.

Ken Scadden and Bob McDougall both generously read through the manuscript at an early stage. I thank them for their helpful comments, although it goes without saying that the responsibility for any errors rests entirely with me.

Finally, I would like to thank editor Anna Rogers and publisher Graham Stewart for the pleasant, professional way in which they steered this book through the many shoals of the pre-publication stages.

The *Wahine* capsizes in truly appalling conditions, rope ladders trailing down her sides – 10 April 1968 – *Evening Post*, courtesy of Wellington Maritime Museum and Gallery

TERMINOLOGY

Units of distance, weight and currency are usually given in the form in which they arise in the sources. This is to minimise editorial intrusion and because expressing pre-decimal sums in dollars (New Zealand adopted the decimal system in 1967) may give misleading impressions of comparability to modern levels of purchasing power. One 1967 pound was equal to two 1967 dollars.

Exceptions are measurements of length and tonnage. Ship dimensions have been metricated (1 foot = .3038 metre), as have land distances (1 mile = 1.6 kilometres). Since, however, distances at sea are still measured in nautical miles (1 nautical mile = 1.852 kilometres), they are expressed so in this book.

I have also followed current practice with tonnage. The weight of cargo has been metricated but the tonnage figures of ships remains unchanged. Ship tonnages are calculated in several ways. Merchant ships (bulk carriers and tankers excepted) are usually measured in terms of gross registered tonnage (GRT). A measurement of volume, not weight (100 feet = 1 ton gross), it measures a ship's enclosed space. Sailing craft are usually measured in terms of net tonnage, calculated in the same way as gross tonnage, but measuring just the cargo space. Naval vessels and small craft are usually measured by displacement tonnage, that is, the weight of water displaced by the vessel. Perverse things, tonnage figures can change with every major refit, especially where passenger ships are concerned. In this book, tonnage figures usually refer to the ship at the time of her accident.

Seafaring was until very recently almost exclusively a male preserve. Gender-specific language has been retained in earlier chapters but eliminated later in the book.

Title page photographs
Upper: The image that television flashed around the world; the *Rainbow Warrior* listing against Marsden Wharf, the banner above her wheelhouse still defiantly demanding a nuclear-free Pacific – 10 July 1985 – *N.Z. Herald*

Lower: Got it! As the *Rona* shows, navigation aids can sometimes be a hazard. The Colonial Sugar Refining Company Ltd's big ship, a regular trader between Auckland, Fiji and Queensland, hit Flat Rock light in the Hauraki Gulf on 26 June 1922. Although damaged, she was refloated and returned to service – *New Zealand Herald*, courtesy of Hooker Bowden

CONTENTS

The little *Wakatu* was bound from Wellington to Kaikoura in thick fog early on the morning of 6 September 1925 when an unusually strong current threw the lightly laden steamer onto the beach at Waipapa Point, Marlborough. The wind and tide carried her far up the shingle beach where she stuck fast, being abandoned later that month. An iron screw steamer of 157 tons, the *Wakatu* had been built at Nelson in 1879.

PREFACE

Shipwrecks are exciting. Even those of us who cannot tell bollards from bollocks find a grim fascination in reading about sudden calamity, great stupidity or the malicious hand of fate. A 'good' wreck can be relied upon to have everything: cruel fate, human drama, bravery (or, even better, abject cowardice), courtroom excitement and legal intrigue aplenty. Not surprisingly, perhaps, younger visitors to the Wellington Maritime Museum and Gallery's well-stocked halls always say that models of the sinking of the *Titanic* or the *Wahine* are the highlights.

Certainly, as a nation of readers we have lapped up shipwreck books. Scarcely a year goes by without at least one hitting the shops. Ever since December 1936, one book in particular, *New Zealand Shipwrecks*, has kept booksellers' cash registers ringing. That year C. W. N. Ingram and P. O. Wheatley brought out *Shipwrecks, New Zealand Disasters 1795–1936*, a monumental work which for the first time listed every known shipwreck. Revised and enlarged editions followed in 1950, 1961, 1972, 1977 and 1984, the later ones under the abbreviated title *New Zealand Shipwrecks* and bearing just the name of Ingram. That rare beast, a truly readable reference work, it has enthralled and informed several generations of New Zealanders. The book has outlived both authors and original publishers and bounced back to life in 1990 under the auspices of a new publisher, Beckett Books Ltd, listing the 2300 ships that have left their bones on our shores since the end of the eighteenth century.

This book makes no attempt to retrace the steps of Ingram or Wheatley. A 65,000-word book trying to cover 2300 wrecks would have to gallop through them at the dizzying rate of one every 28 words or so. Instead, I have tried to give the layperson an overview of some of the more interesting or calamitous wrecks and have attempted to set the individual incidents in their historical context. *Shipwrecks and Maritime Disasters* looks at the conditions faced by mariners down through the decades and links chronologically distant accidents in a thematic order that I hope will interest readers.

Of necessity, this has been a highly subjective selection. My criteria have been personal interest and fair geographical and thematic representation. Instead of covering just the better-known tragedies, I have blended a few of the 'big name' wrecks (*Wahine*, *Wairarapa*, *Rainbow Warrior*) with the stories of lesser-known ones. Since this was commissioned as an illustrated book, the availability of photographs has also played an important part in deciding which wrecks went in and which will have to wait for inclusion in the next volume. If you cannot find a wreck that you want to read about, look up the bibliography (shipwrecks such as the *Hydrabad*, *General Grant*, *Tararua* and HMS *Orpheus* have had their own books) or consult Ingram.

Part 1

HAZARDS OF THE COAST

New Zealand's costliest shipwreck took place on 7 February 1863 when the steam corvette HMS *Orpheus* struck the Manukau bar while attempting to enter port. Of the 259 aboard, 189 lost their lives.

Chapter 1

'HOME PAPERS PLEASE COPY' – PERILS OF THE SEA

The sea has always been New Zealand's highway to the rest of the world. More than 95 percent of our exports leave these shores by ship and, until recently, most people came and left by sea. As this book will show, it was often a dangerous highway.

Who was the first to make landfall the hard way? We will never know. Eastern Polynesians discovered these islands about 1200 years ago and one of these unnamed explorers may have been the first to encounter the welcoming shores of Aotearoa.

If legend is to be believed, the first maritime casualty was the waka atua ('canoe of the gods') *Araiteuru*. Pre-dating even the ancestors of the Maori, the *Araiteuru*'s crew had left an unknown land called Taitewhenua at an unspecified date in the very distant past. After stopping off at Hawaiiki, the traditional setting-off point for the later migrations to Aotearoa, the ancient voyagers sailed south, making landfall at Turanga near present-day Gisborne. There they planted the first kumara before heading further south to Te Wai Pounamu (the South Island).

While off North Otago, however, luck finally ran out for the *Araiteuru*, which had earlier shrugged aside the Pacific's wildest moods. Waterlogged and unwieldy, she got caught up in the fast-flowing current off Shag Point and swept up onto the aptly named Danger Reef, which the Maori later would know as Araiteuru. The kumara, taro and gourds carried aboard were washed up onto nearby Hampden Beach to create the famous Moeraki Boulders.

The Maori memorialised the wreck in stone, in this instance by naming local features after the wreck. *Araiteuru*'s broken mast and sail, turned to stone, are said to be visible near Matakaea (Shag Point) even to this day. The great waves which wrecked her are said to be represented by the range of hills running parallel to the coast. Many carry the names of crew members.

Facts and figures became more accurate after 1642 when the great Dutch navigator, Abel Tasman, rediscovered Aotearoa with the ships *Heemskerck* and *Zeehaen*. Tasman saw only part of New Zealand but did at least put it 'on the map'. James Cook,

2

who followed in his wake on three voyages between 1769 and 1777, charted the coast with more accuracy, filling in most of the more important gaps left on Tasman's sketchy chart.

Exploring uncharted coasts was always dangerous. Cook clawed his way up and down the coast cautiously, taking soundings wherever possible and using his sharpest-eyed men as lookouts. That disaster was only a puff of wind away became clear in December 1769 when French explorer Jean-Francois Marie de Surville almost went ashore in Doubtless Bay, North-land. A storm had carried away the *Saint Jean Baptiste*'s rudder and de Surville was lucky to get away with only the loss of his anchors. Two of these have been recovered recently and are on display at the National Museum and the local museum as memorials to New Zealand's first recorded maritime accident.

Europeans kept clear of New Zealand until the 1790s when entrepreneurs from the nearby penal colony at New South Wales discovered the islands' huge stocks of fur seals. Between 1790 and the early 1820s they ruthlessly exploited first the seals and then whales, with devastating effects on the hapless mammals . . . and sometimes on themselves. Sailing virtually uncharted waters for months at a time was never safe and it is not surprising that the first ship known to have cast her bones on a New Zealand beach was a storeship for the sealers.

That ship was the *Endeavour* – not, as some once thought, Cook's illustrious command, but another craft of entirely different design. Sealing parties had been working from beautiful Dusky Sound in Fiordland for Captain William Wright Brampton since late 1792. By the time the *Endeavour* dropped anchor, a house and a small jetty had been erected and tens of thousands of sealskins had been collected for the China market. An earlier party had even made a start on New Zealand's first Pakeha-designed ship, a 60-ton schooner.

The *Endeavour*, hounded mercilessly by a trans-Tasman gale, limped into the sound in October 1795 with all her pumps working non-stop in a barely successful effort to keep her decayed timbers afloat. A survey found her unseaworthy and any residual debate was settled a few days later when she struck a rock and started taking in more water. When a cable chafed through early in November the old ship was run ashore to prevent her from sinking. The arrival of the *Fancy* brought the sound's European population to over 200. Her crew helped the shore party to finish the schooner (the *Providence*) begun earlier and to convert the *Endeavour*'s longboat into a deep-sea craft (the *Assistance*). All three craft made it back to the Australian colonies early in 1796, carrying with them most of the men. An American whaler picked up the last from Dusky Sound in 1797.

A fair stream of whalers, explorers and missionaries came to grief in the first 40 years of the nineteenth century, but casualties among Pakeha vessels increased dramatically after 1840 when the departure of the New Zealand Company's immigrant ship *Tory* sparked the first serious attempts at settlement.

They used to say that New Zealanders met their deaths

through drink or drowning – or sometimes an injudicious mixture of booze and water. On Otago Harbour one early pub, the Queen's Arms Tavern, acted a de facto lighthouse by 'exhibiting a red light . . . from sun-set to sun-rise for the guidance of persons making for the jetty'.[1] Certainly early drowning rates were extraordinarily high by modern standards. Relatively few people knew how to swim and with small boats being used much as we now use motor vehicles, deaths were common.

People also fell off wharves or slipped into rivers with surprising frequency. Early Dunedin newspapers carried more than one report of watermen finding rats munching on corpses under the first rickety jetty. Upturned dinghies, whalers and canoes accounted for many more. One Port Chalmers rowboat claimed four lives in two accidents in 1850. Even as late as 1866 accidents such as this one reported by the *North Otago Times* were common:

> During some squalls at Port Chalmers last Wednesday two boats capsized. In one were Captain Ridley and one of his sons, who both perished; and in the other two fishermen and a settler named William Geary, the latter of whom was drowned and the other two rescued by Pilot Patten and a volunteer crew. Quite a gloom has been cast over the inhabitants of the port from the melancholy occurrence.[2]

Ports varied in the facilities they had to offer. In the north of New Zealand and on the East Coast of the North Island, steamers continued to visit open roadsteads until well into the twentieth century. Here sacks of kauri gum are being lightered out to a waiting steamer at Ahipara. Masters always kept a watchful eye on the weather under these circumstances. *Northwood Collection, Alexander Turnbull Library, courtesy of Wellington Maritime Museum & Gallery*

Right up until 1928 death by drowning took more New Zealand lives than road accidents.

There were many hazards along the early coastline, some natural, others of human making. The latter were easier to overcome. Maori hostility resulted directly in the loss of some ships (see Chapter 13), but this problem had been overcome by the late 1830s. So, too, had been the Maori custom of stripping wrecks which washed up on tribal shores. Although greatly resented by Pakeha at the time, this was exactly what the British had been doing just a century earlier. Wrecks pillaged in this manner included the brig *Venus* at the Bay of Islands in 1806, the schooner *Parramatta* at the same place two years later, the schooners *Herald* and *Enterprise* at Hokianga Heads in 1828, the brig *Meredith* at Hokianga in 1832, the brig *Byron* at Table Cape, Mahia Peninsula, in the same year, the schooner *Waterloo* near Kapiti in 1833, the barque *Harriet* near Cape Egmont in 1834 and the brigantine *New Zealander* at Table Cape in 1836. Although, in many cases, the wreck was stripped and all or some of the helpless shipwreck victims murdered, there were also several occasions (such as the wrecks of the schooner *Cossack* at Hokianga in 1823 and the ship *Brampton* in the Bay of Islands the same year) where survivors were treated very hospitably by Maori.

There was no shortage of natural hazards in the early days. Since none of the coastline had been charted with any accuracy, early mariners were obliged to feel their way, and several ships ended their days on 'uncharted' rocks. Gradually, however, things improved as explorers' sketch maps gave way to professional charts. Much of this credit must go to the Navy which, since the inter-war period, has put considerable effort into surveying New Zealand waters.[3]

Slowly but surely, the coastline was made a better place for seafarers. Early harbour works were primitive affairs – a signal station here, some buoys there and usually precious little else to guide the mariner. Much was left to private enterprise, although the provincial governments all established harbour departments in the 1850s. Typical of the uphill battles facing early harbourmasters were those fought by Otago's Richard Driver; he complained bitterly about shoddily built beacons and buoys, which were 'mostly worm-eaten and sunken or had gone adrift',[4] and reported that he seldom lit the lamp at the flagstaff because the Government had refused to pay for the oil. Just a month after Driver had penned this angry missive, the immigrant ship *Maori* almost piled up on the rocks, partly because he had been unable to secure a crew for the pilot boat.

Each port had its own peculiarities, but the colony's harbours fell into three broad categories: the major ports, such as Auckland, Wellington and Lyttelton, which were safe natural anchorages and which required little human improvement beyond the provision of wharves and warehouses; the river ports such as Kaiapoi or Greymouth, which provided safety after work on training walls and dredging; and open road-steads such as Oamaru or New Plymouth, which required extensive harbour works before they could be made safe for shipping. The hazards posed by early river ports (Hokitika and Greymouth, for example) and open beach ports (for instance, Oamaru) will be illustrated in Chapters 3 and 4.

Basically, though, many ports were becoming safer places by the 1870s and 1880s. Competition from railways (especially in the South Island) weeded out many of the smallest and most hazardous during this period. The harbour boards which spread like a bureaucratic rash during the 1870s and early 1880s splurged on lavish port development work that straightened out many of the bumps in river channels and threw break-waters between wharves and the open ocean.

By the end of the Victorian era the number of shipwrecks was declining. Ports were safer, ships were more likely to be powered and more services were available to mariners in trouble. Early steamers were not much better than sailing vessels, being underpowered and blessed with boilers that had a nasty habit of bursting when called on to work hard, but by the mid-1870s the much more efficient compound engine was turning the steamship from a 'floating kettle' into the major force in shipping. Steam gave mariners more control over their craft and reduced the possibility of accident.

Small steamers had been acting as tugs since the 1850s but during the 1870s and 1880s the harbour boards finally took a hand in the provision of adequate towage and salvage services. The Otago Provincial Government had subsidised a tug service of sorts since the early 1870s but no one had been happy with the results. The 'official' boat was often raced by private competitors, both leaving smaller ships for what they saw as larger and more remunerative tows. In 1883 the exasperated Otago Harbour Board bought out the business of the Otago Towing Company which had tended to play favourites with the ships of its associate concern, the Union Steam Ship Company. Other major harbour boards also improved their towage fleets about this time, with most owning one or more vessels or at least coming to some arrangement with private contractors.

By this time central government was making the bits of

River ports were next up the scale in sophistication. The smaller ones claimed many steamers and sailing craft on their treacherous bars. Here we see the steamer *Weka* (90 tons, 1883) being refloated at Mokau Heads. *Wellington Maritime Museum & Gallery*

The steam corvette HMS *Orpheus*.

coastline between the ports safer. Following the abolition of the provinces in 1876, the Marine Department (which had replaced the earlier Marine Board in 1866) took control of the ports and anchorages not administered by harbour boards and expanded its lighthouse construction programme.[5] Often the department's work was sadly reactive, forced on it by the most horrific shipping casualties. Lighthouses, the most obvious symbols of coastal improvement, tended to spring up like maritime mushrooms in the wake of disasters. The first permanent lighthouse was completed at Pencarrow, near the entrance to Wellington Harbour, in January 1859.[6]

Typical of the new lights was the one at Waipapa Point, Southland, erected in 1884, three years after the Union Company liner *Tararua* smashed onto a reef with the loss of 131 lives in New Zealand's worst merchant ship disaster. The worst naval one was the wreck of the steam corvette HMS *Orpheus* on the Manukau bar on 7 February 1863, with the loss of 181 lives.)[7]

The Marine Department brought other improvements, most notably the lighthouse tenders *Stella* and *Hinemoa*, which reached New Zealand in 1876. For many years these graceful little steamers helped transport lighthouse kitsets to isolated sites, serviced the lights once they were built, took part in searches for missing ships and transported supplies to depots which were built on some of New Zealand's sub-Antarctic islands, the Kermadecs and the Three Kings Islands. Many seafarers owed their lives to the government steamers.

The supply depots arose in response to some sensational wrecks in New Zealand's inhospitable southern waters. Best known, of course, was the gold-laden ship *General Grant*, which ran onto the west coast of the main island of the Auckland Islands group on 14 May 1866.[8] Of the 83 aboard – 61 passen-

By funding lighthouses, lighthouse tenders and depots for castaways, central government made New Zealand's seas much safer during the last quarter of the nineteenth century. This is the first of the government tenders, the *Stella* (268 tons, 1876).

gers and 22 crew – just 15 survived. Four of these would lose their lives in subsequent attempts to go for help and another would die of illness before the brig *Amherst* rescued them on 21 November 1867 after a year and a half of near-starvation.

As Chapter 6 shows, in the days of sail, ships leaving British ports bound for New Zealand often made the Snares their first landfall, and homeward-bound ships frequented southern waters, hoping to pick up the strong winds common at those latitudes. In foggy or squally weather, several ships ran aground on the bleak little islands, leaving passengers and crews to struggle for survival, often for many months at a time.

The *Hinemoa* established the first depots on the Antipodes and Bounty Islands in 1886. Between then and 1927, when the virtual disappearance of sailing ships rendered these depots obsolete, the *Hinemoa, Stella* and *Tutanekai* (1896) made frequent cruises, restocking depots, maintaining provisions and on occasions rescuing castaways. When the *Hinemoa* called at the Auckland Islands in May 1905, she returned with 22 men from the French barque *Anjou*, which had run aground in February. Two years later she picked up 15 survivors from the big barque *Dundonald*.

What happened when a shipwreck occurred in these early days? The first priority was always the rescue of the passengers and crew. If the vessel was wrecked on an isolated part of the coastline, they had to fend for themselves. If they were lucky, their distress rockets might summon rescuers from nearby settlements or a passing ship might give assistance. If the wreck happened near a major port, there were more reliable remedies at hand. Several towns, most notably Oamaru and Timaru, formed rocket brigades. These bands of hardy volunteers used rocket pistols which fired lines out to the ship. Once this line was secured by the crew (and, as we will see in

Chapter 4, this was often an extremely difficult task), a breeches buoy could be rigged up to help bring the crew ashore. These crude but effective guns plucked hundreds of people from seemingly impossible wrecks.

Then it was a question of attending to the ship and her cargo. Sometimes a ship could be refloated and repaired; Chapters 9 and 15 focus on some of the better-known salvages, but it is worth remembering that many ships lived to founder another day. If, however, the owner's agent decided that the ship was a hopeless case, she would then be 'abandoned to the underwriters'. Her fate was then in the hands of the insurers. If anything larger than sticks of wood remained, the insurance company would put the wreck and her cargo up for auction. By that stage it was all a bit of a gamble. Salvors might purchase £25,000 worth of ship and cargo for just a couple of hundred pounds. If luck was with them and the seas remained calm, they could make a huge profit; on very rare occasions people even salvaged ships written off as lost. But they could just as easily lose their shirts. One storm was all it took to break up even the strongest hull, scattering cargo and wreckage for kilometres.

While all this was going on, the wheels of bureaucracy were usually grinding away. In 1863 the colonial parliament passed the Enquiry into Wrecks Act that empowered the principal Customs officer (or any other person deemed suitable by the Governor) at the port nearest to a shipping casualty to hold a preliminary inquiry into the incident. Then, as now, preliminary inquiries sought to establish the cause of the accident, not who was to blame. If the person conducting the preliminary inquiry thought a more formal inquiry was warranted, he (and it was always a he in those days) could apply for one. Formal investigations were normally presided over by a couple of justices or a resident magistrate.

Six years later the act was amended to enable justices or magistrates to cancel or suspend seafarers' certificates. In 1877, the provisions of the act were incorporated in the Shipping and Seamen's Act and the Marine Department was made the administering body. Later amendments to the act altered details but left the main features intact.

Formal inquiries were held in about a quarter of the casualty cases last century. Magistrates or justices of the peace were almost always assisted by one or two professionals – often the local harbourmaster or another master. Hearings could drag on for days, with each day's proceedings being followed anxiously in the local papers. The courts could exonerate mariners by returning their certificates or could impose a variety of penalties which ranged from reprimands with no suspension of certificates through to suspension of certificates (and with it the mariner's licence to work), accompanied by terms of imprisonment.

Court findings sometimes brought recommendations for major change. As we have already seen, the inquiry into the wreck of the Union Company steamer *Tararua* in April 1881,

Crossing the bar could be a frightening experience. These two photographs were taken aboard the barque *Manurewa* (upper photograph, 371 tons, 1884) as she was being towed across the Whangape bar by the small tug *Ohinemuri* (114 tons, 1891), whose mast and funnel are just visible in the lower photograph.
Wellington Maritime Museum & Gallery

Eventually the open roadsteads and small river ports gave way to sheltered ports protected by stone and concrete breakwaters. This is New Plymouth just before the First World War. *Wellington Maritime Museum & Gallery*

with the loss of 131 of the 151 aboard, resulted in the erection of a lighthouse at Waipapa Point, Southland. The loss of the same company's *Penguin* in February 1909 (see Chapter 11), with 75 dead, eventually produced the Karori Rock automatic light. The loss of a comparatively small ship, the coaster *Ripple*, off Cape Palliser in 1924 with all hands, brought new regulations for the mandatory installation of radio equipment aboard home trade ships.

From the end of the nineteenth century shipwrecks decreased in frequency and severity. By the late 1890s casualties were mostly of a minor nature, more the result of machinery breakdown or berthing accidents, as the following table of Union Company casualties testifies:

UNION STEAM SHIP COMPANY CASUALTIES JANUARY–MAY 1898

Date	Ship	Details
3 Jan	*Te Anau*	Too close inshore while on voyage Napier–Wellington. Master admonished.
12 Jan	*Rosamond*	Minor fire in coals off Cape Campbell. Ship undamaged.
20 Jan	*Corinna*	Broke down off Sinclair Head.
? Jan	*Waihi*	Cylinder cover damaged.
26 Jan	*Croix du Sud*	Cradle broke while on slip. Minor damage.

Date	Ship	Event
1 Feb	*Waikare*	Captain Anderson and three passengers injured in accident while hoisting launch in Preservation Inlet.
3 Feb	*Corinna*	While under pilot struck Nelson wharf, damaging wharf.
9 Feb	*Dingadee*	Damaged windlass while hauling up anchor, Totaranui. Four days to repair.
10 Feb	*Monowai*	Cargo damage from fire in No. 4 hold while on voyage Melbourne–Hobart.
11 Feb	*Rotorua*	Grounded 20 minutes Nelson.
18 Feb	*Corinna*	Stranded four hours Westport while swinging.
12 Mar	*Rosamond*	Touched lightly off Farewell Spit.
23 Mar	*Taieri*	Damaged Newcastle wharf.
25 Mar	*Kawatiri*	Hit North Mole, Napier, while under command of pilot. Ship and mole damaged.
31 Mar	*Omapere*	Damaged Napier wharf.
2 Apr	*Wakatipu*	Hit and sank barque *Laura* at Victoria Wharf, Dunedin.
4 Apr	*Mawhera*	Blown against wharf, Wellington.
9 Apr	*Dingadee*	Grounded Westport; no damage.
27 Apr	*Manawatu*	Collided *Edna*, Manawatu River. Sank.
5 May	*Rotorua*	Damaged Wellington wharf.
10 May	*Herald*	Damaged Timaru wharf.
16 May	*Kawatiri*	Broke shaft; towed into Wellington by *Ohau*.
24 May	*Wareatea*	Lost propeller bales, Macquarie Harbour.
27 May	*Australia*	Wheel chains carried away while crossing Macquarie Harbour bar.
31 May	*Waikare*	Touched bar, Taiaroa Heads.
31 May	*Moana*	Minor fire off San Francisco.

The dramatic wrecks rendered so heroically in the old Victorian lino-cuts or oil paintings were very much in the minority. Far more common was a simple bump with the bowsprit or a few hours' embarrassing drifting about when a shaft snapped.

Technological advances such as radio and radar brought huge improvements in seagoing safety. Radio had been installed in several passenger ships following the loss of the *Titanic* in 1912, three years after New Zealand regulations had made its installation mandatory in passenger vessels more than 45 metres long. Unfortunately many shipowners were at first reluctant to fit it to their smaller passenger/cargo vessels. Gradually, though, the sets began to appear in smaller freighters. Parallel improvements in the meteorological service enabled masters to receive more accurate weather forecasts.

The life story of a wreck. These small snapshots record salvage operations aboard the little steamer *Opua* (575 tons, 1902), which ran aground in fog at Tora, just north-east of Palliser Bay, on 2 October 1926. Although the wreck appeared intact, she was badly holed and could not be saved. These photographs record everything from raising the anchor with a block and tackle to 'brewing up' on deck. The bottom photograph on this page shows the ship as she appeared 30 years later. The *Opua* has proved a remarkably resilient wreck and is still visible.
Wellington Maritime Museum & Gallery

Radio beacons, which enabled ships to pinpoint their location accurately, were commissioned at Cape Maria Van Diemen and Baring Head in 1926 and 1937 respectively. By the outbreak of the Second World War similar beacons had been established at seven other stations. By this time most large inter-colonial (as the trans-Tasman ships were then called) and coastal vessels were fitted with radio direction finding equipment.

The use of radar, the electronic device which enabled mariners to 'see' in the dark or in fog, became widespread during the Second World War. Sets began to appear on New Zealand ships during the 1950s but too slowly to satisfy members of the New Zealand Merchant Service Guild. Some owners took heed of the seafarers but others did not, pleading poverty. It took the magisterial comment that, with radar, the wreck of the *Holmbank* off Banks Peninsula in 1963 (see Chapter 17) would have been avoidable to spur the rest into action. Even so, it was 1970 before the carriage of radar was universal, even aboard 1000-ton ships. It is not a complete guarantee of safety, as the lamentable example of the *Pacific Charger* showed (see Chapter 15), but radar has made a huge difference to improving our sealanes, especially for night navigation within port limits.

The latter part of the twentieth century brought further improvements in shipping safety. The gutting of the coastal shipping trade in the 1960s and 1970s eliminated the smaller ships that had featured so prominently in early casualty returns. Today's modern coastal craft, barely two dozen in number, feature elaborate radar, radio and satellite navigation facilities. Their crews are also much better trained than any of their predecessors. Nowadays, casualties are more likely to be fishing vessels or yachts.

The aids for any ship that does get into distress are very much more sophisticated. Most ports built up fleets of powerful tractor tugs in the 1970s and 1980s. Even ports such as Timaru, Gisborne and New Plymouth, which used to lack adequate towage craft, now boast sophisticated tugs. Backing them up are the resources of the defence forces (whose heli-

Modern ports are much safer places than their predecessors. From the 1960s onwards, New Zealand ports were re-equipped with powerful salvage tugs such as Wellington's *Kupe* (304 tons, 1971). *Wellington Maritime Museum & Gallery*

copters are an integral part of modern search and rescue operations), police launches at Auckland and Wellington and private aircraft.

Yet, as the later chapters of this book will show, the business of steering ships about by day or night is never without danger. The sea is a mighty force that can overcome even the best-equipped ship (*Wahine*); perhaps even more important, human error can always override any margin for error built into even the most sophisticated navigation gear (*Pacific Charger* and *Mikhail Lermontov*). As the foundering of the police launch *Lady Elizabeth* at the entrance to Wellington Harbour demonstrated in 1986, sometimes even the rescuers find themselves in need of rescue.

By the twentieth century shipwrecks had ceased to be common events for large trading vessels; total wrecks had dropped away to just one or two a year by the 1930s. Here we see the Union Company's big trans-Tasman freighter *Waikouaiti* (3926 tons), which went ashore on Dog Island, near Bluff on 28 November 1939 and became a total wreck. No lives were lost. *Wellington Maritime Museum & Gallery*

Notes
1. Gavin McLean, *Otago Harbour: Currents of Controversy*, Dunedin, 1985, p. 306.
2. *North Otago Times*, 27 November 1866.
3. For an account of the naval survey service, see John O'C. Ross, *This Stern Coast*, Wellington, 1969.
4. Gavin McLean, *op. cit.*, p. 35.
5. For a history of the Marine Department see E. R. Martin, *Marine Department Centennial History*, Wellington, 1969.
6. The most recent short history of local lights is Geoffrey B. Churchman, *New Zealand Lighthouses*, Wellington, 1989.
7. Each wreck is well served by at least one author. For the *Tararua*, see Joan MacIntosh, *The Wreck of the Tararua*, Wellington, 1970. For HMS *Orpheus*, see Thayer Fairburn's exhaustive and definitive, *The Orpheus Disaster*, Whakatane, 1987.
8. R. K. Eunson, *The Wreck of the General Grant*, Auckland, 1971.

The progress of 30 years:
Port Chalmers 1848 *(top)*
and the late 1870s *(lower)*.
As this chapter relates, the
period between these dates
was not always
characterised by
humanitarian work
practices, good working
conditions or simple 'British
justice'. *Hocken Library*

Chapter 2

THE HUMAN FACTOR

Last century, seafaring was a nasty, brutish life. Several cases of shipwreck stemmed from fights over standards of living or what crews sometimes saw as draconian behaviour by masters. It is surprising, though, that so few ships were lost because of this. In the early days at least, discipline was a serious problem. There are numerous cases of 'hard-driving' masters driving their crews to near-mutiny and more than a few of booze-befuddled masters being relieved of command by their subordinates.

Magisterial courts of inquiry tended to concern themselves only with the behaviour of the master and his officers. The ordinary seafarer was usually forgotten, by his employer as well as by the court, for he was purely a wage worker. Men signed on a ship at the start of a voyage and were paid off at the end, however that end came about. Until well into this century, seafarers usually received no compensation for loss of personal effects through shipwreck and were usually paid off by the local agent as soon as the ship was abandoned to the underwriters.

One particularly sensational incident took place on 27 April 1864 aboard the migrant ship *Flying Foam*, bound from England to Auckland with almost 150 passengers. The trouble began when a crewman assaulted a second-class passenger. The third officer attempted to apprehend the miscreant but was forced back by the seaman's friends. Worried by the turn of events, the master – in the true blue traditions of British class-consciousness – requested the first-class passengers to arm themselves. This done and the decks cleared of women and children, the master formally requested the handing over of the accused. Between them the chief, second and third mates and the surgeon carried the kicking, screaming, swearing man aft. One seaman threatened them with a knife, but ineffectually, and the alleged offender was secured.

From then until 13 July, when she touched port at Auckland, the *Flying Foam* was a ship divided. On 10 July, with their destination in sight, seamen refused to start bringing up passengers' luggage. They were locked up after several warnings but, unfortunately for the master, five from the next watch struck in sympathy with their incarcerated colleagues.

Ordered to temporary imprisonment in the forecastle, several ostentatiously sharpened their knives on the grindstone as they walked forward. Once there, they amused themselves by smashing fittings and swearing loudly. The carpenter erected a set of stocks but the seamen soon wrecked his handiwork and then set about liberating the men placed in them.

The *Flying Foam* was now largely under the control of the officers and passengers, none of whom had booked for a working holiday. Inexperienced, they probably lost the ship about a fortnight's sailing time by fumbling their way through the motions of hoisting and taking in sail. Much to everyone's relief, the ship reached Auckland, where the Armed Constabulary, summoned to the wharf by the master, dragged 16 sailors off to Mount Eden prison.

The legal system had the dice loaded against the ordinary sailor right from the start. Only from 1845, five years *after* the signing of the Treaty of Waitangi, did English law provide for the *voluntary* examination of a ship's master. Until then, anyone with the right connections or the gift of the gab could take command of a ship, regardless of whether he could read a chart. With the passing of the 1854 Merchant Shipping Act, a hefty 548-clause document, the rights of employers and employees and matters of safety were finally defined in reasonable terms. A year later, following tragedies aboard migrant ships such as the New Zealand-bound *Lloyds*, which lost 65 of its 211 passengers because of poor provisioning and the professional incompetence of both the master and the ship's surgeon, the British Parliament tightened up laws with the passing of the Passengers Act 1855.

Even so, justice in New Zealand was an amateurish affair. Otago's first Resident Magistrate, A. C. Stroude, had no legal training and the justices of the peace who helped him were little better, reflecting upper middle-class prejudices in their approach to sentencing. Elsie Locke, in an unpublished study of early Otago seafaring,[1] records that the magistrates tended to exercise the maximum penalty of 12 weeks' gaol, regardless of circumstances; since labour was always in short supply in the young colony and prisoners were usually sentenced to hard labour that benefited such employers as these very same justices of the peace, it was in the merchants' interests to condemn seamen. When nine striking seamen went inside in 1854 after a protracted 140-day voyage aboard the *Thetis*, claiming that the old craft was unseaworthy, a correspondent to the *Otago Witness* exclaimed in vain that:

> I understand that they are to be put in irons, and sent on board that leaky old tub the *Thetis*, which would have sunk with her valuable cargo in the Indian Ocean but for the activity and energy of these hardy tars who . . . will not cheerfully remain and pump out this old sieve till she drifts to England at the rate of 5½ knots.[2]

When the *Strathallan* arrived in Otago in 1858, after a voyage on which her master, Captain John Todd, spent most of his time rip-roaring drunk, the whole crew struck and was imprisoned for its common sense. It was not unknown for migrants, aware of the incompetence of some early masters, to feed and house seamen taking 'French leave' from colonial gaols.

Another 'Strath boat', the *Strathfieldsaye*, brought more tales of woe into the Port of Otago a few months later, with one settler's diary alleging that the master and purser had conspired to swindle the passengers out of their rations, a not uncommon complaint. Just before entering the heads, Captain James Brown was heard to threaten to shoot any passengers or crew who took exception to his behaviour. Making good his threat, he swung around one of the signalling cannon on the poop and aimed it at his fellow travellers. One shot injured a passenger in the hand. The captain, who had taken up with what some of the migrants described as a cheap whore, was later fined for serious breaches of the Passengers Act. Colonist Daniel Brown recorded bitterly that while 17 *Strathfieldsaye* sailors went to the Dunedin gaol for opposing this maniac, Captains Todd and Brown took passage back to Britain aboard the *Strathallan*, having paid no more than token fines.

Gradually, though, the bigger shipping companies began to weed miscreants out of the ranks and to impose more rigid

The crew's bill of fare aboard a Union Company steamer late last century. Although unexciting by modern standards, it was better than many British townspeople could aspire to, especially in its inclusion of meat three times a day! *Union Steam Ship Company*

Union Steam Ship Company of New Zealand, Limited.

BILL OF FARE FOR CREW.

	BREAKFAST.	DINNER.	TEA.
SUNDAY—	Porridge. Grilled Steak and Onions. Irish Stew.	Soup. Roast Beef or Pork. Potatoes. Vegetables. Plum Pudding.	Cold Meat. Pickles. Potatoes.
MONDAY—	Porridge. Chops. Curry and Rice.	Soup. Boiled Mutton. Potatoes. Rice Pudding.	Cold Meat. Stewed Steak. Potatoes.
TUESDAY—	Porridge. Steak. Potatoes.	Soup. Corned Beef and Carrots. Potatoes. Bread and Butter Pudding.	Cold Meat. Haricot Mutton. Potatoes.
WEDNESDAY	Porridge. Chops or Sausages. Potatoes or Irish Stew.	Soup. Roast Mutton. Potatoes. Sago Pudding.	Cold Meat. Dry Hash.
THURSDAY—	Porridge. Steak and Onions. Curry and Rice.	Soup. Roast Beef. Potatoes. Vegetables. Plum Pudding.	Cold Meat. Cottage Pie.
FRIDAY—	Porridge. Salt or Fresh Fish and Chops. Potatoes.	Pea Soup. Boiled Mutton. Potatoes. Bread and Butter Pudding.	Cold Meat. Hashed Beef. Potatoes.
SATURDAY—	Porridge. Irish Stew. Sausages.	Soup. Corned Beef and Carrots. Potatoes. Rice Pudding.	Cold Meat. Curry and Rice.

COFFEE OR TEA TO BE SERVED WITH MEALS THREE TIMES A DAY—MILK TO BE ADDED IN GALLEY.

This Bill of Fare can be varied by Chief Steward as may be found expedient, but in no case is the number of dishes to be exceeded.

8.6 08.

standards upon their seagoing employees. The reasons are obvious. Although sailing ships could be left to follow the dictates of time and tide, steamships were more complex beasts. Hideously expensive to build and scarcely cheaper to run, they had to be worked hard in order to bring any real return on the shipowners' funds. That meant better and brighter officers and men and higher standards of training and discipline.

The Union Company probably went too far in its attempts to impose order on a way of life that still defied such an approach. Take accidents, for example. Whereas other owners were usually content to rely on the sanctions imposed by the magisterial court of inquiry, Union made it clear that any master whose command met with an accident might as well start packing his seabags.

This became clear in 1883 when one of its most experienced masters, Captain Carey, ran the crack trans-Tasman flyer *Rotomahana* aground on Waipapa Reef. The court absolved him of all blame but the Union Company was not nearly as gentle. On 18 August a special meeting of directors, who were probably still smarting at having to pay Sparrow & Co. £4255 to patch up their flagship, fired a broadside at the hapless Carey:

> The Directors have considered all the circumstances surrounding the recent stranding of the *Rotomahana* while under your command and have come to the conclusion that although the magisterial enquiry exonerated all those on board from blame, on general grounds the responsibility must rest entirely with you – the Master being the officer entrusted with the care of the ship and the lives on board.
>
> In the present case you had a fine night, reliable compasses and a good chart and with these such an accident should have been impossible, while a cast of the lead would have determined your accurate distance from the shore at any moment. There can be little doubt that the disaster was brought about by the steamer's distance from Slope Point at three o'clock having been overestimated and by insufficient allowance having been made subsequently for the inset of the current and probably by a little careless steering.
>
> The Directors are therefore forced to the conclusion that you cannot be held altogether free from responsibility for the accident; having regard, however, for your previous good judgement and discipline displayed on board while the steamer was on the reef – and the fact that there has heretofore been no recognised rule in the Service for dealing with such cases, they have decided to allow your position in the service to remain undisturbed.[3]

But not untainted. A circular sent around the fleet later that day outlined Carey's offence and warned that masters would not be reinstated 'unless the accident is proved to have occurred under such exceptional circumstances as to entirely exonerate him from blame'.[4] The company was as good as its word. For many decades afterwards, any master involved in a serious accident was likely to find himself marched down the gangway and onto the beach.

The demon drink was a problem that the coastal companies never really overcame. Seafaring was a hard life and it is not

Union Steam Ship Company of New Zealand, Limited.

INSTRUCTIONS TO OFFICERS.

1.—Officers when on duty are to appear clean, and neatly dressed in dark blue suit, of cloth or serge with blue cloth cap. (See separate uniform circular).

2.—Officers are requested not to smoke while on duty, nor on Bridge or Quarter deck at any time. Coarse language must not be used.

3.—First Officer must keep the Log Book properly entered up each day, and submit it to the Company's Marine Superintendent for inspection on arrival at Head-quarters.

4.—Second Officer will be responsible for the efficiency of the boats and equipments, life buoys, leads and lines. He must see that the boats are not filled with lumber, and that the fails, &c., are clear for lowering at a moment's notice. Leads and lines to be kept in proper order, and ready for use.

5.—Third Officer (or Carpenter, where no Third Officer) to have blue-lights, rockets, cartridges, and signal guns in proper order, and ready for immediate use.

6.—The Officer on watch must not leave the Bridge, unless absolutely necessary. Officers will relieve each other on the Bridge ; the course to be reported in presence of the relieving Officer. The look-out must be strictly and carefully kept, and the bell struck every half-hour during the night when at sea.

7.—The greatest attention must be paid to the steering, and the Ship's course must not be altered without orders from the Captain, except in case of immediate danger, when the Officer on duty must act promptly, and to the best of his judgment. The Officer on duty must not sit down during his watch, nor enter into conversation with Passengers.

8.—If weather becomes foggy, or if doubtful about anything, the Captain must be called, whether night or day. When meeting any vessel, if uncertain which way she is going, slow or stop the engines until her course is ascertained.

9.—The holds to be sounded regularly, both at sea and in harbour, and the result reported to the Engineer on duty.

10.—The hose to be carefully attended to, and kept handy; one length to be always screwed on to the engine deck pump, in case of fire.

11.—In event of an alarm of fire, no noise must be made, but orders given quietly to the engine-room to turn on deck pump, all hands called, and the hoses properly manned. The Captain to be called meantime.

12.—In case of anyone falling overboard, the engines must be immediately stopped and reversed, and boats lowered to the rescue.

13.—The Government Regulations for the prevention of collisions, which are in the possession of the Officers, are to be strictly and carefully followed.

14.—In all emergencies not provided for in the foregoing instructions Officers are requested to use their best judgment, and to act with energy and prudence for the safety of lives and property under their care.

JAMES MILLS,

Managing Director.

Dunedin, 1st November, 1878.

The Union Company's 'Instructions to Officers' 1878. By the late nineteenth century the major shipping companies had codified practices and improved working conditions enormously. Unfortunately smaller employers were not always so good. *Union Steam Ship Company* surprising that many men sought refuge in the bottle. Many of the hostels clustered around the port areas of most towns sold ferocious concoctions. Firemen, performing a thankless and poorly paid job, were the worst offenders, often going on the bottle en masse and preventing ships from sailing to schedule. This was especially so with the officers and men of the smaller companies when at the smaller ports, far from the prying eyes of their superiors. As Union Company official Robert Strang reported in March 1892, officers usually hit the bottle in the 'outports', being 'too knowing to indulge in any large port'.[5] In February and March of 1892 alone, the company's officers had reported Captain Downie of the *Wareatea* and the officers of the *Taieri* tippling, the first mate of the *Dingadee* being 'the worse for alcohol' and a seaman from the *Orowaiti* having 'got drunk and bit Captain Adams on the nose'.[6]

Most drug- and alcohol-related accidents were relatively minor. In August 1900, for example, the master of the Union Company coaster *Kini* tangled the Normanby Wharf chains while attempting to leave Oamaru Harbour. When Oamaru branch manager C. Monson reached the ship he found the master, Captain Walker, 'in a hopeless state of collapse', after having unwisely mixed whisky with morphine.[7]

Occasionally company officials tempered 'justice' with leniency, requiring erring staff to sign the pledge in order to get a second chance. This did not always work. In November 1905 Strang reported that one of the Union Company's masters, Captain McNair, was drinking heavily, just eight months after signing the pledge under duress. McNair, needless to say, found himself seeking alternative employment.

Every company had to keep a watchful eye on the antics of its seagoing staff. The archives of Napier-based Richardson & Co. contain the following delightfully semi-literate passenger's complaint (1908) against Captain Thompson of the *Kahu*:

> I should like to bring to your notice the goings on on the *Kahu* the night he left Napier the master was silly drunk on the bridge at between 12 midnight and the time she landed her passengers he was so silly that at 4 o'clock in the morning that he had to call the Chief Engineer out to tell him where he was, also the language (filthy) he was using on the bridge where there were 2 female passengers and 2 children laying I should like you to warn him if only for the sake of the passengers that travel by your vessels and the safety of both the crew and the passengers and vessel for on Sunday morning her did not know here he was as we were inside of the light instead of outside.[8]

Richardsons promptly fired Thompson, who had already been the subject of several formal warnings. The company had little option. With lives at stake, not to mention a valuable ship and cargo, such behaviour could not be tolerated.

Drunkenness and poor behaviour lingered on into the early part of the twentieth century, especially with the smaller lines, but by the start of the inter-war period a combination of improved training and higher entry standards had weeded out most of the less capable officers and men. Seamen and firemen still went on 'benders'[9] but by the 1960s the problems had almost disappeared.

Notes
1. Elsie Locke, 'From Forecastle to Gaol', unpublished MS in the possession of the NZ Seafarers' Union.
2. *Ibid.*, p. 11.
3. Circular to Masters, James Mills Papers, USS Co. Archives, Wellington Maritime Museum and Gallery.
4. *Ibid.*
5. R. Strang/A. Cameron, 3 March 1892, Cameron Papers MS 1046/4, Hocken Library.
6. *.Ibid.*
7. C. Monson/J. Mills, 25 August 1900, James Mills Papers, *op. cit.*
8. Richardson & Co. minutes, 19 December 1908, Wellington Maritime Museum and Gallery.
9. For an account of post-war crewing problems, see Gavin McLean, *Masters or Servants? A Short History of the New Zealand Merchant Service Guild*, Wellington, 1990.

Few ports inspired more dread than Hokitika, which claimed a disproportionately large number of victims during the 1860s goldrushes. These photographs show seven ships ashore in 1865, Hokitika's most disastrous year. The lower photograph, taken at the same time, shows three vessels; the three-masted schooner to the right may be the London-owned *Sir Francis Drake*, which struck the bar and then hove up onto the beach while trying to enter port on 29 June 1865. *H. N. Murray and Greymouth Evening Star Collections, Alexander Turnbull Library*

Chapter 3

RIVER WRECKS

Most of New Zealand's mountain-fed rivers are short, shallow and dangerous. Few are navigable for any distance, the Clutha, Wanganui and the Waikato being among the only real exceptions. For the nineteenth-century mariner, hazards lurked everywhere. Dangerous bars – submerged ridges of sand which shifted with each storm – guarded river mouths and provided an unpleasant obstacle course for anyone entering the rivers. Many river mouths moved with the seasons, cutting out fresh entrances whenever storms savaged the coast. Even the rivers themselves were not without their problems. Freshes could scour out banks or bring down debris and snags, fouling propellers and puncturing hulls.

Yet, despite their uninviting nature, these river ports were welcome alternatives to the horrors of open roadsteads (see Chapter 4). In 1868, for example, settlers at Kakanui, North Otago, were scooping out portions of their river, which, as the *Otago Witness* of 21 November admitted, 'at some places did not carry much more water than would be required for floating a duck'.

Most communities were soon doing their best to improve upon the parsimony of nature. Rivers were surveyed, snags and rocks buoyed and wharf sites selected. First to go up were signal stations and simple wooden jetties, which often sufficed for the next decade. Later, those ports which survived railway competition might engage an engineer such as Englishman Sir John Coode to prepare expensive plans for upgrading their harbour works to handle bigger ships. Almost invariably, these centred around straightening up the entrance channel and pushing it out to deeper water between the protective arms of breakwaters or training walls.

Hokitika was one of the more notorious river ports. Although ill-equipped by nature for such a role, Hokitika had unofficial port status conferred upon it in 1864 when miners discovered gold in the hinterland. That December Captain Leach introduced it to the possibilities of commercial shipping when he took the small steamer *Nelson* across the bar and into the shallow, snag-infested river. Leach got away with it but others would not be so lucky.

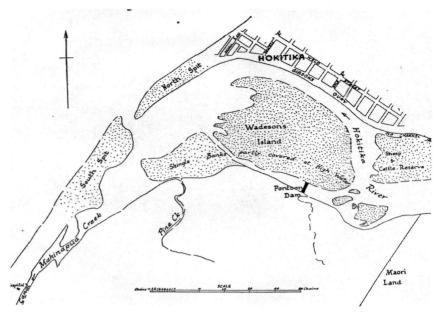

Hokitika Harbour showing both the narrow entrance through the spit and the numerous sandbanks.
Appendices to the Journals of the House of Representatives

Things began optimistically enough. The Canterbury authorities, only too pleased to offer competition to Otago's goldfields, gazetted Hokitika a port in March 1865 and started building wharves, setting aside reserves and knocking together a customs house. By the following year a tolerably good wharf, Gibson Quay, was cluttered with ships of all shapes and sizes, many direct from Australia. Vessels too big to cross the bar (which shifted constantly and could vary in depth from less than a metre to over 2 metres) lay off the entrance while smaller craft shuttled between them and the shore.

Hokitika was a curse of a place, rightly feared by mariners and merchants alike. The holding ground off the bar was poor. Ships forced to anchor there were at the mercy of any storm that might blow in from the Tasman. Neither buoys nor surfboats could be used as landing aids. Then there was the entrance, narrow, shallow and unpredictable even at the best of times. It usually ran to seaward in a north-south direction, forcing vessels entering and leaving to do so broadside-on to the prevailing seas. Even inside the river, skippers had to keep on their guard. Floods frequently swept down the river, diverting the channel away from the wharf and effectively closing the port for weeks on end. Ships could be carried down the river and out over the bar, almost without warning.

Paddle tugs were essential, both to ferry passengers and cargo from large ships out in the roadstead and to help small craft in and out of the port. In August 1865 the Melbourne firm McMeckan Blackwood & Co. set up the first service, charging outrageous fees for the use of its little *Yarra*. Gradually towage and lighterage fees were lowered as Dunedin merchants muscled in on the business but, even so, Hokitika was never a cheap port to work.

The price was paid in lives as well as cash. It was not long

The steamer *Jane Douglas* (95 tons, 1875), tied up at Gibson Quay. Between 1902 and 1907 the *Jane Douglas* had several accidents at Hokitika. The ship was wrecked between Stephens and D'Urville Islands on 10 January 1912. *Wellington Maritime Museum & Gallery*

Despite its unlovely reputation, Hokitika remained open until after the Second World War, although its twentieth-century trade never matched that of the goldrush era. Here we see the three-masted topsail schooner *Eunice* (190 tons, 1902) ashore in May 1907. She became a total wreck at Wanganui September 1917. *Wellington Maritime Museum & Gallery*

before the first wrecks occurred. Between 1865 and 1867 there were no less than 108 strandings – one every 10 days! – 32 of them resulting in total losses. The causes were many and varied: some ships grounded going out, others while coming in, some snapped their moorings during freshes in the rivers, sailing craft lost the wind at a critical point while crossing the bar and, on rare occasions, steamers had their fires doused by heavy seas. All ended up on the bar, some to be refloated and sail again, others to provide firewood for the townsfolk.

Surveying the horizon at the end of the street one day, the local rag waxed eloquent:

From the distance to the river where the *Montezuma* has been cast high and dry on the sands, the picture is one that cannot be equalled in the colony and perhaps not in the world. In one spot the last remnants of the *Oak* may be observed – showing even now how

This photograph shows what it was like to cross the bar at Hokitika. The ship is the small motor vessel *Foxton* (224 tons, 1929). By the time that Hokitika was declared closed to shipping in 1950, it had become badly silted. *Wellington Maritime Museum & Gallery*

Opposite page: The *Lauderdale* (1668 tons, 1889), owned by the Maoriland Steam Shipping Company, joined the list of Greymouth casualties on 27 June 1910 when she touched the bar, lost steerage-way and went ashore, gradually working her way south of the entrance to become a total loss. *Wellington Maritime Museum & Gallery*

well and faithfully she must have been built; further on a confused mass of ruin, a heap of splintered planks and ribs, marks the place where the *Sir Francis Drake* and the *Rosella* finally succumbed to the force of the waves. Yonder can be seen the mast of the *Titania*, and nearer home, what is left of the steamship *New Zealand*.[1]

Philip Ross May, in his booklet *Hokitika: Goldfields Capital*, records that there arose in Hokitika a class known as 'beach rakers', men who found a livelihood by scavenging for material washed off wrecks. Apparently the beach rakers worked in pairs, usually on moonlit nights, using hook and line to drag in anything of value.

Indeed, wrecks kept a good portion of the town in food and drink:

First come the auctioneers, who try to assume a serious aspect (with about the same results as mutes returning from a funeral) as they say aloud, "sad thing, another wreck, I'm afraid"; while inwardly they chuckle to themselves, "Fi fo fum, I smell another sale". They are closely followed by the shipping agents, who affect big sou'-westers and oil-skin coats, and who in virtue of their business are very nautical ashore, and are looked up to as authorities; then come the mass, the consignees, the draymen for jobs . . . with perhaps Thatcher [a goldfields balladeer] to get some fresh material for "a screaming new local".[2]

Space precludes listing every Hokitika wreck here but let us take one day – 9 May 1867 – which shows how easily a single storm could endanger shipping both inside and outside the port.

The first casualty that day was the 148-ton brigantine *Gold-seeker*, which had arrived off the Hokitika bar on the evening of 7 May. She was an old craft, built in 1852 for the Melbourne-Tasmania trade. Bought recently by Hokitika merchants Spence Brothers, and sporting an appropriate name, she carried a mixed load of 200 sheep and general cargo. Since the

WRECK OF THE STAR OF THE SOUTH. 308.J.R.
LOW TIDE

weather looked threatening, her master, Captain Wilkinson, decided to haul offshore under shortened canvas and let the storm blow over. This it did and next day a steamer towed the becalmed *Goldseeker* back to the anchorage.

Unfortunately they missed the tide by an hour. Wilkinson, left on his own again, dropped anchor for the night, expecting to enter the river the next morning. During the night, however, the weather again deteriorated and he had to drop the second anchor. At first they held but, as the westerly gained strength, the *Goldseeker*, her bow held down as she strained at her anchors, started shipping seas. She quickly filled with water. When the pumps showed no sign of coping with the inrush Wilkinson, in an action later criticised by the mate, cut her cables, hoisted sail and ran her up onto the beach to save life. There she broke up.

Greymouth was never as dangerous to enter as Hokitika but, like all West Coast bar harbours, it had to be treated with respect. This photograph shows the wreck of the steamer *Star of the South* (235 tons, 1863) on 22 December 1884. When entering the river in defiance of the harbour signals, the ship was caught by the current and flung right round. Her master, Charles Hodge, hoisted her auxiliary sails and tried to sail upriver but could make no headway and had to abandon his vessel when she struck near the entrance. A flood late in January 1885 swept away the remains. *Wellington Maritime Museum & Gallery*

While all this was going on outside the port entrance, the weather was also affecting shipping alongside the quay. As the *West Coast Times* of 10 May reported:

> Yesterday may be truly considered a black-letter day for the port, as it witnessed the destruction of one fine vessel outside, and whilst that was going on a scene occurred in the river that caused an hour or two's extreme excitement and the most lively apprehensions for the safety of every vessel moored at the Transit Shed, and that of the wharf also, which was at one time threatened with total destruction.
>
> Luckily the crews were stirring, having just turned out at about half-past six, otherwise the most serious results might have ensued. The heavy rains of the past night considerably increased the volume of the river, which at low water rushed down with great force and set full upon the *Bella Vista*, the headmost vessel of those below the shed. She was well moored head and stern, but by some means her bow took a shear off, and the current getting between her and the wharf brought such a strain upon her head lines that the mooring post, unable to bear it, snapped short off, and in an instant she swung across the stream, and grounded bows-on to the shallow bar in mid river. Dropping astern at the same time, she fouled the *Anne Moore*, snapped that vessel's flying jib-boom, and otherwise damaged her head-gear, but not very seriously. The ketch *Florence* was moored outside the *Bella Vista*, and by this sudden change in position found herself in some peril, but her crew moved themselves, smartly, ran lines on shore, and soon got their little vessel out of difficulty, although she also grounded for a time on the middle bar.
>
> Meanwhile the *Bella Vista* lay athwart the stream, her bow on the bar and her stern hanging by the quarter warp, which got under the *Anne Moore*'s bowsprit, and threatened to tear it from the gammoning. The river thus being obstructed, rushed and boiled furiously against the wharf and in less than five minutes worked underneath the piles and washed away tons of the gravel used as the filling-in, and proceeded in its work of destruction with such rapidity that had not the deputy Harbour-Master, who dreading some mishap, was on the alert all night, given orders to cut the *Bella Vista*'s quarter-line, we feel certain that forty or fifty yards of the lower wharf must have gone and the remainder received such serious damage that would have necessitated its almost entire reconstruction. The barque thus released swung to the stream and grounded fore-and-aft, permitting the river to flow onwards in its usual course, and thus saved the wharf.

By the 1870s gold had given way to timber and other less exciting exports. Sir John Coode's plans resulted in modern harbour works by the end of the decade but almost bankrupted the harbour board, which spent the rest of its long existence presiding over a diminishing trade. Hokitika's port declined rapidly after the First World War and was declared closed to shipping in 1950, to the relief of both local administrators and the long-suffering Marine Department. The West Coast's maritime trade settled down to relying on coal and timber exports through the ports of Greymouth and Westport. Yet, even though bigger and better ships handled this business, the rivers, particularly the Grey, continued to exact their toll.

The steamer *Opouri* (570 tons, 1911) was crossing the Greymouth bar late at night on 3 September 1917 when her steering gear failed. Helpless, she was swung around and carried up onto the North Spit Breakwater where she became a total wreck. No lives were lost. *Wellington Maritime Museum & Gallery*

The Union Company had very little luck with the name *Hawea*; the first, as we shall see in Chapter 12, sank at New Plymouth under peculiar circumstances and the second went ashore at Greymouth. The second *Hawea* was a utilitarian-looking cargo carrier of 1758 tons, built at Dumbarton in 1897. Cheap and simple to operate, she was a regular caller at West Coast ports, loading cargo such as coal and timber for destinations on either side of the Tasman.

She was leaving Greymouth for Australian ports on the afternoon of 30 October 1908 when she slammed into a heavy roller while crossing the inner bar. The huge wave struck her port bow, dumping her down onto the seabed and causing her to lose steerage way. Captain J. W. Burgess struggled to regain control but, before he could do so, the steamer crashed into the northern tiphead, grounding amidships and listing alarmingly with huge waves breaking against her. Deck cargo broke loose, endangering the lives of crew members, and only a fortuitous calming of the seas prevented serious injury or death. Later that afternoon the crew made it ashore safely with the use of a line.

Salvage operations were hampered by a dispute between Dunedin-based marine superintendent Col McDonald (reinforcing managing director Charles Holdsworth's line that the question was not whether the ship could be salvaged, but whether it could be done as profitably as simply allowing her to break up and then collecting the insurance money) and J. Daniels, successful salvor of the *Mapourika* a decade earlier (see Chapter 9), over whether to salvage the ship whole or let her break up and salvage just the cargo. The conflict even spilled over into the press, with the *Grey River Argus* spitting that 'to manage a job such as the *Hawea* presented by means of telegrams from business men hundreds of miles apart would be like managing the South African campaign from Downing

Street; and we make no doubt at all that the disappointment in each case was largely due to a like cause'.[3]

By 1 December shore gangs were jettisoning the timber at a rapid clip while others fished it out of the surf and stored it under the rail lines at Cobden Bridge. Daniels was fashioning a canvas cover to put under the ship before refloating her and, with the weather moderating, all looked well. Then Dunedin got its wish; a storm sprang up and pulverised the ship.

Greymouth did not really let up until the mid-1930s. Big ships lost there after 1914 included the *Opouri* (570 tons, lost 3 September 1917), *Perth* (1799 tons, lost 13 November 1921), *Ngahere* (1090 tons, lost 12 May 1924), *Kaponga* (2346 tons, lost 28 May 1932) and *Abel Tasman* (2042 tons, lost 18 July 1936). In nearly every case, the ships grounded on the northern side of the inner bar, gradually worked their way across and were swung onto the north tiphead where the sea soon made short work of them.

One of the last big ships to leave her bones against the tiphead was the Union Company collier *Kaponga*. A big, engines-after collier, less than six years old, she stranded on the bar on 28 May 1932. Her holds bulging with more than 2900 tonnes of coal, the *Kaponga* slipped her moorings at 1530 hours and lined up on the entrance on the first leg of her voyage to Auckland. She was following the same company's *Kalingo* (drawing 5.4 metres) and should have had plenty of clearance. The harbourmaster reported 6.7 metres of water on the bar and she was drawing 5.6 metres after and just under 5.5 metres forward. Conditions were ideal, with good visibility and a very calm sea. What her master, Captain W. A. Gray, did not realise, though, was that the *Kalingo* had lightly touched the inner bar on the way out.

The *Kaponga* struck just opposite the signal station and drifted about two ship's lengths before coming to a halt. So gentle was the impact – evidenced by a loss of headway rather than a bump or jar – that at first only Gray realised that she had struck something. The sea was moderate but the swell swung her bow around to the northward, straddling her across the inner bar, despite Gray's best efforts to keep her bow pointing into the waves. The sea now had her bumping up and down on the sand and the tide was on the turn.

The harbour board tug *Westland* reached the *Kaponga* about three-quarters of an hour later. It got a line to her stern but the rope broke under the strain. Then a crash was heard and it was seen that the *Kaponga* had hit rocks and worked loose her rudder, which now hung broken and useless. The arrival of another rescuer, the small Anchor Company coaster *Titoki*, temporarily raised hopes of a quick escape. The *Titoki* crossed the inner bar safely, backed in and threw the *Kaponga* another line. Unfortunately, the line was lost and, after standing by for a while, the coaster continued on to Westport. Meanwhile, the tug retrieved the broken hawser, picked up a line from the *Kaponga* and steamed upriver to maintain a strain that would keep the *Kaponga*'s bow from veering towards the rocks on the northern tiphead, just 15 metres away. There she stayed while everyone waited for the Union Company's big salvage tug *Terawhiti* to steam down from Wellington.

As a result of working across the seabed, the *Kaponga* started to take in water soon after the grounding, but pumps kept the ingress under control. As night fell, the crew remained aboard, the seas continued to moderate and all felt confident of refloating the ship, which was becoming hogged but was otherwise sound. Flooding was restricted to the fore- and afterpeaks and the engine room remained dry. Everyone wanted to get her off. She was now blocking the port, trapping the Union Company colliers *Komata* and *Karepo* and causing the diversion to Westport of the *Gabriella*, *Kaimai*, *Kanna* and *Kini*.

By the 29th both hope and the ship had been dashed to pieces. The day had begun encouragingly enough. The *Kaponga* had remained fast all night and, the next morning, the Union Company made another salvage attempt. The *Kaimai*, outside the harbour and the *Komata*, inside, pulled away at their hawsers in an attempt to bring the *Kaponga*'s bow upstream so she could be towed into port. They accomplished the first part of the operation, moving her round until she faced upstream, but the hull remained fast amidships and they had to give up when it became obvious that she was wedged tight. Shore labour had started removing coal but had dumped just 40 tonnes before having to give up. By 1800 that evening the sea had risen and big rollers were pushing the ship towards the tiphead where so many other craft had met their fate. Looking overboard, chief engineer O. H. Dillner saw the remains of the *Ngahere*.

The crew rigged up a breeches buoy to the north tiphead and started coming ashore at 0230. By 0420 all had reached shore safely, even though the rolling of the ship had the line whipping up and down violently. Last to leave was Captain Gray, who landed at 0420. 'As his feet touched the ground,' the paper reported, 'the small group standing on the pile of rocks in the pouring rain, with acetylene flares showing up haggard faces, spontaneously cheered.' One man forfeited his right to take ashore a small parcel, instead placing the ship's cat and her three small kittens into a pillow-slip and tucking them under his shirt. All found homes with rescuers.[4]

The morning's tide sent seas washing over the big ship, which by then was listing heavily. The engine room flooded and the fore and after bulkheads collapsed. At that stage the *Terawhiti* was signalled to return to Wellington. Salvage was impossible and, with the wreck up against the breakwater, the channel was once again clear, although temporarily restricted to daylight navigation only. By the end of October the wreck was breaking up. The funnel went overboard at 0300 on 30 October and the stern disappeared, leaving just 10 metres of the bow poking out of the water. It was expected to sink in the next fresh. Large quantities of coal washed up onto the North Beach, to the delight of householders, who cheerfully replenished their cellars.

The court of inquiry found that there had been a discrepancy between Greymouth harbourmaster Captain Frederick William Cox's estimate of the depth of water over the bar, taken earlier that day, and that actually prevailing (5.5 metres). Flummoxed, Cox made an appalling pun when he said, 'I can't fathom it at all.'[5] The explanation was that the soundings had been carried out over too narrow a section of the bar and had failed to detect a patch of shoaling that was building up. The

Westport also had its share of victims. This is the Union Company steamer *Suva* (293 tons, 1877) which was carried onto the breakwater while leaving port on 10 July 1888 at the end of her first trip to Westport. Carried south onto the beach, she broke up within a few weeks. *Wellington Maritime Museum & Gallery*

When the big overseas cargo liner *Port Bowen* went ashore 2 kilometres north of the entrance to Wanganui, she initiated a major salvage operation. Among the small craft involved were the tugs *Toia* and *Terawhiti* (from Wellington) and *Kahanui* (Wanganui) as well as the Wanganui lighter *Morning Light (top)*. When that failed, it was decided to discharge her cargo at low water. The lower photo shows wool being unloaded on trucks; about 3000 bales were discharged in this manner. *Wellington Maritime Museum & Gallery*

Marine Department ordered the harbour board to take soundings over a far wider section of the entrance, to alter the leads and to improve the signalling methods.

The last big craft to leave her bones at Greymouth, the trans-Tasman freighter *Abel Tasman*, did so under unusual circumstances. On 17 and 18 July 1936 it rained as it can only on the West Coast. The Grey River became swollen with muddy water and, by early in the evening of the 18th, it was threatening to top the wharf. This, combined with an unusually strong ebb tide, ripped the *Abel Tasman* from her moorings. Captain W. D. Archibald got steam up as fast as he could and tried to beach her first at Blaketown Lagoon and then at the bight on

Ironically, salvage of the cargo became easier as salvage of the ship looked bleaker. This top photograph shows how far the ship had worked her way up the beach. The lower photograph depicts frozen meat being discharged at high water via wires and slings, which could take 30–40 carcases at a time. *Wellington Maritime Museum & Gallery*

Eventually salvors ran a pierhead out to the *Port Bowen* to make it easier to strip her of fittings and dismantle her for scrap. *Wellington Maritime Museum & Gallery*

the inside of the north breakwater. He failed and the *Abel Tasman*, by now completely out of control, swept down the river towards the bar. While off the north tiphead, she struck the wreckage of the *Kaponga* with a crash, swung across the river and then resumed drifting. Completely at the mercy of the confused currents, she drifted out through the entrance and was swept around to the rocks on the North Beach where she became a complete wreck. Fortunately all hands escaped safely.

Because they served mainly small ships, few of the river ports saw large shipwrecks, but Gisborne and Wanganui each witnessed a large wreck this century. Gisborne's came on 23 September 1912 when a southerly squall blew the 7280-ton steamer *Star of Canada* onto Kaiti Beach. Since her boilers had been closed down for cleaning, her master, Captain J. M. Hart, could do nothing to prevent her from driving ashore where she became a complete wreck. Although she was abandoned by the underwriters on 8 July, the big wreck provided sightseers with something to gawp at for quite a long time.

Wanganui's biggest victim was another overseas cargo liner, the *Port Bowen*. A big 8267-tonner dating from 1919, the *Port Bowen* was making for the anchorage off the entrance shortly after midnight on 19 July 1939 when her master, Captain Francis Bailey, approaching the port too fast and too close, sent her ashore about 2 kilometres north of the harbour entrance. Everyone made it ashore safely but the ship was beyond salvage and, after a long stay on the beach, ended up as scrap metal for the war effort.

Most of the river ports have gone now, victims of silting caused by agricultural clearances in their headwaters, competition from other transport modes or their inability to handle ships large enough to suit modern economics. Most went last century but a few lingered until comparatively recently, expiring in the 1950s (Whakatane) or the 1960s (Patea and Kaiapoi). Greymouth, Westport and Wanganui, although far from prosperous, refuse to lie down and die, handling residual coastal trades and the occasional small overseas ship. Only Gisborne, with its greater depth and bigger swinging basin, maintains any meaningful overseas trade. Yet, as the continuing spate of fishing boat tragedies on the Grey bar shows, these ports remain perilous for the unwary or the unlucky.

Notes
1. For a good introduction to the problems of the port of Hokitika, see Philip Ross May, *Hokitika: Goldfields Capital*, Christchurch, 1964 (from which this extract is taken) and John O'C. Ross, *Pride in Their Ports*, Palmerston North, 1977.
2. Philip Ross May, *op. cit.*, p. 11.
3. Undated *Grey River Argus* clipping, James Mills Papers, USS Co. Archives, Hocken Library.
4. *Dominion*, 30 May 1932.
5. *Ibid.*, 8 June 1932.

Chapter 4

EXPOSED COASTS

For all their shortcomings, river ports at least provided early shipping with some measure of shelter. But not every settlement could lay claim to the dubious shelter of a lagoon or even the shallowest of semi-navigable rivers. Townships such as New Plymouth on the west coast, and Oamaru, Timaru and Napier on the east, sprang up alongside exposed beaches open to the full force of the worst moods of the sea. Their citizens usually faced a simple, but unpalatable choice – either build an artificial harbour from scratch at enormous cost or risk becoming bankrupt backwaters as settlements better endowed by nature picked up trade that might otherwise have gone to them.

Of course, it was never that simple. Roading, housing and commercial building all made big claims on slender purses. Civil leaders had to exercise financial restraint while promising the New Jerusalem. In the beginning at least, more paper than timber or concrete was shifted. In the pioneering period, most communities struggled on as best they could or else resorted to desperate and doomed expedients. Oamaruvians, horrified by the cost of building a breakwater port, and having watched the Pacific wash away their first unprotected jetty, tried to slap together a rather improbable British-style dock in the town's tiny lagoon. Further up the coast, the handful of residents near Temuka also proposed a dock in Milford Lagoon as an alternative to Timaru's troubled port. Napier delayed even longer, making the most of the shallow lagoon port at Port Ahuriri well into the twentieth century. It took the 1931 earthquake to tip the scales in favour of the deepwater breakwater port begun in the 1880s and largely mothballed about 1909. New Plymouth's harbour history was only a little less troubled.

Exposed beaches and open roadsteads are a combination rightly feared by mariners. New Zealand, surrounded on all sides by sea, has one of the most variable climates in the world and sudden changes in weather can overwhelm ships caught too close to land. Although masters always kept a 'weather eye' on the horizon, events sometimes moved too quickly for them to avoid disaster. The early history of all the major breakwater ports is littered with the wreckage of ships skippered by masters caught napping off a lee shore. Typical was the fate of

GREAT REDUCTIONS on previous rates.

October 30th, 1866.

OAMARU BOAT SERVICE.

WE BEG TO CALL ATTENTION to the following REGULATIONS respecting the conduct of the BOAT SERVICE on and after the 10th February :—

1. We cannot be responsible for any loss or damage, arising from whatever cause, during the process of Landing or Shipment ; but every care will be taken to avoid such loss or damage.

2. All Goods must be removed from the Beach as landed, and Charges paid, unless special arrangements are made to the contrary. All parties who do not contract for the delivery of Goods at any place in the Town, will apply for them at our Stores, where they will be Stored at their risk and expense till called for.

3. By special arrangements, Accounts may be rendered and settled Monthly, as heretofore.

TRAILL, ROXBY & CO.
Oamaru, 8th February, 1866.

DISSOLUTION OF PARTNERSHIP.

The landing service, very sensibly, offered no guarantees. *Oamaru Mail & Waitaki Reporter, 1866.*

the little 35-ton schooner *Prince Consort* at Timaru on 20 December 1866. She was lying at anchor in the roadstead when a strong nor'-easter sprang up:

> . . . she was ballasted with about 16 tons of loose shingle, which soon caused a "list" to one side, and a heavy broadside sea eventually put her hopelessly on her beam ends. Three men were on board and two of them, with the efficient aid rendered by the - *Alexandra* lifeboat, were fortunately rescued. Mr Bertram of H.M. Customs, gallantly rescued the third, who was holding on to a spar amid the kelp. The *Prince Consort* soon afterwards drifted on to the rocks and became a complete wreck.[1]

Oamaru, the only one of the major breakwater ports no longer open to commercial shipping, showed just how nasty these exposed roadsteads could be. Just 50 sea miles north of Dunedin, it grew slowly in the early 1850s, earning a precarious living servicing the large sheep runs that sprang up in the hinterland of the Free Church settlement of Dunedin. As a harbour, Oamaru had very little going for it. Cape Wanbrow, a bare, stubby little headland, provided some shelter from cold winter southerlies but no protection whatsoever against the predominant easterlies. And, as the settlers soon discovered, the easterlies could get very strong indeed.

At first the runholders made do with the open beach. Small schooners and cutters made their way cautiously up the coast from Dunedin to pick up the wool clip and drop off pioneering necessities. Everything – pigs, pianos and people – had to be put over the side into large, open surfboats. These sturdy craft were then sent through the breakers in a hair-raising surge of foam to the beach where sweat- and saltspray-soaked townsfolk would sledge them along the beach to a shed near the site of the former gasworks. Writing later in life, one early resident recalled that 'we were carried ashore through the surf by big strong boatmen, who waded out and took the passengers on their backs and carried them ashore'.[2]

An early description of the surfboat service had this to say about the mechanics of the operation:

> A stout hawser rope through slots at the bow and stern of a boat called the tender which was moored several chains off-shore, was secured to stanchions above the beach. A surf boat returning from a vessel arrived alongside the hawser and the bow oarsman would ship his oar and secure the hawser with a short boathook and hold the bow until the other oarsmen had swung the boat bow to seaward. Then the hawser would be shipped into slots at the bow and stern, and the crew would proceed to haul the boat hand over hand until the stern grounded on the beach. Then the boat would be firmly secured to the hawser so that the bow still remained afloat. By this time the shore crew would have waded out alongside and the cargo would be discharged. Having taken the return load the crew would grasp the hawser and a number of the shore crew would be ready to apply pressure to the stern of the boat as each wave lifted the bows; so that by united push and pull the boat was launched into deep water, the oarsman continuing to haul on the hawser until they arrived just behind the tender, when the hawser was cast off and the boat rowed to the waiting ship.[3]

Surfboats unloading cargo at Oamaru, about 1864. Such scenes were repeated throughout New Zealand until ports either died or developed breakwaters and sheltered wharves. *North Otago Museum*

Nothing was guaranteed, though, and the first sight of threatening clouds or a shift in the wind could spell the end of operations while the ship made for the safety of the open sea.

This had happened in 1854 on what was to have been the first of a series of regular visits by the 20-ton schooner *Anne Jane*. Otago merchant Johnny Jones had sent her up there in response to a request from local settlers. Although she left Dunedin in fine weather, conditions began to deteriorate as soon as she came within sight of the anchorage at Oamaru. When the wind showed no signs of abating, her master scurried back to Moeraki, 25 nautical miles to the south, where the local Maori feted their surprise guests. After enjoying this hospitality for a few days, the schooner's crew got underway, only to be driven back by a second storm. After another pleasant sojourn, the *Anne Jane* made a third attempt, this time escorted up the coast by every available Maori boat and canoe. On this happier occasion she managed to drop anchor and unload the stores which by now were desperately needed by the settlers, as an early correspondent explained:

> It is worthy of relation that during this 14 days' passage the settlers had had a bad time, and experienced very great anxiety as to the fate of the boat on account of scarcity of food, etc., at Oamaru. From the summit of the hill of Cape Wanbrow the settlers had watched the first approach of the boat and the anticipated arrival, but they were utterly at a loss for the reason of her turning round and heading for Moeraki. In order to prevent a recurrence of these little pleasantries, a deputation of the few settlers journeyed to Dunedin and interviewed Johnny Jones upon matters of shipping interest to the community.[4]

The whole voyage had taken 14 days. The same thing would happen in February 1862 when the 1742-ton full-rigged ship *Young America*, the first big ship to call at the 'port', had to flee to Port Chalmers in the face of a gale, leaving behind her anchor. On this occasion at least, locals could take some delight from the fact that the big ship managed to run aground in Otago Harbour.

The weather often defeated even the simplest shipping arrangements. In 1857, for example, when Charles Traill went to Timaru to pick up a whaleboat for the Oamaru landing service, he found that none of his northern neighbours wanted to help him sail her south, having feasted for many months on a diet of horror stories about the Oamaru anchorage. Able to get oars but unable to lay hands on sails, he jumped in, rowed the little craft offshore and then rigged up his blanket for the journey south. Fortunately the elements for once played fair with the lone sailor. Early the next morning a favourable breeze had him off Oamaru, where a large stone lashed to a rope served him as an anchor.

Trade gradually built up and more and more vessels found themselves obliged to take their chances off the beaches. Experienced masters preferred to unload during the day and scuttle back to the smaller but better protected Moeraki anchorage to shelter during the night. The threat from easterly gales was just too great to risk lying off the town during the night. The Otago Provincial Government had licensed someone to operate the boating service and a derrick had been put above the beach but, given the slenderness of the public purse, nothing else had been done to make the place any safer. Indeed, provincial harbourmaster William Thompson, himself a former skipper of the Dunedin–Oamaru trader *Geelong*, hated the place, explaining, to all who would listen, his preference for Moeraki.

Events soon gave him plenty of ammunition. On 10 October 1860 a gale sprang up, trapping four ships in the bay. Three managed to beat their way out to the open sea and safety but one, the brand-new 28-ton schooner *Oamaru Lass*, owned by Oamaru resident Captain Dwight, missed her opportunity and had to be run ashore. Fortunately the seas abated quickly and the little craft was refloated a few days later, with only minor damage. She survived until May 1869 when, under the name *Nora*, she went missing between Wellington and Lyttelton.

History almost repeated itself just a few days later when another south-east gale again sent shipping scattering. One schooner, the *Hawkhead*, made it to safety but minus her master, William Smith, who was swept overboard. Another vessel, a barque, was slow to respond and came so close to the breakers that residents could hear the shouts of her crew over the crashing of the waves. Only by extraordinary seamanship and long, skilful tacks did she escape.

Improvements were slow in coming. In November 1860 the Otago Provincial Government, bereft of sense as well as funds, had the hulk *Thomas and Henry* moored off the beach as a floating store. Fit for nothing, she merely added another hazard to the anchorage. Visiting masters had tired of chasing her up and down the coast long before the authorities towed her back south in February 1861.

The 1860s saw the establishment of the first rescue service, organised by Captain William Sewell, newly appointed head of the landing service. Its primitive but effective rescue gear was a large basket containing a light line and a heavy rope. This was taken to the beach by dray whenever danger threatened. Once there, the light line, which was attached to the heavy rope, was fired by a special gun. A rocket took line and rope out to the threatened ship, whose crew then pulled the rope aboard and rigged up a breeches buoy which could be used to get passengers and crew ashore through the surf.

Needless to say, it was never a pleasant ride. The rocket brigade (as the rescue service was generally termed) had one of its biggest tests on 27 August 1873 when two ships were dashed to pieces on the beach. Three seamen had been snatched from one, the 231-ton brig *Scotsman*, when a woman started the frantic journey. By then the waves were really pushing the *Scotsman* about, with the unfortunate result that the rope slackened and dumped her down into the boiling surf every time a wave crashed into the vessel. For several long, unforgettable moments the poor woman had to endure being submerged beneath the cold winter waves or jerked high up into the air. Eventually she made it ashore, dazed and drenched but alive.

Six years earlier, the local press had made mincemeat of the provincial government's other life-saving device, the lifeboat.

The barque *Premier* ashore at Oamaru in 1871. Owned at Oamaru, the 296-ton, nine-year-old vessel cost her owner dearly since she was insured for £1,500, barely half her value. *North Otago Museum*

A well-found, 10-oared, 10-metre-long craft arrived at Oamaru in May 1867. She had been sent there for the protection of shipping but was herself almost lost on her first test just six days later, when the locals tried to launch her to help the schooner *Mary Ann Christina*, which had signalled that she was sinking. Since no carriage or slipway had been provided, the bottom of the lifeboat was stove in when the rescue volunteers tried to launch her on makeshift wooden rollers. The schooner managed to patch herself up and limp back to port a few days later. The lifeboat was not so lucky, being abandoned and eventually swept by the sea into the lagoon, where it was quietly forgotten.

The smoky arrival of the province's first steam service in 1859 had improved matters slightly but even these vessels preferred to spend the night at Moeraki. Moorings laid by the provincial government also provided little security. The overseas ship *Star of Tasmania* broke them in 1864 and it remained a general rule that ships deserted the anchorage whenever a south-easter set in, leaving the newspapers to mutter indignantly about ships cruising 'off the port'.

It was only a matter of time before ships began to leave their bones on the beach. The 170-ton brigantine *Robert and Betsy* was the first fatality. Carrying a cargo of timber from Auckland, she piled up on the beach on the night of 5 April 1862 after parting her cable. No lives were lost but the ship soon became matchwood, littering the beach for quite a distance.

Three years later the 383-ton barque *Gazehound* followed suit. On 13 April, after two days of riding out a strong south-easterly gale, she broke loose from her moorings. Her master hastily put up canvas but when the wind died away she drifted ashore, striking about breakfast time. By midday the London-

Although the brigantine *Emulous* looks intact on the Oamaru foreshore in this May 1874 photograph, storms soon battered her into a total wreck. Of 157 tons register, the *Emulous* had been built at Hartsport, Hampshire in 1866. *North Otago Museum*

owned barque had broken up, scattering her cargo of 638 bales of wool up and down the beach. Fortunately all hands made it ashore unharmed.

In 1867 eight ships piled up on the beaches around the town, four becoming total losses. The first, the 86-ton schooner *Stately*, went ashore when a heavy sea swept the anchorage on 14 March. Six ships had been hugging the shore but four had managed to get away in time. The other casualty, the schooner *Vixen*, hit the beach but was refloated. The *Oamaru Times*, reporting yet another incident, did not mince its words:

> the *Stately* was thought to have been in comparative safety, the sea having subdued considerably; and after 11 o'clock an attempt was made to clear out of port. This unfortunately was beyond his power, and about 12 o'clock Captain Short had the misfortune to find his fine craft going fast ashore, which she did close by the Landing Place, and, as ill-luck would have it, amongst some rocks which abound there. . . . Various opinions have been passed as to the course pursued by the master; many considering that he was perfectly justified in holding on to the moorings, they being reckoned quite sufficient and secure for a vessel very much larger than the *Stately*. . . . Be that as it may, we have the fact before us – the moorings have been found shamefully insecure.[5]

Just a few months later, on 31 July, another sextet was sent scattering when a heavy south-east gale powered in. This time three made it to sea and safety. Of the others, the small cutter *Hope* and the schooner *Midlothian* were beached but later recovered. The principal casualty was the 133-ton brigantine *Vistula*. Her master felt that she lacked sufficient ballast and had to take her chances at the moorings. Just a fortnight later the schooner *Banshee* joined the casualty list. She was got off, battered but safe; others would not be so lucky.

On 23–24 November a heavy gale raised a tremendous sea along the east coast of Otago. As usual, Oamaru got the worst of it. The first victim was the 195-ton brig *Highlander*. Heavily laden with a cargo of New South Wales coal, she parted her cables and hit the shore where her old timbers soon became so much debris. Unluckier by far was the local schooner *Caroline*. This well-found little craft had made it out to sea and looked safe until the gale split her sails. Unable to gain an offing and filling with water from wave damage to her skylight and poop, she was run ashore to save life. She grounded alongside the remnants of the *Vistula* and quickly broke up.

The next year, 1868, was even more devastating, the casualties including the overseas ships *Star of Tasmania* and *Water Nymph*, the ketch *Otago* (see Chapter 5) and, perhaps most important of all, the town's brand-spanking-new jetty.

The jetty, exposed to the Pacific's worst caprices, was an act of stupidity almost without parallel in the history of New Zealand port construction. Designed on the cheap, but not built cheaply (like all such projects, costs blew out during construction), it proved almost useless during its brief months of life. Locals, only too painfully aware what the waves could do to any unprotected structure along their coastline, cried out for a sea wall. However, the cost was prohibitive and the provincial government's engineer had already recommended closing the port and running a railway line to Moeraki when disaster struck.

The tragedy at last forced everyone to look at a proper solution. After a short period of political bloodletting and 'indignation meetings', the townsfolk decided to improve on nature and dredge out a dock in the lagoon. The creek and lagoon were small and narrow but engineers and contractors believed that a satisfactory dock could be built. Protected at its entrance by twin sea walls (in much the same manner as training walls at river ports) and by a fairly respectable sea wall running off Cape Wanbrow, it would enable reasonably substantial (300-ton) ships to discharge their cargo right in the heart of the commercial district in complete safety. That was the theory, anyway.

Work began in April 1871 when contractors started lining both sides of the lagoon with heavy concrete blocks and fitting mooring chains. Then, with both walls to the entrance in place, they started digging the proposed channel. Again, though, fate intervened. Red-faced engineers quickly discovered that the digging was undermining the dock walls, which started to slide out of alignment. Work came to an abrupt and embarrassed halt. Weeks later the Pacific settled the matter for once and for all. A heavy storm swept over the shingle bank, scattering the blocks like children's toys. For the second time in three years, Oamaru's port lay in ruins.

Six months later, the first total wreck in three years, that of the brigantine *Emulous*, reminded residents that a permanent solution to the rapidly expanding town's transport woes would have to be found. This time they settled on the now obvious solution – a large artificial harbour protected by a long stone breakwater. Fortunately Oamaru's now bigger population base (it was New Zealand's ninth largest centre in 1878, after Dunedin, Christchurch, Wellington, Auckland, Nelson, Invercargill, Thames and Napier) meant that there was more money to throw at the problem. Work on the wrecked dock halted forever and the contractors started later that year on the 564-metre-long breakwater, approximately in line with the outer sea wall of the dock scheme. Construction work continued until 1884, often in the face of appalling conditions, and at considerable risk to contractors but, long before its completion, shipping was taking advantage of the shelter afforded by its finished portions.

This was reflected in the rapid fall-off in the number of fatal wrecks at the port. The *Premier* (wrecked twice in 1871, first on 31 July and then, fatally, on 29 September) had been followed onto the beach in 1872 by the schooner *Margaret Campbell* and the brigs *Emile* and *Scotsman*. In 1874 the number of total wrecks was again three – the schooner *Ocean Wave* and brigantine *Emulous* on the night of 2–3 May and the schooner *United Brothers*. The curious fate of the *Emulous* echoed that of the *Premier* several years earlier. Stranded but refloated, she was

The 3rd of May 1874 was a bleak day for the port of Oamaru with the three-master schooner *Ocean Wave* (*left*) and the brigantine *Emulous* (*right*) up on the beach. Neither sailed again. *North Otago Museum*

prepared for the voyage down to Port Chalmers for more permanent repairs. Three times she ventured out to sea, only to be beaten back to Oamaru. On the fourth time, on 11 October, fate intervened for the last time. Forced back when just 8 nautical miles from safety, the unlucky brigantine was pounded apart just 3 miles north of Oamaru later that day.

By 1875 the breakwater had advanced far enough into the bay to offer reasonable shelter for most craft visiting the port. With the opening of the first wharf (Macandrew Wharf) that year, fewer ships now had to take their chances out in the roadstead. At the same time, the more widespread use of steamships meant that far fewer of the port's traders were so vulnerable to the whims of wind and tide.

Shipping casualties fell away dramatically. There was only one total wreck at Oamaru in 1875, that of the fine three-masted schooner *Elderslie* in May, but no more ships came to grief until June 1879, when the ketch *Franklin Belle* broke adrift while lying off Normanby Wharf and hit the beach. Four years later, Oamaru's last major shipwreck occurred when the Otago fishing schooner *Friendship* hit the beach while trying to enter port in bad weather.

For the next 91 years that the port was open to commercial shipping, no more trading vessels would be wrecked at Oamaru. Here, as at Timaru, New Plymouth and Napier, the breakwater port, though expensive, proved its worth. A measure of its success is that none of these ports has witnessed a major total wreck this century.

The nearest thing was in 1964 when the big New Zealand Shipping Company/Hain freighter *Treneglos* (9976 tons, 1963) ran aground 1¼ miles south of Timaru. The *Treneglos* had just

48

The salvage of the *Treneglos* took five days and the best efforts of the Otago Harbour Board's then-new tug *Otago* (502 tons). Litigation over the salvage claim took much longer! The *Treneglos*, last of a distinguished line for this famous Cornish company, finished her days at the hands of Chinese shipbreakers in 1985.
Langwood Studios and S. A. Bremford

left the South Canterbury port on 12 November and was heading for Dunedin to complete loading for Britain when she struck rocks just a short distance north of where the *Elginshire* (4579 tons, 1891) had gone ashore in March 1892. For the next five days the *Treneglos* lay pinned to the rocks until the Otago Harbour Board tug *Otago* (502 tons, 1956) pulled her clear. Damage was extensive and took several months to repair.

Notes
1. *North Otago Times*, 25 December 1866.
2. *Beginnings: Early History of North Otago*, Oamaru Mail, Oamaru, 1934 and 1978, p. 132.
3. *Ibid.*, p. 50.
4. *Ibid.*, p. 33.
5. *Oamaru Mail and Waitaki Reporter*, 19 March 1867.

Part 2

EARLY WRECKS

By the time that this photograph was taken in the 1890s, shipwrecks were just a memory at Oamaru. The first jetty, swept away in the disaster of 1868, was located near the start of the breakwater, just off the right-hand edge of the photograph. *Gavin McLean*

Timaru shared the same coastline and the same problems as Oamaru, also losing many early traders. These photographs show the wreck of the brig *Fairy Queen* (214 tons, 1863), which was blown ashore in heavy seas and strong winds on 27 August 1873, along with the schooner *Duke of Edinburgh* and the ketch *Wanderer*. *The Duke* escaped with severe damage but the other two broke up. *Bascard Collection, Alexander Turnbull Library*

Chapter 5

SEVERAL AT ONCE – OAMARU 1868 AND TIMARU 1882

'The late hour at which our notice was penned and the circumstance that our reporter himself was well nigh drowned, must be our excuse for so meagre details of a disaster the most serious which has ever visited this port,' the *Oamaru Times and Waitaki Reporter* apologised to its readers on the morning of Tuesday 4 February 1868. It need not have bothered. With all the clean-up work facing them, many of the townspeople would not have had time to pore over their four-page newspapers.

The storm that swept onto the North Otago coast on 3 February 1868 was one of the worst ever to strike the province. It buffeted anchorages from the Catlins in the south to Lyttelton in the north before striking inland. Howling east-south-east winds and pouring rain caused rivers from South Otago to North Canterbury to burst their banks, flooding farmland, sweeping away isolated settlers, demolishing bridges, damaging buildings and wrecking business premises. Many people, by no means all of them seafarers, lost their lives on 3–4 February.

It all began innocently enough with the Oamaru beachmaster, Captain William Sewell, running up the Blue Peter. This was the traditional safety warning for shipping in the bay to head out to open sea. At the time four ships were lying off the township, the big overseas woolships *Star of Tasmania* and *Water Nymph*, the ketch *Otago* and the schooner *Emu*. The *Star of Tasmania* was a fine, clipper-rigged ship of 623 tons register. Built by Hall's Aberdeen yard 12 years before, the *Star* had been calling at Oamaru for several years to collect the annual wool clip for the London market. The *Water Nymph*, at 548 tons register, was slightly smaller. She had started life in 1855 as a corvette for the French Navy but had been bought while still on the stocks and adapted to mercantile purposes. She had a reputation for fast passages. Her owner at the time of her loss was the renowned English firm, Shaw Savill and Company.

The *Star* had 22 people aboard: the master, two officers, 10 ABs, one ordinary seaman, the cook, carpenter, steward and boatswain, a woman passenger and her two children and, lastly, a boy named McLean. Before the day was out, the two Baker children and three seamen, who included David Petrie of Arbroath, Scotland and William Brooks of London, would lose their lives in Oamaru's worst maritime disaster.

The smaller craft were better placed for a quick getaway. At 1330, just half an hour after reading the signal, the *Emu* spread her canvas and worked out. Hauling as close to the wind as possible, she was soon out of sight of land. Half an hour later the *Otago* set her mainsail, staysail and jib and also stood out.

The larger ships stayed put. It was later discovered that the *Star*, at least, could not make out the signals on the flagstaff. Worse, she blocked the *Water Nymph*'s escape route. In frustration Sewell shouted commands to the *Water Nymph*, which was lying to leeward of the *Star*, to run out before it was too late. The wind blew his words back in his face. At 1530 he ran up another signal to 'proceed to sea without delay'.[1] Locals, aware of the tell-tale signs of impending disaster, began to worry. A large crowd had already begun to gather down at the anchorage when Sewell noticed the *Star of Tasmania* dragging her chains.

The Otago Provincial Government moorings to which she had made fast offered little security. The *Star* had broken them on an earlier visit, as had other ships. The provincial government's chartered schooner *Caroline* had relaid them whenever necessary but no one could pretend that they were a substitute for a proper breakwater. Some idea of the low esteem in which they were held can be gauged from an *Oamaru Times* report of 2 April 1867:

> Another instance of the absolute inefficiency of the present moorings in our Bay was afforded on Tuesday last, when during the smart southerly gale that was blowing the barque *A.W. Stevens* went adrift. Parting with the moorings the chief officer (Captain Brown being on shore at the time), to ensure the safety of the vessel, cut the hawser springs, slipped 75 fathoms of the best bower chain, got up sail and stood to sea. The Captain, accompanied by Captain Sewell, at once followed the vessel in a boat and overtook her about three hours after the accident. A party of ladies were on board at the time on a visit to Mrs Brown; they were landed on Saturday.

On 3 February 1868 the moorings were again found sadly wanting. Later in the afternoon they snapped, sending the *Star of Tasmania* drifting about 400–500 metres before her master, Captain William Culbert, brought her up by dropping the starboard anchor. The forecastle party set about fishing up the broken chain and then dropped the port anchor. It held, but only briefly. Suddenly both anchor cables parted with a jolt and the big ship drove shorewards rapidly.

The crew made desperate attempts to hoist sail. By now, though, the *Star*'s decks were being swept by huge rollers which sent deck cargo crashing everywhere; it was suicidal to even think about working the ship. All hands took to the rigging and braced themselves for the final crash onto the beach which took place at about 1900 hours. The *Star of Tasmania* fetched up broadside-on, opposite the Presbyterian church with her head to the southward. In the words of the newspaper correspondent sheltering on the spray-lashed beach:

> There was by now an awful sea on, the breakers being of a magnitude never before seen on this part of the coast. The vessel rolled to and fro upon the shingle, and being heavily laden, strained and creaked as the enormous masses of water struck her and knocked her about. In a very few minutes the copper on the starboard side was torn off her timbers, and the water pouring through her seams showed that the port bilge had been driven in. Wave after wave leaped clean over her, and the vessel finally fell over on her port side, her masts quickly afterwards falling into the sea.

Now the real drama began. Rightly suspecting that the *Star of Tasmania* would not long remain intact, the passengers and crew crawled forward to the starboard bow. Some had very close escapes during this short journey, the luckiest being Captain Culbert, who leaped off the *Star*'s poop just as it started to break up. Less fortunate were two of the child passengers, who drowned in their berths. As a refuge, though, the forecastle had its limitations. The seas were crashing over the full length of the helpless ship, bow included. Each wave brought with it a deadly combination of bales of wool, iron tanks, spars, planks and timbers. While struggling forward, both Culbert and the mate were struck by wreckage.

On shore, the would-be rescuers could offer little besides sympathy:

> To add to the miseries of the scene it was raining as we never saw it rain before, the water coming down in torrents and making it impossible to look towards the vessel. The spray, too, came over in great white sheets, and struck upon the faces of the hundreds who were gathered upon the beach in the hope of rendering assistance to the unfortunate crew, with a cutting violence which made it appear as though it were a shower of needles.

Several times the rescuers tried to get a line to the ship but each time the wind, by now shrieking onto the land at gale force, frustrated them, even though they were just 10–12 metres from the *Star of Tasmania*.

At that point Stevens, the *Star*'s mate, leaped from the forecastle and struck out for the shore. He was lost to sight, then glimpsed again when a receding wave showed him on his hands and knees about halfway between ship and shore. Another wave was just rearing up, bristling with dozens of pieces of timber and debris, when several bystanders, judging the moment perfectly, rushed in and dragged him ashore, the sea sucking at their feet as they raced the last life-saving metres. A huge cheer went up but Stevens could only shout in dismay, 'The line! The line! I've lost the line!' He had gone over the side with a line but had had to let go of it during his struggles in the surf. Two other crewmen, following his example, also leaped into the surf and were dragged ashore more through good luck than planning.

The next death occurred when a fourth man unwisely followed his shipmates. Judging his moment poorly, he got caught up in the undertow, was swept around past the bow and carried out to sea. A fifth would-be swimmer repeated the same error, being dragged out past the bow, desperately clutching a bale of wool. Shocked by the sight of the man being swept to certain death, the onlookers shouted orders to the others not to try any further jumps. A boatman named George Mackenzie then made the first of many attempts to get a line aboard. Time and time again he waded out into the boiling surf and hurled his line, only to have it fall short. He continued this dangerous dance with death until sheer exhaustion took over.

To add to the misery of the survivors, darkness was now falling. Townsfolk brought up a drayload of firewood, oakum and turpentine and soon had the beach lit up by the glow of an immense bonfire. At that point, police sergeant Bullen waded back into the surf, a rope fastened around his waist for security. Like Mackenzie's, his initial efforts were in vain. One throw did put the end of the rope on the forecastle but in the darkness no one saw it in time and it fell overboard. Then a wave washed Bullen off his feet and he had to struggle to avoid being washed away.

Still, no one wanted to admit defeat yet. Captain Steward of the Volunteers tried to fire a line to the ship, using a rifle and a stout fishing line in lieu of the rocket gun which was not available. It failed, the line and ramrod parting company. While Steward had been taking pot-shots into the dark, another even more muddle-headed group dragged up the useless lifeboat we last met in Chapter 4. One look at the surf convinced its proponents of their folly, however, and the boat stayed on the shingle.

George Mackenzie, his breath recovered, then threw himself back into the surf. It looked as though his bravery would again go unrewarded until 2240 hours, when the rope finally hit the *Star*'s deck and was scooped up by a crewman. He made it fast, allowing the first rescuer, boating company employee Duncan Young, to clamber aboard just minutes later, amid loud cheering from the beach. Stevens followed, returning with young master McLean, whose parents lived in the town, clinging to his shoulders. One by one the rest of the passengers and crew slid down the lifeline through rain and saltspray to the safety of the beach. Stevens returned for the one woman passenger, Mrs Baker, whom he also slung over his shoulder. Let the newspaper take up the story:

> He then commenced descending the life-line with his burden, but just as he reached the water an immense wave dashed over the vessel and hid them for a moment from view. As the wave retired Stevens was seen hanging to the rope with Mrs Baker still clinging to him. Again a wave submerged them, and it was feared that they must both be carried away, but on its subsidence they were found to still be safe and in a few moments Stevens had got near enough to grasp the helping hands held out to him, and the lady and her preserver were brought safely ashore amid loud cheers. The first words uttered by the brave woman were "Never mind me, save the poor, dear Captain".

By now only two sailors, Duncan Young and Captain Culbert remained aboard. Both sailors made it ashore safely, to be followed by Culbert. Last off was hero of the night, Duncan Young. In a manner later generations of Hollywood fans would have appreciated, he ran to the waist of the ship, jumped on a portion of her mast which was wedged underneath the keel and plunged ashore just as a wave retired. He hit terra firma to the cheers of hundreds of drenched but happy onlookers.

Other dramas had been in progress while all this was going on. The *Water Nymph*, which had been moored closer to the shore, started dragging her anchor about half an hour after the *Star of Tasmania* struck the beach. The *Star* had effectively blocked her until then, but now it was too late to contemplate escape. At about 1700 the *Water Nymph*'s master, Captain Edwin Babot, dropped his other pick, praying that it would hold. But, as with the *Star of Tasmania*, no weight of anchors could hold a vessel under such trying conditions. Within minutes both anchor cables had parted and Babot was ordering the crew to put on all canvas in order to drive the ship as far up the beach as possible. The *Water Nymph* struck the beach about 100 metres north of the *Star of Tasmania*, with her bow pointing northward. The canvas canted her onto her port side, allowing the crew to escape safely with all their effects.

Captain Babot, master of the ill-fated *Water Nymph*. *White Wings*

The landing place at Oamaru in the early 1870s, showing the surfboats up on the beach and the cables leading out into the sea. The narrow-gauge railway in the left foreground was a sign of better things to come – the construction site of the long-awaited breakwater that would preclude the chance of another *Star of Tasmania* storm ever again wreaking such damage on the port. *North Otago Museum*

The ketch *Otago*, which we left clawing her way out to sea under close-reefed canvas, also came to grief that night. She had almost made good her escape by 1730 hours when her rudderhead carried away, leaving her unmanageable. Her master, Captain Campbell, lowered the mainsail and pointed her at the shore. She hit the beach approximately 13 kilometres north of Oamaru. She grounded bow-on but so strong were the breakers that within minutes everything about decks had been wrenched free and the hull was starting to break apart. All hands scrambled ashore, but only with great difficulty and minus all their possessions. The *Otago* broke up almost instantly, scattering her cargo of 160 bags of coal and stacks of timber far and wide. In the morning nothing could be seen of her but her name board and a few spars and planks.

The morning dawned on a port in complete ruins. The brand-new jetty, built only months before with no protection from the sea, was just so much firewood, its T-end missing and the approachway badly undermined. Its decking was splintered and scattered everywhere. So were most of the surfboats of the Oamaru Landing Service and Traill, Roxby & Co. Wreckage from bridges, buildings and the three ships stretched from Oamaru up the coast to Timaru where the same gale had driven the well-known 142-ton paddle steamer *William Miskin* ashore and completely demolished her. Normally her engines would have guaranteed her safety but at 0130 the seas washing over the ship extinguished her boiler fires, leaving her as helpless as the Oamaru sailers. The pumps failed and the anchors parted about an hour later, sending the ship up onto the shingle, just missing a rocky promontory. Fortunately only one man lost his life in the Timaru wreck, but it was a warning that the South Canterbury port was just as vulnerable should nature ever turn this nasty again.

It did. Timaru shared a coastline similar to that of Oamaru and a list of troubles almost as long. Like its southern rival, the town had dithered, debated and dallied while the wrecks piled up along its beaches. Like Oamaru, it was finally getting around to building an expensive artificial breakwater port during the early 1880s.

In May 1882 some might have been forgiven for thinking that it was all a bit too late. Timaru had not been kind to shipping that year. First up onto the rocks, on 14 January, had been the big iron-hulled, full-rigged ship *City of Cashmere*. After parting her cable in light seas (something that at first went unnoticed by those aboard) she drifted up onto the beach about 6 kilometres from the port. An attempt to intercept her and tow her to safety with the steam launch *Lillie Durham* failed and she had to be left to drift. The rocket brigade rescued her crew and the big ship went to pieces the next day.

The next casualty was another big craft, the 1047-ton barque *Duke of Sutherland*, which had arrived from Algoa Bay on 25 March to load wheat. Cargo handling had been delayed by shortages of boats and labour and the master had been complaining to the Timaru Harbour Board about being left for so long in such a dangerous position. He failed to jump the queue and the *Duke of Sutherland* was still lying in the roadstead on the evening of 2 May 1882 when disaster struck.

Although it was very low water, she was drawing about 5.5 metres in an anchorage that had about 8.5 metres of water at low tide. Larger ships had already used that spot without incident. A heavy sea had been running all day but as all the ships anchored off the partly built breakwater were riding their anchors easily, there were no fears for their safety. Shortly after 1700 hours, however, blue lights and rockets indicated that something was amiss aboard the *Duke of Sutherland*. Harbourmaster Captain James Mills called out the rocket brigade in readiness. But, because the steamer *Waitaki* had passed her just moments before without observing any signs of trouble, no one was too worried at first.

An hour later a boat containing men from the *Duke* pulled alongside the landing steps with bad news. They revealed that at about 1700 an unusually big sea had dumped the stern of their ship on the seabed. Captain Henry Rowlands, who was in his cabin at the time, went topside, certain that his command had been struck by a spar or similar floating object. He was still looking for it a few minutes later when the *Duke of Sutherland* repeated the performance, but this time with a much heavier crash. Now there was no room for further doubts. Rowlands immediately sent up distress signals that were answered by another overseas trader, the ship *Ben Venue*. Her master, Captain William McGowan, at once dispatched a boat.

By the time the *Ben Venue*'s lifeboat pulled alongside, Rowlands's men had discovered that the impact of the ship's striking had carried away her rudder post. Water was pouring in and the *Duke* was plainly settling by the stern. By 2000, when most of the crew was ordered into the boats, the water was up to her 'tween decks. Mills and Rowlands later rowed back out to see what could be done to save her. Harbour board diver William Collis opened the lazarette hatch and discovered 'a considerable quantity of water in the ship',[2] although he could not discover the source of the leak. While Collis was exploring, Rowlands and Mills had succeeded in getting the pumps working again. For several hours they managed to keep up with the inrush of water.

Mills's biggest fear was that the *Duke of Sutherland* might sink right in the middle of the entrance to the port. At 0400 he ran a line to the *Ben Venue* and had the big barque hauled well to the northward. Then the cable was slipped and the *Duke* abandoned to drift down towards Caroline Bay in order to keep her clear of the other vessels in the roadstead. The heavy sea rapidly carried her away and cast her up on the beach just under half a kilometre from her original anchorage. Being exceptionally strongly built, she remained almost intact until 1600 when her deck collapsed and she fell over onto her starboard side, her main topmast and most of her yards coming away. While a growing crowd of hundreds watched, Rowlands secured many of her spars, all of her boats and other valuable items.

Lamenting the event, the *Timaru Herald* commented that:

> The mishap to the *Duke of Sutherland* is a most unfortunate one, coming so soon as it does after the wreck of the *City of Cashmere*. We are glad to learn that our Harbor [sic] Master has, from first to last, objected to large vessels being brought so close in, and that only a few days ago, although urgently pressed to do so, he refused to bring the ship *City of Perth* nearer the Landing Service than she at present lies. The hardship in the present case, so far as the vessel

and the port is concerned, is that she was like the *City of Cashmere*, all but ready for sea, and but for the want of working appliances on the part of the Harbor [*sic*] Board, would ere this have been on her way to England.

Twelve days later it was the turn of the *City of Perth* and the *Ben Venue*. Early on the morning of 14 May conditions at the port started to deteriorate, showing the old pattern that, to local eyes, always spelled trouble – big seas running with huge rollers showing far out to the horizon. To make it worse, the day remained calm and sunny.

The 999-ton *Ben Venue*, caught lying stern-on to the sea, was soon shipping big rollers over her stern. These hammer blows caused her cargo to shift and the ship to list to starboard. By now she was in serious trouble. At 0900 hours a third anchor was dropped to replace the second, which had parted minutes before. Four hours later both cables had parted and Captain MacGowan had ordered the crew to abandon their ship. An hour after that the *Ben Venue*, her bow still pointed towards the shore, struck under the cliffs at Caroline Bay, where she turned broadside-on, her shattered decks facing seawards.

Her crew made for the *City of Perth*. No sooner had they scrambled aboard than their place of refuge began to get into trouble, parting her cables. Both crews took to the boats, leaving the *City of Perth* to ground alongside the *Ben Venue* on an even keel. For the thousands of Timaru people gathered on the cliffs above, the two big craft presented an awesome spectacle as the breakers sent spray flying over their rigging. Amazingly, the *City of Perth* was almost undamaged and would be refloated later to become the New Zealand Shipping Company's *Turakina*.

Meanwhile, high drama had been acted out among the breakers. Mills disapproved of the decision to abandon the *City of Perth* and, seeing an improvement in the weather, decided to do something to save her. Accompanied in a separate gig by the master of the *City of Perth*, Captain C. Macdonald, Mills headed out for her in a whaler, with the intention of halting her drift. They scrambled onto her deck just as the last cable parted. Admitting that it was hopeless, Mills ordered some of his men into one of the *City of Perth*'s lifeboats and then directed the three small craft back to shore.

Just short of the lee of the breakwater, tragedy struck when a heavy sea swamped the lifeboat and threw most of its occupants into the water. Mills steered his whaleboat straight for the men but was himself swamped by another rogue sea. The third boat kept clear of trouble a little longer but eventually she also succumbed to the force of the breakers. Her capsize left almost 40 men struggling in the mountainous seas.

What a sight it must have been! Although the seas were rough, the skies were still clear and the wind light. The Timaru lifeboat *Alexandra* was launched and now made for the boats at full speed. Her dramatic mercy dash, which involved three capsizes and rightings, was the stuff of good Victorian melodrama. She drew alongside the men struggling in the water

One of the most dramatic pictures ever taken of a New Zealand shipwreck, with the *City of Perth* and the *Ben Venue* being battered by the breakers at Caroline Bay, Timaru on 14 May 1882. *Wellington Maritime Museum & Gallery*

Incredibly, the *City of Perth* survived her ordeal and, repaired and sold to new owners, re-entered service as the New Zealand Shipping Company's *Turakina*. *Wellington Maritime Museum & Gallery*

and plucked as many as possible from their peril. But for some it was already too late. The spill had cost the lives of two of the crew of the *City of Perth* and five Timaru watermen. Two seamen suffered serious injury and Mills would die of injuries later that day.

That was the last such wrecking at Timaru. Within a few years the breakwater was complete and the casualty rate had fallen away to almost nothing.

Notes
1. The account of the gale of February 1868 is drawn from the *Oamaru Times and Waitaki Reporter* of 4 and 8 February 1868.
2. The Timaru wreck accounts are based on contemporary issues of the *Timaru Herald* and Sir Henry Brett, *White Wings* Vol. 1, Auckland, 1924, pp. 129–132.

Dismasting at sea, although not common, was rightly feared by mariners. These cards, prepared by enterprising Port Chalmers photograph D. A. de Maus, depict one of the most celebrated examples, that of the ship *Dallam Tower* (1499 tons, 1866). In mid-July 1873 the ship was en route from London for Port Chalmers when a hurricane dismasted her, stove in her hatches and threw her on her beam ends. All navigational instruments were washed overboard, along with most deck fittings and the crew's gear. But, under the command of the enterprising first mate, George Donald McDonald, the crew manned the pumps and rode out the storm, fashioning three crude jury masts from spare yards and wreckage. Fortunately strong following winds favoured the *Dallam Tower* from then on and the battered ship limped into Melbourne some weeks later after an epic voyage of 2000 miles under jury rig. When the ship eventually made it back to London the master, Captain John Davies, whom one passenger criticised for not taking in sail soon enough, was dismissed. *Wellington Maritime Museum & Gallery*

"DALLAM TOWER" BEGINNING OF THE STORM.

"DALLAM TOWER" STORM AT IT'S HEIGHT.

"DALLAM TOWER" UNDER JURY MASTS.

Chapter 6

WITHOUT TRACE

When a ship hits rocks or sinks within sight of the shore there are no insoluble questions of what happened, where and when. Usually the only tasks that remain are to count the survivors, file the insurance claim and establish responsibility for the accident. After a bit of legal bickering the authorities can close their files. In the days of sail, though, a surprising number of ships simply vanished without trace, leaving behind a host of unanswered questions.

Before the advent of homing beacons, radar and air searches, it was all too common for a ship to disappear from the face of the ocean. After a few weeks beyond her expected arrival time she might be listed as overdue by the shipping company; if she was on a coastal voyage, other ships might be sent out to look for her. In the case of the Home trade ships, nothing more could be done than request other ships to keep a lookout for the missing craft as they crossed her anticipated route. In the southern oceans, of course, this was as hopeless as looking for the proverbial needle in a haystack. A few months later an insurance company or a court of inquiry would declare her 'missing'. And that was that.

When we think of ships lost at sea, images come to mind of mid-ocean catastrophes, big clippers bowling headlong into huge icebergs or foundering in the teeth of oceanic storms of unimaginable violence. In fact, the sea, unpredictable always, claimed at least as many New Zealand coasters as Home trade ships. Many little coastal craft shuttling between anchorages only a few nautical miles apart disappeared without leaving so much as a plank or lifebuoy to mark their passing. To give the example of just one port, Oamaru experienced three such losses between 1875 and 1883. Two went down in 1875 alone. The first, the 75-ton schooner *Euphrosyne*, sailed from Dunedin for Oamaru with a load of coal on 14 March and simply vanished without trace. With her went a crew of six men. Despite an extensive sea and shore search not a fragment of wood was ever discovered. How could a well-found craft disappear during a voyage of 50 nautical miles along a comparatively well-settled coastline?

On 9 July another ship, this time the 186-ton brig *Chanticleer*, sailed from Oamaru into oblivion, taking with her 10 people.

Right: The *Dunedin*, which carved her niche in New Zealand history by carrying the first successful shipment of refrigerated meat to Britain in 1882. This photograph, taken at the old Port Chalmers graving dock, shows her as she appeared during her moment of glory, ship-rigged and with a black hull. *Wellington Maritime Museum & Gallery*

Below: This historic photograph shows the *Dunedin* (now painted in Shaw Savill & Albion colours) leaving Oamaru Harbour in 1885, where she would be a frequent visitor until her loss. Other ships in this scene include the steamers *Elderslie* and *Korowai* at Sumpter Wharf, the brig *Zaima* at Normanby Wharf, the steamer *Mawhera* at Cross Wharf and the barque *Excelsior* at Macandrew Wharf. *Hocken Library*

She was bound for Hobart but never made her destination and is presumed to have foundered at sea with all hands. Three years later another small vessel disappeared after leaving the North Otago port on a coastal trip. The ship concerned was the 10-year-old schooner *Fiery Cross* (72 tons). Laden with wheat, she sailed for Onehunga in the company of the brigantine *Oamaru* (which was owned by the same person), but although the *Oamaru* arrived in port safely, nothing more was heard of the *Fiery Cross*.

By far the most famous vessel to go missing from Oamaru was the barque *Dunedin* of frozen meat fame. Built in 1874 by Robert Duncan & Co. of Glasgow as a full-rigged ship for Patrick Henderson, the *Dunedin* (1320 tons) spent seven years on the New Zealand run with migrants and general cargo before being selected to carry the first trial shipment of refrigerated meat to Britain. Fitted with a Bell-Coleman cold air plant, she loaded the historic first shipment of meat at the Port of Otago. A machinery fault meant the first load had to be dumped on the local market, but the problem was soon rectified and the ship loaded another shipment from the Totara

Estate (outside Oamaru), sailing from Port Chalmers on 15 February 1882. She delivered her cargo to London 98 days later. The success of this shipment marked the beginning of the New Zealand agricultural industry and was a key to the economic recovery of the 1890s.

The *Dunedin* returned on several occasions and, following the completion of the Oamaru harbour works, became a regular caller at the North Otago port, loading frozen meat, rabbit skins and other general cargo direct from the district. By 1890 she no longer carried migrants and had been cut down to barque rig, but was still in fine order. At 0130 hours on 20 March 1890 the barque left Oamaru in tow of the Union Company collier *Wareatea*, bound for London direct. She was never seen again. Oamaru harbourmaster William Sewell had no doubts about her seaworthiness; her master, Captain Roberts, had remarked to him the day before that the ship had never been in better fettle, having 80 tonnes more stiffening than on previous voyages.[1] At the time she carried a complement of 34. She was spoken to once before reaching Cape Horn and was believed to have foundered in a storm or hit an iceberg, several of which were reported at the time by other ships.

Ice was a hazard never far from the minds of passengers and crew alike. Since the 1850s masters on the Australasian run had been taking their ships down into previously little-frequented southern waters in order to obtain favourable winds. They did this in belated response to the 1847 publication by John Thomas Towson, a scientific examiner of masters and mates at Liverpool, of a small but radical book which stated what we now know to be obvious – that because the earth is a sphere, the shortest distance between any two points must be a curve. Three years later, Captain Godfrey, in the *Constance*, tested the new theory by swinging further south – the so-called composite great circle route – where he picked up favourable winds and made a record passage to Adelaide. At first others were reluctant to follow him into these cold and dangerous waters but the 1850s Australian goldrushes brought demands for record passages and the southern route, with all its perils and freezing temperatures, became the normal one for people migrating to the Australasian colonies.

Once down in southern latitudes, mariners ran for up to 2000 miles whenever the ice permitted. They encountered many hazards: fierce storms, the danger of collision in fog and, of course, icebergs by the thousands. The last-named were one of the greatest threats imaginable to sailing ships. Many migrant ships reported terrifying encounters with 'continent-sized' icebergs and fields that seemed to stretch to the horizon in all directions. Whenever fog-bound in ice-infested waters, masters took careful readings of water temperature (low temperatures betrayed the presence of 'bergs) and beefed up the lookouts but, no matter how careful they were, danger still existed whenever icebergs were nearby.

Typical was the experience of the renowned *Margaret Galbraith*. Home-bound in 1893, the ship had entered warmer waters and had relaxed her guard, even though the weather was squally and a mist hung about. Suddenly, the lookout spotted the weak sunlight glinting off a huge iceberg right in the path of the ship. Her master promptly swung away but a seaman recalled that 'as we swung up into the wind you could have jumped from our quarter on to the ice that had so nearly been our doom'.[2] When the mist cleared, the ship found itself in the midst of a huge field of icebergs of all shapes and sizes. It was a miracle that she had avoided them for so long. For the next four nerve-wracking days the ship threaded her way through a field that included some ice pinnacles nearly 100 metres tall. The biggest, encountered a few days later, was thought to be 75 kilometres long and 300–350 metres high. Other ships encountering these dangerous floating islands that season, the *Turakina, Loch Torridon, Cutty Sark, Brier Holme* and *Charles Racine*, all agreed with these estimates.

Other New Zealand traders had similar adventures. The *Electra*, caught in an ice-field in 1869, could see nothing but mountainous icebergs in all directions. In early 1895 the *Himalaya* had to dodge them for almost 2000 miles. The *Matoaka*, which avoided them successfully in 1867 on a run from London to Lyttelton, is believed to have gone down after striking one two years later on a return voyage from the same New Zealand port.

Perhaps the strangest tale in our maritime history concerns a likely victim of these icebergs, the *Marlborough*. But for the lack of convincing, well-documented evidence she might have carried off the title of New Zealand's *Marie Celeste*. The - *Marlborough* was another fine product of Robert Duncan's shipbuilding skills. Launched in June 1876 for John Leslie and retained in his ownership, although for practical purposes virtually part of the Shaw Savill & Albion fleet, she was a fine full-rigged flyer of 1124 tons. Between 1876 and 1889 she completed 14 safe and speedy passages out to New Zealand.

On 11 January 1890 she sailed from Lyttelton for Britain in excellent condition. This was the last anyone heard of her. After a decent interval Lloyds listed her as 'missing' and it was presumed that she had blundered into an iceberg in southern waters and gone down with all hands (29 crew and one passenger). Or had she?

In 1919, according to Sir Henry Brett, British newspapers carried a most extraordinary report of the alleged rediscovery of the long-lost ship off the coast of Cape Horn. The master of a vessel bound from Lyttelton to Britain was quoted as saying:

> We were off the rocky coves near Punta Arenas, keeping near the land for shelter. The coves are deep and silent, the sailing is difficult and dangerous. It was a weirdly wild evening, with the red orb of the sun setting on the horizon. The stillness was uncanny. There was a shining green light reflected on the jagged rocks on our right. We rounded a point into a cleft rock. Before us, a mile or more across the water, stood a sailing vessel, with the barest shreds of canvas fluttering in the breeze.

We signalled and hove to. No answer came. We searched the "stranger" with our glasses. Not a soul could we see; not a movement of any sort. Masts and yards were picked out in green – the green of decay. The vessel lay as if in a cradle. It recalled "the Frozen Pirate", a novel that I read years ago. I conjured up the vessel of the novel, with her rakish masts and the outline of her six small cannon traced with snow. At last we came up. There was no sign of life on board. After an interval our first mate, with a number of the crew, boarded her. The sight that met their gaze was thrilling. Below the wheel lay the skeleton of a man. Treading warily on the rotten decks, which cracked and broke in pieces as they walked, they encountered three skeletons in the hatchway. In the mess-room were the remains of ten bodies, and six others were found, one alone, possibly the captain, on the bridge. There was an uncanny stillness around and a dank smell of mould which made the flesh creep. A few remnants of books were discovered in the captain's cabin, and a rusty cutlass. Nothing more weird in the history of the sea can ever have been seen. The first mate examined the still faint letters on the bow, and after much trouble read "Marlborough, Glasgow".[3]

Fact or fiction? We shall never know for sure but instinct, backed up by a little research, suggests that this is just another seafarer's tall tale. The cutlass sounds suspiciously Hollywood and the port of registry was usually found inscribed on the stern, although another report, from a French book, *Mysteries of*

A de Maus shot of another interesting ship, the *Marlborough*. Logic suggests that she went missing in 1890 after striking ice in southern waters; some, though, say that she was found adrift off South America, her decks covered with the skeletons of her crew. *Wellington Maritime Museum & Gallery*

Long-distance sailing, especially at southern latitudes, brought many hazards. Here the *Sam Mendel* (1034 tons, 1861) lies at Port Chalmers looking pretty sorry for herself after losing her bowsprit and foremast in a tornado-like wind in southern waters on 10 August 1881. The mast snapped less than a metre above the deck, forcing the crew to cut away some of the rest of her rigging in order to save the mainmast. Although the *Sam Mendel* experienced several stormy passages, she survived until 1908–09 when she was broken up at Genoa. *De Maus photograph, Wellington Maritime Museum & Gallery*

the Sea by Robert de la Croix, dates the sighting as 1913 and reports the words 'Marlborough, Glasgow' as being on the stern. The *London Evening Standard* report gave the alleged discoverer as Captain G. Hadrup of the barque *British Isles* but no person of that name is known to have commanded that ship. Furthermore, as shipping enthusiast Duncan Haws points out, the claim to have found skeletons in the poop-house of the *Marlborough* is unlikely since that ship did not have such a structure; nor did she have painted ports (a Shaw Savill & Albion trademark) since she was owned by Shaw Savill associate company John Leslie, whose ships sported a black hull.[4] Still, it is a good story!

Notes
1. Oamaru Harbour Board Annual Report, 1890.
2. Sir Henry Brett, *White Wings*, Vol. 1, Auckland, 1924, p. 56.
3. *Ibid.*, p. 117.
4. Duncan Haws, *Merchant Fleets 10: Shaw Savill & Albion*, Burwash, 1987, p. 33.

Chapter 7

COLLISION!

Some Victorian journalists loved nothing better than a good wallow in purple prose. Reporting the mass funeral of victims of the sinking of the *Pride of the Yarra* in 1863, the *Otago Daily Times* described the bodies as:

> delicately handled, as sacred though now-deserted temples in which the divine spirit had dwelt; delicately coffined, they were borne to the house of God where the burial service of the church was impressively performed by the ministers of their own faith; and followed by thousands of reverent mourners, amongst whom there was not a dry eye, they were carried to their last resting place in that "God's acre" where their remains will never be disturbed by sacrilegious hands.[1]

The accident alluded to took place in July 1863 and, in terms of human life, it was the most costly two-ship collision ever to take place in New Zealand waters. It involved two small harbour steamers, the *Pride of the Yarra* and the *Favourite*, and its disastrous consequences (the loss of 12 passengers) stopped the small town of Dunedin in its tracks.

The first participant, the 24-ton screw steamer *Pride of the Yarra*, had earned herself an invidious reputation in the four brief years that she had been part of the harbour fleet. In June 1859, just months after entering service, she had got herself into what could easily have been a fatal scrape off Grassy Point when her boiler collapsed without warning. Completely helpless and with her fires dead, she drifted up onto a sandbank where she sank. Only the shallowness of the water prevented heavy loss of life because her owner, one of the so-called pillars of the local business community, William Hunter Reynolds, had not fitted her with even the most basic life-saving equipment. Her passengers had to huddle together on her upper deck for warmth until rescued the next morning. Although the local papers campaigned for harbour steamers to carry life-saving equipment, the *Pride* still lacked lifebelts or a lifeboat as late as March 1860, by which time two drownings had taken place from her.

These misadventures paled into insignificance on the evening of 6 July 1863 when, in the florid words of the *Otago Daily Times*, 'two of the port steamers, proceeding at full speed in opposite directions, came into violent collision, and, amid the darkness, the confusion and the general terror which prevailed, the more tender vessel of the two filled and sunk, taking down with her many of the human freight and leaving other waifs upon the waters to battle desperately for life – some with success, others with hopeless effort to avert their fearful fate.'[2]

At about 1800 hours the *Pride of the Yarra* embarked between 40 and 50 people at Port Chalmers, some from the jetty, the others from the steamer *William Miskin* (see Chapter 4), which had just arrived from Invercargill. Included in that number was one nine-strong family group which had arrived from London the day before aboard the migrant ship *Matoaka*. So foggy and dark was it that even the master had difficulty estimating how many were aboard his 23-metre-long craft. Most were up on the chilly deck but a number, including the majority of the women and the children, had sought 'the fatal shelter of the cabin'.[3] They included Mrs Campbell, wife of the newly appointed principal of the new high school, her two maid-servants, Fanny Finch and Mary Roberts, her husband, the Reverend M. Campbell, their five children, Mrs Henderson and several gentlemen. Ironically, they had taken the *Pride of the Yarra* at the behest of Captain Dickie, the deputy harbour-master, who reasoned that the *Pride*'s ability to come alongside the *Matoaka* would avoid the danger of transferring into small boats. As the night was particularly cold, another small knot of men huddled together in the unlit, partially filled forward hold.

Although the *Pride of the Yarra* was known as the fastest boat in the port (9 knots), her regular master, Captain Spence, was at the wheel that night and he had an experienced and steady helmsman at the wheel. As she passed Sawyer's Bay, at the start of the upper harbour, the lights of another ship were observed. It was the paddle steamer *Favourite*, heading for Port Chalmers where she earned her keep as a tug. She was under the command of Captain Adams and steered by C. Murray, both of whom were on the bridge. Accompanying them was one of the port pilots. Both craft were displaying their navigation lights, the *Pride* one at her masthead showing the usual colours, and the *Favourite* a masthead light together with the usual port and starboard lamps. Visibility was poor and, as later testimony would show, the wind was blowing the *Pride*'s funnel smoke in such a way as to obscure her from the - *Favourite*'s lookout.

The *Favourite* was keeping so far to starboard that her port lights were concealed from Spence's view. Since she appeared to be maintaining this course, he ported the *Pride*'s helm (it being usual practice to allow a vessel to pass on the port side) and kept her as far to the starboard side of the channel – which at that point was delineated by a bluff, rocky headline – as was prudent. Even that was insufficient, though, and minutes later passengers heard his desperate cry of 'For God's sake, reverse the engines'. This was done, but too late to avert the tragedy. The *Favourite*, later described as 'a terrible engine of destruc-

Port Chalmers less than a decade after the fateful collision between the *Pride of the Yarra* and the *Favourite*. The ship in the foreground of this battered old 1872 glass plate photograph is the trans-Tasman trader *Omeo* (821 tons, 1858), occupying the graving dock. In the background can be seen a typical harbour ferry of the era, the *Golden Age* (113 tons, 1862). *Alexander Turnbull Library, courtesy of Graham Stewart*

tion' by some of the *Pride*'s passengers, did likewise but also too late. With a grim inevitability she ploughed straight into the smaller craft, catching her nearly in line with her mast, cutting right through her port side and listing her over.

'As the water was heard to rush into the vessel's hold and as the deck was felt to subside below the fickle surface, the crowd on deck advanced with all the rapidity which love of life could inspire, to the point of attachment between the two vessels,' a survivor later reported.[4] In fact, it was a mad scramble, because the *Pride*, lacking any watertight bulkheads, was sinking very fast. Unfortunately, the extra weight of these desperate people scrambling forward only drove the shattered bow deeper down into the water. A lucky few made it over the *Favourite*'s bulwarks with little more than wet feet but most were left floundering in the harbour water's chilly grip, clinging to each other and crying out frantically to the crew of the *Favourite*, now scrambling forward to render whatever assistance they could.

Not so lucky were those below decks in the *Pride*. The men in the hold made it to safety by the smallest of margins, the first one out being up to his neck in water by the time he started moving. Less fortunate were the saloon passengers. Captain Wilson from the *William Miskin* and Thomas Kingston, who were seated closest to the door, shot out with only seconds to spare, making their way out just as the water pouring in reached chest-height. Captain Spence pulled out a lame man, the skipper of the cutter *Alpha*, but could reach no one else before his vessel slipped beneath the waves. As for the Campbell family, 'so happy in the knowledge of arrival at their new home . . . cribbed, cabined and confined, they had not even the drowning man's hope'.[5]

The *Pride* filled fast, lurched once and then sank into the harbour depths, taking with her both the dead and the living. Because the *Favourite*, like so many early harbour craft, did not carry a boat, she was ill-equipped to help the people left in the icy water; 'round the stricken steamer a fearful carnival of death was enacting, and the scathless victor in the fearful

Unfortunately, no photographs survive of either the *Pride of the Yarra* or the *Favourite*. This photograph, taken at Dunedin, shows a typical Otago Harbour ferry of the era, the *Golden Age*. Although bigger than most at 113 tons, the *Golden Age* shows the rough and ready nature of such ships. Her register was closed in 1884 after a long period of idleness. *Alexander Turnbull Library*

encounter had to stand supinely by,' the editorial writer would lament a couple of days later.[6] One man floated free and was hailed by the *Favourite* but when a line was thrown to him he did not have the strength to take hold of it. The crew heard him utter one pitiful gasp before he sank from view. The *Favourite* lingered for another half-hour, then steamed for Port Chalmers where she broke the sad news. Her shaken passengers were transferred to the *Golden Age* for passage up to Dunedin.

Next day the provincial harbour staff and the police used a diver to recover bodies from the wreck. That man reported finding the bodies of the children gathered around the mother, Mrs Campbell clutching her infant with one hand and that of her husband with the other. When removing these corpses, he was careful to wrap the body of the infant with a shawl before sending it up to the surface. The tragedy stunned Dunedin, which had been looking forward to Campbell's arrival for a long time. The public funeral which followed on Thursday brought the town to a complete standstill. Two thousand mourners, almost the complete population, attended and the procession stretched for almost 2 kilometres.

The inquiry convicted the master and mate of the *Favourite* of manslaughter and severely censured Captain Spence for driving his ship at excessive speed. The harbourmaster tightened up safety procedures and larger, better-equipped ferries replaced the pioneering craft in the next couple of years. The *Pride of the Yarra* was raised and beached but never sailed again. When a survey revealed the extent of the damage, she was condemned and broken up.

Last century collisions were frequent but usually fairly trifling.

In most cases they amounted to little more than a snapped bowsprit, some battered bulwarks or a few stoven planks. In the rare instances that one of the participants sank, it was usually in a harbour or river where salvage was comparatively easy.

Typical was the fleet of the Auckland-based Northern Steam Ship Company. Formed in 1881 from a number of concerns controlled by Alexander McGregor, its small steamers serviced the Northland, Hauraki Gulf and Bay of Plenty trades that the Union Company considered beneath its dignity. At first it had no easy monopoly and the NSS Co. had to contend with competition from single-ship steam companies as well as from the more numerous scows and schooners.[7]

McGregor had already come a cropper in 1879 when one of his ships, the *Glenelg* (289 tons, 1878) challenged the rival *Rose Casey* (132 tons, 1878) to a race out of Auckland. She sprinted after her rival and had almost caught up with her when the German warship *Albatross*, lying peacefully at anchor in the stream, loomed into view. The *Rose Casey* was giving no ground, so the *Glenelg* smashed into the warship's gig, which was off her stern at the time. McGregor had to apologise and offer the Germans a replacement boat. Racing was one of the great unpardonable sins and officially, at least, shipping companies took a dim view of it. It did happen, though, and it led to the occasional accident. In February 1888 the Northern Company's *Gairloch* (211 tons, 1847), trying to beat the Seamen's Union's *Bellinger* (225 tons, 1884) into Waitara, hit the north training wall; days later the same company's *Clansman* (591 tons, 1884) ran down the cutter *Mana* (32 tons, 1875) off Mercury Island.

Northern's worst collision involved two of its steamers, the *Wellington* (366 tons, 1863) and the *MacGregor* (256 tons, 1881). It took place off Kawau Island on the night of 11 May 1885. The *Wellington* was steaming at about 11 knots with her topsail and trysail set when she spotted the *MacGregor*'s white masthead light off her bow. Chief officer Stephenson starboarded his helm and called the master to the bridge, but the *Wellington*, a notoriously 'cranky' ship, did not respond in time to avoid the collision. She slammed into the *MacGregor* amidships, shattering a few of her own bow plates but nearly cutting the newer ship in two. The *MacGregor*'s second officer sustained serious injuries (which would require hospitalisation) from falling timber but the rest of the crew escaped unharmed.

The salvage of the *MacGregor* took nine weeks, £3,700 and a great deal of ingenuity. The first attempt to lift her failed when one of the chains wrapped under her hull broke. On 29 May the ketch *Fanny Thornton* (80 tons, 1877) and the cutter *Gazelle* (24 tons, 1864) got her up using these chains but at great cost to the elderly *Gazelle* which sank and herself had to be salvaged. The *MacGregor* finally made it back to Auckland on 15 July.

Ironically, most of the more serious collisions with a New Zealand significance occurred at the other end of the world, in the English Channel. Then, as now, the 'ditch' was a crowded place, with hundreds of coasting and cross-channel craft threading their way through the lines of big migrant ships, West Indiamen or stately trans-Atlantic flyers. When the fog settled in or squalls slashed visibility to just a few metres, it could be a very menacing stretch of water.

Several New Zealand-bound ships went down still within sight of the Old World. One of the most dramatic collisions occurred on 17 September 1883 when the full-rigger *St Leonards*, a fine veteran of the New Zealand migrant trade, was struck by a steamer in foggy conditions 18 miles east of Start Point. In the words of the *St Leonards*'s mate, the ship 'struck us amidships, crunching through the *St Leonards* as if she was a bonnet box'.[8] The 'bonnet box' went down within nine minutes. Excellent training and superb discipline ensured that all 62 aboard the ship were saved. Five years later another Shaw Savill charter, the *Killochran*, went down in the final stages of an eventful voyage back to England from Auckland.

The worst New Zealand-linked Channel disaster, though, happened on Tuesday 11 September 1877 when the *Avalanche* collided with the *Forest*. The *Avalanche*, a Shaw Savill vessel, was a full-rigged iron ship of 1161 tons. She was just three years old. Outward-bound from London for Wellington (to which she had already made three voyages) and fully laden with general cargo, she carried, along with 34 crew, 59 passengers seeking their fortunes in the New World. The *Forest* was a wooden ship of 1422 tons. Built at Hansport, Nova Scotia in 1873, she carried a crew of 21. Of the more than 110 (estimates of the combined totals vary from 114 to 122) people aboard the two craft, only 12 would survive.

The voyage had gone badly almost from the start. The *Avalanche* had slipped out of the East India Docks on the 8th but had not got very far before running into trouble. The next day, while being towed down the river by a steam tug, she had collected the bows of a barque with her bowsprit. Repairs took two days. By 2100 hours on the 11th she was underway again and south-west of Portland. A south-west gale was blowing but visibility was good when the *Avalanche*, close-hauled on the port tack and doing about 6–7 knots, saw on her starboard bow the red light of the *Forest*. It was a dangerous situation and one that called for the *Avalanche* to give way, either by going about on the starboard tack or by passing astern of the *Forest*. She did turn to starboard, but too late to avoid the *Forest*, which had also altered course.

The *Forest* sliced deep into the *Avalanche*'s port side, amidships, striking the migrant ship four times in all. Right from the start there was no doubt that she was doomed. The *Avalanche* sank within minutes, taking with her all but a few lucky people who happened to be on deck at the time of the collision. Some managed to clamber across to the *Forest* but most went down with the ship or drowned shortly afterwards in the huge seas.

The *Forest* was also mortally wounded and lowered her three boats. Only one boat, carrying 12 exhausted survivors (nine from the *Forest* and three from the *Avalanche*), made it through the night. The *Forest* capsized during the night. Found floating upside down in the Channel, she was destroyed by HMS *Defence* in order to prevent her from becoming a hazard to shipping.

Serious collisions have been rare this century, especially for large trading vessels, which, even before the days of radar, demonstrated commendable skill at keeping out of trouble. When these accidents *have* happened, they have usually done so under pretty bizarre circumstances.

One of the strangest took place in broad daylight on Wellington Harbour during wartime. The ships involved were the Union Company's inter-island ferry *Wahine* and the Navy's auxiliary minesweeper HMNZS *South Sea*. The *Wahine* was no stranger to Wellington Harbour, having been the mainstay of the Wellington–Lyttelton run since 1913. Her master, Captain Alexander Howie, knew the port equally well. The *South Sea* (312 tons), commanded by Temporary Lieutenant Peter Bradley, was the former steam trawler *Ferriby*, built in England in 1912. Requisitioned by the Navy as an anti-submarine mine-sweeping trawler, she was on patrol duty inside the harbour at the time of her loss.

The weather was fine with good visibility as the *Wahine* pulled away from Fryatt Quay at 0824 hours on Saturday 19 December 1942 and put on a good turn of speed. Six minutes later, just abreast of Point Jerningham, Howie became worried that the minesweeper, heading in from her picket line off Somes Island, looked as though she might be on a collision course. Bradley had seen the ferry but overestimated his own speed and thought that he had time to clear her safely. At 0831 Howie altered course to starboard and sounded the whistle. Another minute later, with the *South Sea* now moving at about 6 knots and sheering slightly to port, he put *Wahine*'s engines full astern. This had cut her speed to about 8 knots by the time that she sliced into the small minesweeper two minutes later; the impact was still considerable, however, throwing two men off the stern of the *South Sea* and into the water and knocking unconscious the warship's helmsman. The ferry had struck the minesweeper just aft of her bridge, opening a big hole in her starboard side.

Rescue craft appeared on the scene within minutes. The scow *The Portland* plucked the two ratings from the water and the remainder were able to step across to other craft without too much difficulty. The tug *Toia* and the minesweeper HMNZS *Rata*, their pumps working furiously, tried to keep the *South Sea* afloat long enough to tow her into shallow water but to no avail; HMNZS *South Sea* sank off Point Halswell at 0920 in about 24 metres of water. The *Wahine*, after careful examination, continued her voyage. Too important to take off the vital ferry run, she had to put up with her damaged bow until mid-January 1943 when she could be patched up at Lyttelton.

Although it considered salvaging the old minesweeper, the Navy settled for the easier and cheaper alternative of stripping the wreck of its vital fittings. Between January and March 1943 it removed her guns, depth charges, radio gear and other valuable items of equipment. It then lowered an old depth charge and blasted away the higher parts of the *South Sea*'s superstructure to minimise the danger to shipping. She still rests there today, safely out of the way of the keels of modern shipping but still surprisingly intact.

Because of the wartime need for security and the fact that a court of inquiry had no jurisdiction over a naval vessel, there was no formal marine court of inquiry. The Navy did hold its

Wartime secrecy prevented waterfront photographers from recording the *Wahine/South Sea* collision. These photographs show the *Wahine* at Wellington after a berthing accident there in heavy fog in June 1936. *Wellington Maritime Museum & Gallery*

own inquiry in December 1942. It found that Bradley had erred in not taking any bearings of the *Wahine* and that he had not acted in accordance with articles 22 and 23 of the Regulations for Preventing Collisions at Sea. Howie might have avoided the collision by turning to port rather than starboard (i.e. by turning towards the minesweeper), but this would have been against the regulations and all the instincts of seamanship, since the Union Company master did not know that the warship captain had not realised that a collision was impending. The Union Company later presented the Navy with a bill for almost £5,000.[9]

Wellington featured again less than a decade later when Shaw Savill & Albion's big refrigerated cargo liner *Taranaki* rammed the Union Company freighter *Waipiata* off Seatoun, just inside the heads, on 5 May 1950. No one was injured but both ships suffered extensive damage.

It was a cold, wintry day with a strong southerly sweeping in patches of heavy, misty rain. The *Waipiata*, a big 2847-ton, 1930s-vintage engines-aft coaster, was inbound from Oamaru with a cargo of mainly foodstuffs and the *Taranaki* (8695 tons, 1928) was heading out, bound for Hamburg and London with six passengers and a large cargo. Both ships were in the hands of experienced men. The *Taranaki*'s master, H. J. Bennett, was one of the few seagoing masters with a square-rigged vessel's qualifications on his ticket. He had commanded submarines in the First World War and had been with Shaw Savill since 1932,

Left: The Union Company coaster *Waipiata* seen in happier days. A big, 'three island' type, the *Waipiata* maintained what has been termed the 'main trunk' service of the coastal trade, the east Coast general cargo service. *Wellington Maritime Museum & Gallery*

Below: Shaw Savill & Albion's *Taranaki* was one of a quartet of outstanding motor ships delivered during the late 1920s. So good was this type that for almost two decades cargo ships built for the company displayed generally similar profiles. *Wellington Maritime Museum & Gallery*

Two views of the *Taranaki* and the *Waipiata* locked together in the dark. Note how low the *Waipiata* is in the water. *Wellington Maritime Museum & Gallery*

apart from a break for further war service. Captain J. MacNeil had been with the Union Company for 25 years and had commanded the *Wingatui* and the *Karu*.

The bigger ship slammed into the *Waipiata* immediately forward of her bridge, smashing its starboard wing to pieces. A seaman rushing up on deck was greeted by 'a frightening view of a ship's bow towering over our bridge, cloaked in steam from our fractured pipes'.[10] Captain MacNeil swung out the lifeboats while the *Taranaki* rigged nets and floodlights just in case the *Waipiata*, which was settling by the bow, sank. The *Taranaki*'s

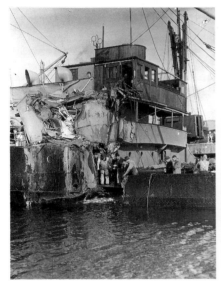

Top: The *Waipiata* alongside the Clyde Quay Wharf the next day, down by the bow and with her stern partly out of the water. *Wellington Maritime Museum & Gallery*

Left: When the ships had been separated and taken back to the shelter of the inner harbour, it was time to begin assessing the damage more closely. This photograph, taken on 8 May 1950, shows that the *Waipiata*'s starboard bridge cab has been wrenched away and the hull fractured abreast the No. 2 hold. Dominion, *courtesy of Wellington Maritime Museum & Gallery*

Right: Six days later the camera revealed what happened beneath the waterline. This photograph, taken aboard the Jubilee floating dock, shows both the huge gash to the ship's side and some of the mess in the hold. Dominion, *courtesy of Wellington Maritime Museum & Gallery*

passengers, seated at dinner, had felt the impact as little more than a sudden roll. The *Waipiata*'s 31 crew members put on their lifebelts but remained calm. Calmest of all was Mary, the *Waipiata*'s grey-flecked cat. When it seemed as though the ship might go, seamen tried to put her aboard the pilot launch but were met with stubborn resistance from the animal, who refused to leave her home. When put ashore the next day she returned promptly, as if to say 'after all the crew hasn't been paid off yet'.[1]

Fortunately the *Waipiata* stabilised with her foredeck awash. The pilot boat crew made an unsuccessful attempt to prise the two ships apart, then gave up, wisely deciding that the undignified embrace was all that was preventing the coaster from foundering. Meanwhile, the water poured into the *Waipiata*. Her forepeak, chain locker and No. 1 and No. 2 holds flooded as the coaster settled in the water with less than a metre of freeboard at the No. 1 hold. Fortunately, crates of acid stowed in the deck cargo remained intact. Had they burst, the crew would have been unable to keep the ship afloat.

As the *Waipiata* showed no signs of settling any further, the harbourmaster, Captain D. M. Todd, decided to bring in both ships 'as they lay'. And so, with the *Waipiata* hanging across her bows, the *Taranaki* crawled up the harbour stern first at just a few knots, burning two red towing lights. Word of the accident spread so fast that a traffic officer had to be sent along the Oriental Bay waterfront to control traffic. The trip to the Clyde Quay Wharf took about five hours, finishing at midnight. In the final manoeuvring, the *Waipiata* provided some assistance by bringing her own engine into play. Slowly and tenderly, she was edged around until she lay alongside the wharf in the normal fashion, her sunken bows pointing out to sea.

There the tugs *Taioma* and *Tapuhi* made more futile attempts to separate the ships from their bizarre embrace. The only results of their efforts were broken mooring lines, bent forecastle railings on the *Waipiata* and high blood pressure for some. Eventually workmen using oxyacetylene gear made some impression and the *Taranaki* and *Waipiata* were separated at about 0800 on the 6th. During this dangerous task, paint in the *Taranaki*'s bow locker caught fire but the fire brigade extinguished it before any real damage was done. Once freed, the *Waipiata* settled bow first on the bottom alongside the wharf, her forward holds an unappetising mush of cereals, peas and Bournvita.

She had come off very much the worse for the encounter, being sliced in two almost to the keel. The No. 2 hold had been penetrated to a depth of at least 2 metres and flooding had affected both holds as well as the forepeak. The *Taranaki* had also smashed in the second officer's cabin, which lay beneath the starboard bridge cab. Had second officer Athol Hansen been asleep at the time, he would almost certainly have been killed. The *Taranaki* had taken a little water through her damaged bow but most of the damage had occurred above the waterline. She entered the Jubilee floating dock in June 1950 and reappeared four months later sporting a new stem. Then it was the *Waipiata*'s turn.

The court of inquiry, held at Wellington in June under the chairmanship of A. A. McLachlan, SM, heard much conflicting evidence. It found that both masters were unusually tardy in acting under the provisions of the Regulations for the Prevention of Collisions at Sea and apportioned the blame three-quarters to MacNeil and one quarter to Bennett. Had MacNeil applied ordinary cautionary measures eight minutes earlier, by moving to starboard in accordance with the 'end-on rule', collision would have been avoided; had either done so even four minutes later, slowing up, stopping or going astern, no damage would have been done. MacNeil had probably mistaken a green section of the Somes Island light for the *Taranaki*'s green light and had compounded his error by pressing on even after he suspected that something was wrong. Certificates were restored to both men.

The *Taranaki*'s damage was almost superficial in comparison. *Evening Post, courtesy of Wellington Maritime Museum & Gallery*

Notes

1. *Otago Daily Times*, 10 July 1863.
2. *Ibid*.
3. *Ibid*.
4. *Ibid*.
5. *Ibid*.
6. *Ibid*.
7. Information on the Northern Company collisions is taken from an excellent article, C. F. Amodeo, 'A Trial of Strength', *New Zealand Marine News*, Vol. 31, No. 3, 1981, pp. 71–91 and Vol. 32, No. 4, 1981, pp. 111–137.
8. Sir Henry Brett, *op. cit.*, p. 68 and J. P. C. Watt, 'The *Avalanche* Story', *New Zealand Marine News*, Vol. 28, No. 3, 1978, pp. 93–99.
9. For information on the loss of the *South Sea* see R. J. McDougall, 'The Unfinished Voyage of HMNZS *South Sea*', *New Zealand Marine News*, Vol. 33, No. 3, 1983, pp. 67–77 and Vol. 34, No. 2, 1984, pp. 47–48.
10. Colin Thompson, 'The *Taranaki–Waipiata* Collision', *New Zealand Marine News*, Vol. 37, No. 4, 1987, pp. 154–156.
11. *Southern Cross*, 8 May 1950.

A rare photograph of the
ill-fated *Cospatrick*.
*Wellington Maritime Museum
& Gallery*

Chapter 8

FIRE!

Of all the perils that confronted a nineteenth-century ship, fire, especially far from the comforting sight of land, was undoubtedly the most frightening. It takes little imagination to realise that small, closely subdivided wooden ships, lit only by the naked flame, were grave fire risks at the best of times, and death traps once fire broke out. The officers of the better-run ships conducted regular fire drills but fire-fighting equipment was rudimentary. Cargo stowage was unscientific by modern standards and highly dangerous once a fire broke out; it was nothing to have petroleum products scattered among more innocuous general cargo. Because of the fear of fire, few lights were left burning at night untended, adding to the gloom of the passage. On well-run immigrant ships, late-night fire patrol duties were often added to the tedium of shipboard tasks for passengers and crew alike.

The blackest spectre – literally and metaphorically – that haunted nineteenth-century imaginations was that of the New Zealand immigrant ship *Cospatrick*, burned at sea on 17 November 1874, with the loss of almost 470 lives. This disaster symbolised the worst fate that the sea had in store. In the words of veteran shipping journalist Sir Henry Brett, it 'caused a thrill of horror throughout the Empire and particularly in Auckland, for which the vessel was bound'.[1]

The *Cospatrick*, a 1220-ton full-rigged ship, on just her second voyage to New Zealand, was several hundred sea miles west of Cape Good Hope when fire broke out in the forepart of the ship. Captain Elmslie (also spelt Elmsley in some reports) had 473 passengers and crew aboard his ship at the time. (If that does not seem crowded, remember that the 65,863-ton liner *Queen Elizabeth II* was designed to carry 1400 passengers.)

The fire defeated the best efforts of passengers and crew alike. Boatswain Henry McDonald, awakened from his slumbers by the dreaded cry 'Fire!', ran forward to find great clouds of smoke issuing from the forepeak. The bosun's locker, crammed full of inflammables such as oakum, rope, varnish and paint, was well and truly alight. The crew got the hoses going, spraying the forepeak with seawater, but made no impression on the flames. Soon the *Cospatrick* lost steerageway and, her head to the wind, was ablaze from stem to stern as the breeze fanned the flames aft. Within an hour and a half of the discovery of the first wisps of smoke, the magnificent *Cospatrick* was clearly doomed.

According to McDonald, 'dreadful scenes followed, for a panic broke out among the emigrants'.[2] The first boat launched was immediately swamped by the crowd of 'demented men and women that jumped into it'.[3] The longboat went up in flames and only two boats made it into the water safely. One sank in a gale four days later, leaving just one afloat, carrying 41 frightened and poorly equipped passengers and crew. In the meantime, the occupants of both craft could only watch the last moments of the *Cospatrick*, powerless to assist their friends and colleagues. As McDonald recalled: 'The main and mizzen masts fell, and many of those who had crowded aft were crushed to death. Then the stern was blown out. That was the end, and the shrieks of the survivors were silenced suddenly in the roaring flames.'[4]

Yes, as McDonald would later admit, the ones who perished in the cauldron were perhaps the luckiest. The hapless inhabitants of the two boats lacked clothes, food or sails and were hundreds of miles from land, entirely at the mercy of the wind and currents. On the 20th a gale separated the boats, with fatal consequences for the occupants of one. Before long, though, the crew of the surviving boat had little energy or inclination left to mourn the dead. Without food or water they began to succumb one by one. One man, steering, fell overboard and drowned. Three went mad through lack of water and died. The others threw their bodies overboard.

Four more died on the 24th, three of them as raving madmen. Early the next morning, a steamer passed within 50 metres without spotting the boat; another man died that day. Two more died the next day. Although the survivors threw one body overboard, they were by now too weak to get rid of the other corpse, which they had to leave rotting in the bottom of the boat. Just five remained alive and drinking seawater was fast threatening their remaining shreds of sanity. Fortunately at that stage the steamer *British Sceptre* put in a timely appearance and hoisted the desperate survivors aboard.

Even at anchor, safe and sound in their ports of destination, wooden sailing ships remained vulnerable to destruction by fire. One was the migrant ship *Montmorency*, which caught fire in the Napier roadstead in March 1867. A 688-tonner dating from 1855, the *Montmorency*, a former Black Ball liner, was described as 'remarkably roomy between decks, was a favourite Vessel for the conveyance of immigrants' and was alleged 'to have carried more immigrants in her day than any other British ship'. Since reaching Napier on the 24th she had discharged her passengers and their luggage but had not made a start on her cargo of 400 tons of general merchandise for Napier merchants.

Just minutes before midnight on 27 March a watchman discovered smoke and sounded the alarm. Within minutes the

Edward Cotter.   Thomas Lewis.   Henry McDonald.
Mrs. Elmslie.   Master Elmslie.   Captain A. Elmslie.

CAPTAIN ELMSLEY AND SURVIVORS.

A contemporary sketch of the *Cospatrick* survivors. *White Wings*

chief officer (the master, Captain Josiah Hudson MacKenzie, was ashore at the time) and the crew were on deck. As soon as he went forward, the chief officer found his way barred by thick smoke billowing out through the hatchway. He ordered his men to pass down a hose and to prise apart the hatchcover; this revealed flames coming from the port side. The chief officer, boatswain and sailmaker went down into the hold, playing the hose on the fire, but the thick, choking clouds of smoke and the heat of the deck soon forced them back. They closed up the hatchcover again in order to deprive the fire of as much oxygen as possible and warned the crew to prepare to leave the ship. While they were doing this, the chief went aft to burn blue lights and fire several rockets in an attempt to attract attention.

Within minutes the flames had spread from the hatches to the spare spars stacked on the decks. The *Montmorency*'s position was now hopeless. Some of the seamen attempted to go below to fetch their possessions but were forced back by the flames; the ship's carpenter's efforts to scuttle the ship were foiled by the same smoke and flames, and by the swell. By 0030 the flames were licking the poop. More rockets burst over the anchorage, but drew no response. The chief officer then ordered the crew to take to the boats, leaving just the second officer, the port customs officer and himself aboard.

By now, as the *Hawke's Bay Herald* of 30 March recorded, the flames had been noticed by an officer of the barracks:

> The cargo included over 100 casks of spirits, and a quantity of other goods of an inflammable character, and the volume of fire which shot up to heaven was immense, as well as singular in appearance. This sight is described as grand in the extreme, although of course such as to create a feeling of deep sorrow for such a calamity. After the fire reached the deck the fore-rigging was the first to be ignited; then the main yard, causing the main top sail to drop down on the poop. Soon after, the chief officer and the two others who remained on board were forced to drop over the stern into the boats.[5]

The boat, accompanied by one commandeered by the port pilot, again tried to scuttle the *Montmorency* but once again without success. Next they attempted to unshackle her from her moorings, but could get only one of her cables freed before being compelled to abandon their attempt. All they could do was lie off her and watch the masts fall. They splashed overboard about 0430; the foremast went first, over the starboard bow, to be followed, in quick succession, by the others.

All day the wreck smouldered while crowds gathered on the hill to watch. At one point the *Star of the South*, responding to an order from the provincial deputy superintendent, tried to unshackle the remaining mooring and tow the *Montmorency* away from the anchorage she was endangering, but she failed and herself suffered minor damage. By the next day the charred remains of the *Montmorency* were up on the beach between the spit and the bluff. The cause of the fire was not established; some thought that it may have been smouldering for a long time at sea but this seems unlikely in view of the fact that an inspection the day before had produced no evidence of any trouble.

Total loss by fire became less common as the number of steel-hulled ships grew and knowledge of safe stowage of dangerous goods increased. Even so, accidents still happened. This was largely because of the greater demand for motor spirits ('benzine'). Modern-style coastal tankers really only date from the 1950s. Until then, motor spirits, carried in the ubiquitous tins that inventive Kiwis hammered into all sorts of shapes, formed a part of almost every ship's cargo. Although Shell put a small coastal tanker, the *Paua*, on the coast in the late 1920s, even she handled her cargo in cased form.

One victim of such cargo was the little coaster *Moa*. Built at England in 1864 and altered several times during her adventurous career, the 185-ton steamer was approaching the entrance to Wanganui River at 1000 hours on 3 February 1914 when an explosion rocked her. Within minutes she was alight from stem to stern – not surprising given that her cargo included over 5000 cases of kerosene, motor spirit, benzine and turpentine.

So quickly did the flames race along the deck that the lifeboats were engulfed before the crew could reach them. They

The little coaster *Moa* had many scrapes during a very long career. This photograph shows her ashore at Gisborne in April 1894. *Wellington Maritime Museum & Gallery*

threw lifebelts and pieces of wood in the water and leaped for their lives, swimming towards the *Arapawa* which was approaching as close as safety permitted. So strong was the heat that the other little ship, herself loaded with over 4000 cases of benzine, had to keep her distance. Nevertheless, her boats picked up all the crew of the *Moa* apart from the fireman, William Kennedy, who had perished in the initial blast. As for the fiery torch that was once the *Moa*, the winds took hold of her and blew her ashore, just a few kilometres south of the southern breakwater. There she burned all day until about 2000 when a huge explosion seemed to put out the flames.

Four years later another little coaster full of benzine almost set the city of Wellington alight. This was the Westland Shipping Company's 185-ton *Defender*. On 2 August 1918 the little ship, which had been on the coast for almost 15 years, was moved from Queen's Wharf to King's Wharf where she started to trans-ship 1200 cases of benzine to a larger vessel. At about 1100 hours this work came to an abrupt halt when someone noticed smoke coming from her forehold. When the crew's fire-fighting efforts failed, the harbourmaster, aware that he had a potential floating timebomb on his hands, ordered the tug *Karaka* to tow the *Defender* away from the wharves. Taking up the story, the *Evening Post* recorded that:

> So far the flames, though raging under the battened hatches, had not been visible above the deck but almost immediately after the vessel had been towed clear of the larger vessel and the wharf a few minutes after noon, a dense volume of black smoke, followed by a rush of roaring flames, burst from the fore hatch and rapidly increased.[6]

While city workers held their breaths and motorists and cyclists scampered out onto the Hutt Road to watch, the *Karaka*, escorted by the Union Company tug *Terawhiti* and the launch *Uta*, towed the blazing hulk across the harbour. Just off Lepers' Island, near the northern tip of Somes Island, the *Karaka* slipped the tow and let the *Defender* drift onto the rocks. At 1325 a huge explosion rocked the city, to be followed by another a quarter of an hour later. The fire was then left to burn itself out.

Fifteen days later the crew putting the steamer *Aorere* through her trial paces reported little of the *Defender* poking above the water apart from one davit and a length of blackened superstructure. An effort was being mounted to recover her machinery.

Twentieth-century innovations in ship design (steel hulls, electric light and, more recently, smoke detectors) have greatly diminished, although not eliminated, the risk of shipboard fire. Few ships have been lost through fire, although many lives have been lost through fires which have damaged vessels. In the 1950s, two well-known coasters suffered serious fire damage. The first, Richardsons' *Pateke* (785 tons), caught fire at Lyttelton on 10 December 1955. By the time the local fire brigade had brought the fire in her accommodation under control, £26,000 worth of damage had been done to the year-old ship and three sleeping seamen had made the closest of escapes.

Four years later another new coaster went up, this time with fatal consequences. Like the *Pateke*, she was a modern (1957), well-appointed ship of the very latest design – the Holm Shipping Company's 845-ton flagship *Holmburn* – and the place was again Lyttelton.[7] The *Holmburn* had been loading general cargo for Lyttelton throughout the afternoon of 7 May. Just before midnight steward John MacIntyre noticed smoke coming from a fire in her starboard side, near the engine room. MacIntyre and the cook, William Griffiths, fought their way through the crews' quarters at great risk to themselves, waking their sleeping shipmates as they went. Two men leaped into the sea to escape but neither MacIntyre nor Griffiths could reach the part of the superstructure where the master, Captain

The coaster *Holmburn* aground on a sandbank in the Manukau Harbour in the early 1970s. *J. F. Holm/Wellington Maritime Museum & Gallery*

Derek Crabtree, and the chief steward, A. J. Hempstalk, were still asleep. Both were burned to death. By the time the fire brigade put in an appearance, the *Holmburn* was well ablaze and smoke from her fires was billowing across the harbour.

One firefighter was injured while bringing the fire under control but by 0400 hours on 8 May, the last embers were being put out. It had been a close thing. The *Holmburn* was listing to starboard against the wharf, her accommodation area battered and blackened. Repairs would take months and cost tens of thousands of pounds. The court of inquiry expressed its suspicions that drink, a cigarette butt and poor fire safety training lay behind the incident but could not pinpoint a definite cause for the fire, which was not fought intelligently by the crew. As a result of this incident the coastal companies tightened up fire safety and, wherever possible, altered the accommodation plans of their ships.

In 1969 another fire captured the headlines, this one aboard the Shaw Savill & Albion liner *Gothic*. Built in 1948, the 15,911-ton *Gothic* had made a name for herself as the stand-in royal yacht in 1953. Although de-rated for cargo-only operations by the late 1960s, she was still a most impressive ship. On 2 August, while she was deep into the Pacific on a voyage from Bluff to Liverpool via Panama and carrying refrigerated cargo and general cargo, the *Gothic*'s smoke alarms began to ring. A serious fire was raging in the smoke room and adjoining galley. Probably started by a dropped cigarette butt, it soon spread once the cold sea spray blew in the overheated windows. Unfortunately the *Gothic* was heading into the wind; this

Twisted, blackened steelwork attests to the fury of the fire. Although patched up, the *Gothic* did not last long, going to the breakers soon afterwards. *Wellington Maritime Museum & Gallery*

These aerial photographs of the *Gothic* limping back to Wellington Harbour show how the fire swept through her bridgework; seven people died in the blaze. *Evening Post/Wellington Maritime Museum & Gallery*

pushed the fire back through the former passenger accommodation in the direction of No. 3 hold, which was packed with wool.

Captain Agnew turned around his battered command and helped his crew bring the flames under control. Three hours later they succeeded. By then seven people, including two young boys travelling with their father, had died. With much of her superstructure wrecked, the *Gothic* turned back for New Zealand, her master navigating by means of a chart and compass whipped out of one of the lifeboats. Late on 6 August she limped into Wellington Harbour under naval escort. She was given a rudimentary patch-up but sent for breaking up the following year.

That fire still sinks ships was brought home twice during the 1970s. The first incident took place off the Northland coast on 3 September 1975 when the 3614-ton French islands trader *Capitaine Bougainville* reported an engine room fire shortly after leaving Auckland Harbour on the first stage of a routine voyage back to the Solomons via Sydney and Port Moresby. Aboard were 37 men, women and children. She was an old ship, dating from 1955 but, like most Sofrana-Uniline ships, well maintained.

The crew soon lost control of the fire, but as the engines still worked, master Captain Jean Raymond Thomas kept going, heading close to the shore where he hoped to anchor and await

daylight and rescuers. Later that day he was anchored 2 miles off Whananaki, near the entrance to Whangarei Harbour. But by then, the smoke was so dense that there was no alternative to abandoning ship in the dark.

All made it off the *Capitaine Bougainville* safely but the heavy sea running meant conditions were difficult for those in the boats. Both lifeboats and one liferaft capsized; some scrambled back aboard but 16 did not and perished, either drowning in the icy waters or succumbing to exposure. A Northland Harbour Board tug took the still-burning ship, by now a constructive total loss, in tow and had her alongside the wharf by 1530. There the fire was finally put out.

The second trading vessel to go down in New Zealand waters recently as a result of fire did so off Banks Peninsula on 10 June 1978. The vessel concerned was the attractive little 19-year-old Tongan trader *Kemphaan*. She had cleared Timaru for her home port of Nuku'alofa with a cargo of frozen meat and general cargo and was making her way home in fine weather and good visibility. Just off Le Bons Bay, Banks Peninsula, smoke was observed billowing from the 460-ton freighter's engine room. Her 12-man crew stood to fight the fire but it spread so quickly that there was not even time to send a distress message. By the time that the crew abandoned ship in a liferaft and the ship's boat, one man was dead and another was nursing serious burns over much of his body.

It took the crew of the lifeboat eight hours to reach shore to raise the alarm. An RNZAF Iroquois helicopter lifted the injured man from the drifting liferaft and flew him to Christchurch hospital where he died later. Salvage craft from the Lyttelton Harbour Board dampened the fires and took the stricken ship into port where her flames burst forth with a renewed vigour. Worried that the ship, by now dangerously full of the water used to fight the fire, might sink in the harbour, the board ordered her to be towed to Purau Bay where she sat on the mud. A constructive total loss, the *Kemphaan* was sunk as a target by the air force a few days later.

Notes
1. The account of the loss of the *Cospatrick* is taken mainly from Sir Henry Brett, *White Wings*, Vol. 1, Auckland, 1924, pp. 62–64.
2. *Ibid*.
3. *Ibid*.
4. *Ibid*.
5. The account of the loss of the *Montmorency* is taken from a 30 March 1867 *Hawke's Bay Herald* story reproduced in the *Oamaru Times and Waitaki Reporter* of 12 April 1867.
6. The *Defender's* story is based on *Evening Post* reports of 2 August and 19 August 1918.
7. The account of the *Holmburn* fire is based on Union Company files held by the Wellington Maritime Museum and Gallery.

The *Taranaki* at Picton.
Wellington Maritime Museum & Gallery

Chapter 9

SUCCESSFUL SALVAGES

In August 1868 when word reached Wellington that their flagship, the *Taranaki*, had sunk in Tory Channel, the directors of the New Zealand Steam Navigation Company (NZSN Co.) probably reached for the key to the liquor cabinet. No one could blame them. In the two and a half years that she had graced the coast, the magnificent *Taranaki* had lost them money hand over fist. Certainly, she was attractive to look at, fast and big, but that cut little ice with the struggling company's accountants. Her government mail contract had failed and an exploratory voyage to Hokitika was no more successful. In July 1867 she had snapped a propeller shaft in Poverty Bay and only the timely arrival of the *Lord Ashley* had prevented her from drifting onto the rocks. Even so, the tow down the coast had been long and eventful, with the line snapping at least once with nearly fatal consequences. She was in the wars again as soon as October when she smashed into the Bluff Wharf.[1]

The Tory Channel calamity happened at 1630 on 19 August when a sudden tidal eddy thrust her onto Boat Harbour Rock at the entrance to the channel just as she was finishing a regular voyage from Lyttelton to Picton. Refusing to answer her helm, the *Taranaki* struck the rock on her port side, starting several iron hull plates and shearing off her propeller. Captain Francis tried to beach her by using the ship's boats to tow her but had to abandon the attempt, along with his ship, just two hours later, when the water level began rising too quickly to control. Seven hours after striking the rock she sank stern-first in about 30 metres of water in Bowdens Bay.

The NZSN Co. went down a few months later, filing for voluntary liquidation. Meanwhile the *Taranaki* settled deeper into the mud, rumours flew about her harbouring a stash of bullion and at least one diver lost his life while poking and prodding about the underwater hulk. Of one thing everyone was certain – salvage would not be easy. Since the *Taranaki* had sunk into about 1.5 metres of mud, the usual method of passing chains underneath a wreck and raising her by pulling on them was out of the question. In March 1869 the old NZSN Co. sold the salvage rights to a Wellington consortium which duly renamed itself the Wreck Recovery Company. Later that year it announced ambitious plans to *screw* the wreck to the surface.

The graceful steamer *Taranaki* at Port Chalmers during the early 1870s. *Harraway Collection, Hocken Library*

This was a new technique, pioneered the year before in Belfast Lough on the paddle steamer *Wolf* by John Weild, a salvage expert. Under this method, steel chains were hooked onto the sunken wreck; the chains were screwed over pulleys set up on a floating raft of iron tanks and the ship was brought slowly to the surface where she could be pumped out and repaired sufficiently to get her to port.

This really was shooting for the stars in the colonial New Zealand of 1868. The *Taranaki* was entombed more than twice as deeply as the *Wolf* had been and the site was washed by stronger tidal movements which would pose quite an obstacle to divers. Still, Seagar and Thirkell, the enthusiasts behind the Wreck Recovery Company, were bubbling with enthusiasm and the company's directors believed that the ship and cargo would fetch a tidy sum.

They hired the steamer *Ladybird* to position four pontoons – two each side – over the wreck. Seagar and Thirkell rested 22 sets of kahikatea cross-beams between the pontoons, with two lifting rods, a lifting screw and a 1.5-metre lever attached to each beam set. They would be used to ratchet the ship up slowly in small stages, taking care at each stage to maintain the *Taranaki*'s balance. The best estimates were for each 0.6-metre lift to take three hours, with another hour being required to reset fittings for the next step. From time to time the *Ladybird* would pull the *Taranaki* into shallower water.

Divers, working from an underwater cage and spending up to two hours at a time below, first removed anchors, chains and other heavy fittings before securing the iron hooks into the *Taranaki*'s portholes. After three weeks everything was in place and the company was itching to put its theory to the practical test.

Lifting started on 7 August. That day the salvors moved the *Taranaki* about 15 metres sideways and 1.5 metres closer to the surface. The first 18 metres were relatively easy; then things got hard. An underwater bank caused many problems before the *Ladybird* could continue towing the wreck towards the

The Union Company coastal
steamer *Arahura* (1596 tons,
1905) entering Greymouth's
narrow river. Although
usually safe enough, in
poor weather, with little
visibility, the river was very
dangerous. *Wellington
Maritime Museum & Gallery*

shore. For a while it was a race against time because the
pontoons were starting to leak and the cross-beams were
warping under the strain of the waterlogged hulk. By 23
September, though, that obstacle had been overcome and the
forehold was being pulled out of the water. Seven days later
the *Taranaki*, battered and sullied, but afloat nonetheless, was
ready to be brought back to Wellington.

Teredo (shipworm) had feasted on her decking and water
pressure had collapsed the boiler, but otherwise she was in
pretty good shape. The Wreck Recovery Company patched her
up and had her running again but the company was soon in
financial straits. The sale of her cargo fetched much less than
expected. The *Taranaki* was sold to the New Zealand Steam
Shipping Company (NZSS Co.) in 1871, and joined the Union
Company in 1876 when that line bought out the NZSS Co. That
year she had a very close escape off Shag Point in North Otago,
hitting the notorious Danger Reef. A short while afterwards, a
heavy sea off North Cape caused extensive damage to her
fittings.

Her end came on 29 November 1878 in the Bay of Plenty. It
was a misty morning when the ship ploughed into Karewa
Island near the entrance to Tauranga Harbour. All 75 passengers and 32 crew got off safely but the ship broke in two the
following night and became a total loss.

Of all the difficult passenger runs maintained by the Union
Company last century, the West Coast service was undoubtedly the most dangerous. Even the two specialised shallow-
draught steamers built in 1898 and 1905, the *Mapourika* and
Arahura, had their work cut out to maintain a service to the
shallow West Coast bar harbours that we encountered in
Chapter 3. Time and again, they barely scraped their way
across the shallows, to the alarm of passengers and observers
alike. Often they would lie 'bar-bound' off one of the river ports
for days at a stretch, unable to enter. Travelling to these ports
was always a bit of an adventure.

The *Mapourika* (1203 tons) was one of two near-sister ships built by the Union Company in 1898 for its West Coast passenger services. The other was the *Rotoiti* (1159 tons), built to maintain the run between Onehunga and New Plymouth. The *Mapourika* traded on an even tougher run, between Wellington, Nelson, Westport and Greymouth. She was a handsome little single-funnel ship, with a straight stem and elliptical stern, 67 metres long, 10 metres in the beam and with a draught of just under 4.5 metres. Triple expansion engines pushed her along at a shade over 11 knots.

As the first ship built for the West Coast service in over a decade and almost twice the size of her predecessors, the *Mapourika* excited great interest. She arrived at Wellington on 25 August and entered service in mid-September, quickly establishing herself as a firm favourite with travellers. One of the people most delighted to see her was Judge Ward, who frequently travelled south on his district court circuit. A man of great height and enormous girth, usually forced to bunk down on smoking room floors, Ward had a special berth fitted for him in the new ship.

At about 0100 hours on 1 October 1898 the *Mapourika* was lining herself up for another entry into Greymouth. On the bridge was Captain McLean, formerly the master of the *Mawhera* and the *Penguin* and a man with considerable experience working the West Coast bar harbours. The first officer was Mr Liddell. Although the night was dark, the weather was fine and the sea over the bar only moderate.

McLean increased speed to half-speed and came in in line with the lights. A heavy sea was running, but not enough to trouble the *Mapourika*; there was sufficient water over the bar to accommodate her with ease. Just as she was three ship's lengths from the southern tiphead, though, a huge 'blind roller' slammed into her about amidships. The timing was awful. With both her helm and her propeller out of the water, the *Mapourika* hung in the air for what seemed like a minute, then plunged, striking the seabed and becoming unmanageable.

McLean ordered full speed ahead but got no response from his ship. Then another big sea struck the *Mapourika* and started carrying her towards the northern tiphead. McLean ordered 'full astern' but could do nothing to avert the disaster staring him in the face. Her propeller racing full astern, the *Mapourika* was carried onto the northern tiphead, gradually working her way up onto the northern beach. She struck with such force that a 20-tonne concrete block was split in half.

McLean remained calm and passengers reported just the briefest of panics as they made their way up on deck. Fortunately the ship's stern had run so far up the beach that everyone was able to scramble ashore safely, carrying their luggage and the mails. At first, though, the outlook for the ship did not look at all promising. An initial wire report painted a pessimistic scene:

Considerable excitement was caused in Wellington this morning by

These two photographs, show the *Mapourika* ashore near the tiphead, being pounded by the waves. In the lower photograph note the brave – or foolish! – person crossing by the ropes that so tenuously connect her to the shore. *Wellington Maritime Museum & Gallery*

the receipt of a telegram from Greymouth stating that the fine new steamer *Mapourika*, which recently came out from Home to the order of the Union Steam Ship Company, had gone ashore after crossing the Grey Bar and was likely to become a total wreck. . . . She now lies on the north side of the north groin, with her bows on the rocks. . . . She has holes in the bows.[2]

Despite relief that no one had been drowned, the Greymouth business community took on a gloomy air in the next few days. The big new ship had been a symbol of progress and prosperity and everyone feared that the Union Company might never risk such a valuable ship there again. The *Grey River Argus*, sensitive to criticism of the port's appalling wreck record, called for a full and careful inquiry.

The inquiry, conducted the following week at Greymouth by Mr Stratford, SM, was a quiet affair. Although the Greymouth harbourmaster, possibly overly anxious to protect the reputation of his port, 'considered the *Mapourika* unsuitable to that trade, because she drew so much water and had so much of her propeller blades out of the water',[3] Stratford found that the accident had been caused by the ship becoming unmanageable when it struck the seabed after being hit by a blind roller. Such rollers were not uncommon, especially in summer months; earlier one had practically turned the lightly laden steamer *Janet Nicoll* around. The bar had been safe and the master perfectly justified in entering under those conditions.

Although many wrote the *Mapourika* off as finished, the Union Company's branch manager, W. A. Kennedy, was made of sterner stuff. After all, he had rescued another of the company's steamers, the *Mawhera*, from an identical predicament in the same spot a few years earlier by dragging her across the beach and relaunching her in a more sheltered spot. The job had taken months and cost a fortune but it had saved a valuable ship. Kennedy reasoned that it was worth attempting with this brand-new ship and summoned J. Daniel, foreman of the company's workshops, down to Greymouth to assist him.

One thing was certain – the ship had to be moved fast. She was in a very dangerous position, with her submerged bow in deep water and her stern on the rocks. The speed of the river at that point and the heavy surf that was continually running made it impossible to risk using tugs to pull her off. Daniel ran out five hawsers to the stern and one to each side of the bow to swing the stern further away from the breakwater. But at first he could do nothing about the bow which, being in such deep water, was completely at the mercy of the waves. A heavy south-wester sprang up on the 5th and caused the *Mapourika* to bump heavily, further holing her bows. Fortunately the engine room remained watertight and steam was working again by then.

At first nothing went well. Daniel had requested pumps and additional men from Wellington but bar conditions prevented the ship carrying them, the *Wainui*, from entering Greymouth. She had to steam up to Westport to transfer them to the *Haupiri* for the delayed trip down. In the meantime he had made an unsuccessful attempt to move the ship using a steam winch. On the 10th the ropes broke four times.

Kennedy got the pumps working on the night of the 12th and soon had the forepart pumped out. Men were then sent in to shovel out the 150 tonnes of shingle that had worked its way into the hull while others, assisted by divers, patched the holes on the badly fractured port side. By now it was literally a race against time. A heavy storm on 17–18 October threw the ship farther up the beach, twisting her stern and punching more holes and dents in her plates. Then, using steam winches and muscle power, Kennedy and Daniel hauled the ship out of the water. By 20 October she was high and dry, out of harm's way.

Daniel's men then removed the rest of her damaged cargo (over £300 worth for indignant Hokitika merchants who complained vociferously about it not being removed earlier) and

By late October to early November (*upper photograph*) the *Mapourika* had been winched up onto the beach. She was now safe from the threat of the waves. The next step was the fitting of a wooden framework (*lower photograph*) to enable jacks to lift her onto wooden rails that would then be used to take her across the breakwater and into the river for a safe relaunching. *Wellington Maritime Museum & Gallery*

repaired the extensive hull damage. In order to get the *Mapourika* out of the way and over to the other beach for launching, they now started the laborious job of levelling a section of the beach and removing part of the breakwater wall, made up of the same 20-tonne concrete blocks that had arrested her headlong dash.

This took four months. Daniel had the *Mapourika* lifted onto wooden skids and manoeuvred about 100 metres across the beach to a point where she could be relaunched into the more placid waters of the Grey River. The big launch day was 10 March 1899. An estimated 6000 people crowded the break-

By December the *Mapourika* had been jacked up by 3 metres and was being eased gradually across the beach. As these photographs show, it was a massive task.·
Wellington Maritime Museum & Gallery

water and beaches to watch the *Mapourika* slip faultlessly down the skids and into the water. At the ceremony, Union's managing director, James Mills, slightly touchy about press criticism that his company had followed its usual policy of firing masters unlucky enough to lose their ships, hit out:

> All he had to say was that if the waters were difficult to navigate the company did not enforce that law [summary dismissal] but considered the circumstances. Where there was land on one side and

3,000 miles of open ocean on the other the matter was different, and in the interests of the shareholders and of the general public – whose lives and property were entrusted to them – the company could not act otherwise than they [sic] did.[4]

This was not the end of the *Mapourika*'s narrow squeaks. In August 1900 she ran ashore at Picton and was again the subject of a major salvage exercise. Other minor accidents occurred at regular intervals. In 1907 the company's Greymouth agent, D. Carter, informed Dunedin that the ship had had a very similar escape. The account of the whole incident, hushed up at the time, is worth reproducing in full:

> I now confirm my telegram of this morning advising that the above vessel had a very narrow escape from stranding whilst negotiating the Bar inwards last night. I thought it better to let you know of this by telegram, as in such small places as this the Newspapers are inclined to make "Scareheads" of such things, which are also telegraphed over N.Z. although in present instance I do not think this will take place as the editor of *Argus* mentioning the matter this afternoon I assured him that the incident was being made too much of, and in any case the reputation of the port would be at stake were much made of the occurrence, in view of this he said that if it was referred to at all, it would not be enlarged upon . . .
>
> Vessel left Westport at 9, P.M. Thursday, Weather at that time here being N.W. increasing wind and sea, *Koonya* got in at 8.30 P.M. but at 10 P.M. a whole gale from the same direction was blowing and Bar rapidly became impassable and remained so all through Friday, with very thick weather, *Mapourika* being first sighted at 1 P.M. that day, Signal staff shewing "Put to sea" at this time there was a very heavy sea, and strong fresh, this continued until about 9 A.M. Saturday when the wind lightened and sea rapidly decreased and continued to do so, so much so that when we received your

Launching into the river took place in March 1899. This photograph of the *Mapourika* crossing the Greymouth bar, taken six years later in 1905, shows what ships have to contend with at these bar harbours; the risk of bow or stern striking the seabed is always present. *Wellington Maritime Museum & Gallery* urgent telegram at 11.30 that morning to signal her back to Westport Capt Connor assured us that the Bar would be workable that night and so it proved. Before Connor went off duty that evening I asked him when he anticipated the vessel would get in, and he said about 9 P.M. (H.W. 11.7 p.m.) The Deputy harbour-master came on duty and Connor told him that if he felt the least doubt about letting her in to ring him up and he would come down to the tip head and himself decide (He did not feel the slightest doubt himself, except as to the time she would get in) Macpherson in company with Capt Drewette went down to the tip and it was decided that it was perfectly safe to let her in and she got the signals, all went well, (the ship coming up to it in good position) until she got inside the line of the tip heads, when she was caught by a sea and sheered over to port in the direction of the tip to the Eastward, Capt gave her all the steam he could command, and port helm and fortunately she answered to it and came back into position again and came up to the wharf without further incident . . .

Capt Drewette was of the opinion that the bar was quite safe to work when *Mapourika* got the signals, and said that vessels had come in under far worse conditions before . . . I saw the Capt (Clift) when the vessel reached the wharf, and he was somewhat severe in his strictures on Macpherson, in his presence, feeling that he had given the signals when the bar was unsafe, but at the time he was not in a condition to calmly view the matter . . .

The opinion of Drewette and Macpherson is that the vessel was caught at a bad time with a heavy roller and the influence of the slight fresh at the same time being felt she took the sheer . . .[5]

The *Mapourika* crashed into King's Wharf, Wellington, on 20 July 1918 while berthing, causing about £40 worth of damage. On 2 August she grounded briefly on a sandbank in Nelson Harbour but was refloated undamaged. On 14 May of the same year she had a particularly trying voyage from Nelson to Wellington. A workman working in the storeroom had closed the porthole without securing it. Out at sea, the strait was rough and the porthole came open again, flooding the room and damaging stores. By the time that this was discovered, the after hold was awash and the cabins were being threatened. Listing slightly, and less manageable than usual, the *Mapourika* concluded a very unfortunate voyage by crashing into Queen's Wharf. She got off unscathed but the wharf suffered about £500 worth of damage.

Sold to the Anchor Shipping and Foundry Company of Nelson in 1921 as the *Ngaio* and laid up in 1930, the *Mapourika* was dismantled in the mid-1930s.

Notes

1. The account of the two wrecks of the *Taranaki* is based on C. W. N. Ingram, *op. cit.*, p. 190, and C. F. Amodeo, 'The "Unsinkable" S.S. *Taranaki*', *New Zealand Marine News*, Vol. 33, No. 4, 1983, pp. 104–120.
2. *Evening Post*, 1 October 1898.
3. *Ibid.*, 12 October 1898.
4. *Ibid.*, 16 March 1989.
5. D. Carter/C. Holdsworth, 31 March 1907, James Mills Papers, USS Co. Archives, Hocken Library.

Chapter 10

THE WRECK OF THE WAIRARAPA

As the party from the *Argyle* clambered over the rocks and waded round the jutting points to reach the spot, they found the bodies stretched out full length on the hard rocks. One of the women, both of whom had belts fastened around them, was entirely naked. The other wore a tattered chemise. The savage sharks had attacked the body of the former, which presented a shocking spectacle, the calf of one leg and a big piece out of her side having been bitten away. The younger girl was apparently 14 or 15 years of age, and looked a most pitiable object as she lay with upturned face on the sea-worn shingle, her eyes staring vacantly into space and her mouth filled with sand. The men in the party had to turn away their heads to hide their emotions as they took in the situation.[1]

That report, sent down the wire to the *Otago Daily Times* for its issue of 5 November 1894, was just a sampling of coverage of the wreck which probably generated better press copy than any other in the nineteenth century. The repercussions were still flying thick and fast a month later when the court of inquiry was attacking the master, his officers and crew. 'This conduct

The *Wairarapa* photographed at her home port of Dunedin in December 1893. The crowded wharves reflect the importance of sea transport last century. *Wellington Maritime Museum & Gallery*

Another, undated view of the *Wairarapa. Wellington Maritime Museum & Gallery*

seems inhuman and inexplicable,' the court thundered. 'Of Mr Fenwick, the purser, all we can say is that he saved himself.' The court was, of course, referring to New Zealand's third most costly shipwreck, that of the Union Company steamer *Wairarapa*, which ploughed headlong into Great Barrier Island in the first minutes of 29 October 1894 with the loss of 121 (some reports said 125) lives.

The *Wairarapa* was a steel screw passenger steamer of 1786 tons. Although no longer in the front ranks of the ever-expanding Union Company fleet, she was by no means obsolete. Built in 1882 at Dumbarton as one of the batch of six generally similar ships, she and her sister craft were still the mainstay of the Union Company's trans-Tasman passenger/cargo service more than a decade later. With a top service speed of about 13 knots, the *Wairarapa* was, together with the *Manapouri*, one of the first vessels in the world to boast incandescent lighting. Each of these steady if unspectacular vessels could carry about 200 passengers in various classes in a very fair measure of comfort. The Union Company had had its fill of 'flyers' with the celebrated *Rotomahana* of 1879 and had thereafter opted for safe, reliable workhorses of the *Te Anau/ Wairarapa* type.

Nevertheless, the *Wairarapa*'s career had not exactly been incident-free. In February 1884, while unofficially racing the *Adelaide* off the Australian coastline, she had been struck by the Australian ship, sustaining about £1,000 worth of damage. The funny side to the story came when one man, thinking the *Adelaide* was sinking, leaped aboard the *Wairarapa*! Less than a year later she was again in the news. Early on the morning of 1 November 1885, while en route from Napier to Gisborne, the ship caught fire amidships.

The flames spotted coming from the staircase leading to the

A close-up of the bridge and funnel of the *Wairarapa*. The open, exposed bridge was typical of even large steamers of the time. The steam whistle on the funnel, just visible behind the ventilator, is shown on page 106. *Wellington Maritime Museum & Gallery*

main deck immediately indicated that the linen locker and boot room were ablaze. No one died but the second stewardess burned herself badly while helping women passengers to the top deck. As the fire quickly burned out of control, Captain H. W. H. Chatfield raced to Gisborne where the fire was eventually brought under control. Even so, it had been a close thing. The ship had sustained fire damage along a third of her length and would require several weeks in the Port Chalmers dock and £6,000 worth of repairs before again being ready for service.

On 24 October the *Wairarapa* left Sydney on the start of what should have been another regular voyage across the 'Union Company lake'. Aboard her were 95 saloon and 90 steerage passengers and 65 crew, the majority of the passengers being Australian. On the bridge was one of the Union Company's most senior masters, 55-year-old Captain John McIntosh. McIntosh, who had taken over from Chatfield, had commanded the *Wairarapa* for several years. His ship was fresh out of the Port Chalmers dock and was in perfect order.

The uneventful voyage was drawing to a close on 28 October when the *Wairarapa* began picking her way down the Northland coast. A thick fog hung about all the way but for some reason McIntosh, usually the most prudent of masters, flouted the company's standing orders by maintaining full speed and by refraining from using the fog horn – allegedly through fear of awakening those passengers who had gone to bed early so as to arrive refreshed in Auckland the following morning. It was a recipe for disaster. By the end of the day, some of the passengers and crew had been openly questioning such reckless speed.

At precisely eight minutes past midnight on the morning of 29 October the *Wairarapa*, still steaming at full speed, slammed into a 200-metre-high cliff about a kilometre east of Miners Head at the barren and forbidding tip of Great Barrier Island. McIntosh, who had earlier resisted his officers' requests to reduce speed, further compounded the problem by immediately ordering the engines to be reversed. This reduced the *Wairarapa*'s rush up the beach to the comparative safety of dry land. Although her bow was just a couple of metres from the cliff, the steepness of the bank made it impossible for anyone to come ashore via the bow. There she rested on a narrow rock shelf under assault from the waves.

Conditions were terrible. A heavy sea was washing the wreck and the night – still thick with fog – was pitch dark. Even the officers had no idea where they were, believing themselves to be on the Hen and Chicken Islands. Passengers and crew huddled on the cold decks, unable to see anything in the foggy dark but all too aware of the fearful sound of waves breaking against the cliffs nearby. Gradually their numbers thinned as waves snatched more and more away, sweeping them overboard and out into the dark. More went about 11 minutes later when the ship, sitting on a ledge of rock, slipped off and slid further into the water. Sixteen horses in their stalls, part of the deck cargo, broke loose at this point. They drowned but killed or stunned several of the passengers in their desperate struggles.

Typical was the experience of young Annie Howsea, who was travelling with her 70-year-old grandmother, Mrs Forbach, and W. Baker, a gentleman friend. When the alarm sounded the girl got up and assisted her grandmother onto the deck where the three were given lifebelts. They slipped these on just in time because minutes later a huge wave sent all three over the side into the water. There they clung together until Forbach slipped out of her belt and Baker disappeared from sight. The same thing very nearly happened to Annie, who had to struggle to tighten her belt. For a long time the old woman clung to her granddaughter, imploring her not to leave her and saying that if it had to be, they should meet death together bravely. Some time later in the night she died. Annie held onto her for as long as possible but later had to let go. After being in the water for a long time, she was picked up by a passing boat and taken ashore.[2]

Individual passengers and crew members displayed incredible courage. The three stewardesses were everywhere, helping women and children into lifebelts and even giving their own belts to those without them. Dunedin jeweller A. J. Lumley surrendered his to stewardess E. Grindrod before going over the side. Luck was with him. He was pulled into a boat by a fireman named Neill and taken to Whangapoua Bay where another boat, under third officer William Johnston, was waiting.[3]

Some quick-thinking crew saved several lives by cutting loose the liferafts and pushing them towards people struggling in the water. All but two of the boats were smashed before they could reach shore. Those two stood by until daylight, plucking

Mrs McDonald and Miss MacQuaid, two of the three *Wairarapa* stewardesses whose bravery in the face of death was lauded by the newspapers. Although seafaring last century was almost exclusively a male preserve, the larger passenger ships employed small numbers of stewardesses to attend to women passengers. *Wellington Maritime Museum & Gallery*

swimmers from the water wherever possible. Within a few hours the only people still alive aboard the wreck were those clinging to the fore and main rigging.

The bridge, symbol of McIntosh's shattered authority, did not last long. For a short while – probably no more than quarter of an hour – 40 or so people shuffled about on the bridge before it, too, collapsed and was washed overboard, taking everyone with it. One man reported that one great wave washed over them all, scattering them into the surf. He made it ashore after three-quarters of an hour but most were not so lucky. One particularly unfortunate woman succumbed to the hoof-blow of a drowning horse.

McIntosh had remained on the bridge after the collision but was not present when it collapsed. Just minutes earlier he had climbed onto the port rail and plunged head-first into the sea.[4]

Dawn brought an awful sight. Let the November issue of the *New Zealand Times* speak for itself:

> When daylight came a shocking scene presented itself to the gaze of the survivors. Straight ahead rose up a frowning perpendicular cliff, the ill-fated steamer on her port side, bows elevated, a perfect wreck, and quite close to the cliff, dead bodies mingled with the wreckage and deck cargo, while the sea for a considerable distance around was covered with flotsam of all descriptions – portions of deck-houses, cases of fruit, horse-stalls, etc.[5]

Two extremely brave seamen (one of whom was second steward Kendall) swan ashore with a rope and succeeded in bringing ashore all the rest of the survivors, except for two who lost hold of the rope and were carried away. Last to leave was steerage passenger John Austin. He had scrambled back on board earlier when the third lifeboat had capsized and had joined two Chinese men in the rigging. He soon realised that this was a temporary reprieve and that it would be suicide to remain there for long. Eventually he managed to persuade them to leave their perilous perch. 'The Chinese did not savee for a long time,' the paper reported, 'but before they could venture into the water they stripped, and sent their clothes in front of them.'[6]

There the survivors, most of them very scantily clad, huddled on the rocks, sustained by nothing more nourishing than a few oranges washed up alongside them. Conditions remained awful. The sharpness of the rocks and the absence of boots prevented most of the men from doing much to help swimmers caught in the surf. Instead, they had to watch the heavy waves toss these poor unfortunates about among the rocks.

While they endured these further trials, the rest of New Zealand grew apprehensive. The *Manapouri* had spoken to the *Wairarapa* at 1800 hours on the 26th but nothing further had been heard of her. By 1 November, the Auckland papers were reporting that 'some anxiety is felt regarding her'.[7] This had been heightened on the morning of the previous day when the same company's *Rotomahana*, which had left Sydney 24 hours after the *Wairarapa*, turned up safely.

By 1 October, the Dunedin headquarters of the Union Company was clearly worried. It instructed two other trans-Tasman liners, the *Waihora* and *Wakatipu*, to search the neighbourhood of North Cape and the Three Kings (*Waihora*) and to the southward (*Wakatipu*). Even at this late stage, though, no one suspected the worst. Machinery and shaftings were still unreliable and it would not have been the first (or last) time that a ship was left drifting around the Tasman for days or even weeks.

Then came dramatic news. The *Wairarapa* had run ashore at Great Barrier, almost in sight of her destination, and most of her passengers and crew were feared dead. Local settlers and Maori reported bodies in the sea and all along the coast of the beautiful but inhospitable island shoreline.

Later the Union Company's stewardesses erected a memorial in Dunedin to commemorate their co-workers' heroism. This composite print by local photographer de Maus features photographs of the stewardesses and the monument superimposed over a painting of the wreck. *Wellington Maritime Museum & Gallery*

When the coastal steamer *Argyle* steamed out to Great Barrier on Wednesday with Thomas Henderson, the Union Company's Auckland branch manager, and a party that included an undertaker aboard, she called first at Fitzroy Harbour. There the postmaster informed Henderson that the bodies of two women had already been buried; the Maori of Catherine Bay had interred about a dozen corpses. Estimates of the death toll varied widely. One settler had made the tally 137, of which 40–50 had already been accounted for. The later best estimate was 125 casualties; some 40 bodies were never found.

There were some pathetic sights. On Tuesday rescuers had plucked the body of a woman in a lifebelt out of Fitzroy Harbour; in her lifeless hands she still clutched the body of a tiny baby. The *Argyle* rescued third officer Johnston from a small boat and then passed the floating bridge of the steamer off Catherine Bay, fishing out bodies as she went. There Henderson learned that local settlers had snatched 19 bodies from the surf, dragging them above the wave line.

Collecting the bodies was not a task for the faint-hearted. The first corpse of an unnamed man was found with a lifebelt under his arms; his only clothing was a portion of his nightshirt. Almost beside him was a dead horse. About 100 metres further on, the landing party found its second corpse, that of a young woman. And so on. . . . As each body was found, planks, hammers and nails were produced and rough, makeshift coffins were knocked up while others in the party

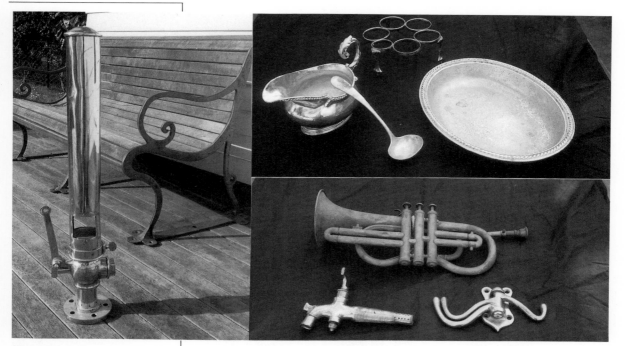

The *Wairarapa* wreck site continues to attract divers. These photographs, taken by Auckland diver Grant Ogle, show relics recovered from the site. *Top right*: tableware; *lower right*: a cornet, tap and coat hooks; *left*: the steam whistle from the funnel. The seat in the background is made of material recovered from the site of two Union Company wrecks, the *Wairarapa* and the *Waikare* (Dusky Sound, 1910). *Grant Ogle*

took careful note of the appearance of the bodies, clothing, rings, etc. Several bodies showed the marks of their rough encounters with the rocks. Just around the corner, the men came upon bodies lying under bright red pohutukawa.

The unpleasant job of searching for and collecting bodies went on for days. Identifying them and contacting next of kin took even longer. Passenger lists did not tally and confusion reigned for some time. Each day the colony's press carried reports on new bodies, items found and, increasingly rarely, of people confirmed safe and sound. As late as 30 November the *Otago Daily Times* carried details of Oamaru survivor David Hastie's wallet, of documents and letters belonging to Charles White from Sydney and of a reported dispute over the ownership of 133 sovereigns found on the body of George Bird.

Given all this raw material, it was only to be expected that the court of inquiry would go to town. Judge H. W. Northcroft, assisted by Captains M. T. Clayton and Andrew, had no doubt that the real cause of the disaster must be laid at the feet of Captain McIntosh. The *Wairarapa* had overrun her distance on her east-south-east course, with McIntosh failing to make due allowance for the speed at which she was travelling or the current and set of the sea, both of which were pushing him off course. 'I am of the opinion that the S.S. *Wairarapa* was lost through Captain McIntosh and the first and second officers not taking a correct point of departure at the Three Kings, and not allowing for a current which, by the first and second officers' evidence, they should have been aware was running to the south and south-east,' he concluded.[8]

Concluding that 'the so-called boat drill is a mere farce', Northcroft roasted the officers and men for failing to take advantage of the 11 minutes between initial impact and the heavy list to port. He accused them of allowing the abandonment of the ship to degenerate into a free-for-all, 'not having even had this farcical boat drill for over six months.'[9] (McIntosh had suspended it during winter months, reasoning that the longstanding crew knew its job well enough.)

Northcroft then railed against their inability to meet 'what might have been expected of them, what we always expect of British seamen worthy of that name when there are women, children and passengers in peril'.[10] Quoting the evidence of several crewmen, he condemned McIntosh for suggesting that officers and men made for the comparative safety of the rigging while passengers remained on the wave-tossed decks. In concluding this section of his report, Northcroft quoted carpenter Peter H. Thompson: 'It was thought that the ship was going down, and my impression was that it seemed to be everybody for himself.'[11]

Referring to the chief officer's conduct in letting the raft with 12 people float towards the Needles while he retained two serviceable boats at Whangapoua, the court said that 'no censure we can pass is severe enough'. His three-day delay in searching the coastline between the wreck and Whangapoua was described as 'inhuman and inexplicable', especially in view of the fact that many of the bodies later found floating in the water were wearing lifebelts. How many of them might have been saved if a steamer had appeared earlier?

Also slated were the second and fourth officers and the purser, of whom Northcroft said, 'All I can say is that he saved himself'. The only ones praised were the engineers, the stewards and the stewardesses, especially Mrs McDonald and Miss Macquaid, each of whom was last seen giving her lifebelt to a female passenger. 'The conduct of these noble and self-sacrificing women is beyond human praise,' he concluded.[12]

The court's practical recommendations were for all boats to be uncovered and swung out in foggy weather and for the rafts to be launched at the first possible opportunity rather than left until all the boats had been launched. Costs were divided between the various parties.

The Union Company conducted its own inquiry, the results of which were presented to the board by managing director James Mills in a highly confidential report dated 10 January 1895. This document, which was never released to the public, makes interesting reading. Although one could suspect Mills of bias, it should be remembered that he was no protector of the incompetent; furthermore, the fact that the report was never made public means that it was not intended to have any propaganda value.

Mills agreed with the court's basic findings, attributing the loss to McIntosh's 'recklessness'. Like so many others, Mills was puzzled by this. As he acknowledged, McIntosh 'had the reputation of being a careful and prudent navigator', with a loyal following who would often travel in the *Wairarapa* because of his track record. Mills could only put it down to the captain's recent health problems. McIntosh had suffered from repeated attacks of influenza in recent months. While at Port Chalmers in September–October, when the ship was undergoing a refit, he had applied for a short leave of absence and had taken a train to Lake Wakatipu for a rest. Only later did the company learn that McIntosh had 'consulted Dr Coughtrey about his health, informing him that he felt at times that his nerves were shaken, and that at times he did not feel confidence in his own judgement'.[13] Clearly the man had had some sort of break-down during the voyage.

Mills disagreed with other findings, especially the one which said that the crew should have had time to swing out the boats just after striking. With just eight (six crewmen and two catering staff) on deck at the time and most of the rest below or asleep, Mills believed that little more could have been done before the ship's list made the safe launching of boats imprac-tical. The list made it impossible to launch the starboard boats and the collapse of the funnel had destroyed another boat.

He also pooh-poohed the finding that it had been everyone for themselves. 'We cannot conclude that, though the chief officer merits to some extent the censure passed upon him, and perhaps, also the second officer and purser, the ship's company as a whole behaved exceedingly well under very trying circumstances, and did not deserve the sweeping criti-cism passed upon them by the court, while in individual cases great heroism was displayed.'[14]

Mills reserved his greatest criticism for the chief officer, second officer and purser Fenwick. The second officer he almost excused on the grounds of age. The chief, however, was roasted for not providing a better example to passengers and subordinates. He was also criticised for not dispatching a Maori boat to the mainland on Tuesday to summon aid. Both officers lost their jobs. Fenwick had been worried by McIntosh's actions and had slept fully clothed in the saloon. After the wreck he had done nothing to compile a list of survivors or help with the identification of bodies.

Mills's final remarks make interesting reading.

In reviewing all the circumstances connected with this unfortunate disaster, it must be borne in mind that the catastrophe was of a sudden and overwhelming nature, the ship heeling over within a few minutes after striking, and her decks being swept by heavy seas on a rough night, the darkness of which was rendered even more intense by the prevailing fog . . . correspondents in the newspapers have urged that, under certain conditions, the officers should have the right to set the master's authority on one side, and themselves take charge of the ship. This is a point to which I have given much consideration. I find it is the almost universal practice in our fleet for masters to consult with their chief officers at all times in cases of doubt. I hesitate, however, to recommend any regu-lation authorising officers to interfere with the supreme authority of the master . . . such a regulation would lead to divided authority, and in many cases would undoubtedly be a source of danger rather than the contrary. One of our new rules, however, will convey an

Left: The wreck of the *Wairarapa* exerted a morbid fascination over the inhabitants of the small colony. This 'special' was rushed out by Dunedin's *Otago Daily Times*. Union Steam Ship Company Archives, *Wellington Maritime Museum & Gallery*

*Right:*The cover of the report containing the Union Steam Ship Company's internal inquiry into the wreck. Needless to say, it never saw the light of day. *Union Steam Ship Company Archives, Wellington Maritime Museum & Gallery*

instruction to officers, providing that in cases where a master is taking a course that is dangerous, or in defiance of the Company's regulations, they shall present the same to the master and record the fact of such record, to be subsequently forwarded in writing to the Marine Superintendent. I feel sure that this will afford sufficient check upon recklessness on the part of masters, while at the same time it will not in any way relieve them of their responsibility.

Mills also questioned reports that McIntosh had been racing his ship, aiming for a record passage. The fuel- and safety-minded Mills had always drummed it into the heads of his masters that their ships were not to be raced under any circumstances. McIntosh had no incentive to try for a fast passage.

And what of the *Wairarapa*? Even as late as the 1930s she would continue to fatten her file in the Union Company building as relatives tried to track down information about former passengers or crew. Rumours about the ship's safe being loaded into a boat and then lost in the surf drew the curious. In November 1923 W. E. Vear and J. McKinnon, working from the scow *Katie S.*, and against the wishes of the Union Company, bought the *Wairarapa* from the Minister of Marine and started diving on her and the wreck of the nearby American schooner *Cecilia Sudden*. Using generous amounts of dynamite, they brought up about 40 tonnes of materials, including the four propellers, some of the shafting, a 6-tonne condenser and other material. They found several horse skeletons on the seabed but no human ones and no sign of the safe.

One of the boilers was found some distance away, full of crayfish.

As recently as 1979, divers-cum-authors Steve Locker-Lampson and Ian Francis reported that the old ship was badly broken up but still a wreck of importance. The starboard side is still semi-intact and large pieces of wreckage abound. Indeed, the compass had been recovered a decade earlier, still in working order.[15]

```
                              COPY.

                      D R O M A N A.
                      14th N o v, 1894.


      M R  D. MILLS.
            Melbourne.
                Dear Sir,-

                    I wish to ask you for further particulars
      of the body of one of the passengers that was wrecked  in the
      "WAIRARAPA" a tall stout man with brown beard and one of the
      thumb nails growing over the end of the thumb as described in
      the Argus on the 8th inst, that is known to be the body of J_
      Talbot.   I wish to know if his clothes were on him or if they
      have been found as he had some title deeds on him, also a watch
      of Stewart Dawson & Co, and Mackintosh branded Foy & Gibson.
                    I may also mention I am left a widow with 3 little
      children.
                Kindly enquire and let me know.
                    K. TALBOT.
```

This letter, sent to the Union Company, underlines the personal losses experienced by the dependants of shipwreck victims in the days when social welfare benefits were almost non-existent. Shipping companies seldom made *ex gratia* payments. *Union Steam Ship Company Archives, Wellington Maritime Museum & Gallery*

Notes

1. Information for this chapter is based on newspaper clippings and original documents from the Union Company papers held by the Wellington Maritime Museum and Gallery. Also useful was Steve Locker-Lampson and Ian Francis, *Eight Minutes Past Midnight*, Wellington, 1981.
2. *Otago Daily Times*, 3 November 1894.
3. *Ibid.*, 14 November.
4. *Ibid.*, 3 November.
5. Press clipping, '*Wairarapa* File', Union Company papers, *op. cit.*
6. *Otago Daily Times*, 3 November 1894.
7. *Auckland Star*, 29 October 1894.
8. 'Report of the Court of Inquiry', printed as a supplement to the *Otago Witness*, 13 December 1894.
9. *Ibid.*
10. *Ibid.*
11. *Ibid.*
12. *Ibid.*
13. James Mills, 'Finding of the Court of Inquiry in the Matter of the Wreck of S.S. *Wairarapa* Together With Memorandum Prepared by Managing-Director For the Consideration of the Board and List of Lost and Saved', Dunedin, 10 January 1895, Union Company papers, *op. cit.*
14. *Ibid.*
15. Steve Locker-Lampson and Ian Francis, *The Wreck Book*, Wellington, 1979, pp. 96–97.

Chapter 11

THE PENGUIN

> During the whole morning and all the afternoon the Union Company was crowded with people eager for the latest word about the missing and the saved. Anxious relatives or friends of passengers and members of the crew clustered around the notice boards and swept from room to room. Some, when the wires and messengers failed to bring news about the safety of a father, a mother, or child, hoped on for better tidings but the hope of some broke down, and the sounds of women's sobbing rose above the murmur of many voices asking, answering, wondering about the chances.

This report, from the *Evening Post* of 13 February 1909, heralded news of worse things to come – one of the costliest shipwrecks in the short history of the colony. The victim of the catastrophe was the *Penguin*, the regular ferry between the capital and Picton and Nelson. Although the initial fears that all but 13 of the 105 aboard had drowned would be disproved, there was no question that the accident, which claimed 75 lives, was a disaster.

At first the likeable little *Penguin* seemed an unlikely victim. True, she was rather long in the tooth, having started life at Glasgow as long ago as 1864. Since coming to New Zealand in 1879 for the Union Company to replace the wrecked *Taupo*, however, the *Penguin* had been maintained immaculately by

The *Penguin* at Port Chalmers early in her career. This view shows her pretty much as built. *Harraway Collection, Hocken Library*

114

Like most nineteenth-century coasters, the *Penguin* experienced several minor mishaps. This photograph, which gives an excellent view of the hull form of the ship, was taken during a stranding at Nelson. *Nelson Provincial Museum*

the company's meticulous repair staff. The outwardly non-descript little 824-ton steamer had plied along many of the company's most important routes.

An 1892 re-engining with compound engines lowered fuel bills while pushing the *Penguin*'s maximum speed up to 13 knots. Three years later she started making once-weekly return voyages between Wellington and Lyttelton, the start of the later famous 'steamer express service'. In 1902, after a brief stint in Australian waters, the *Penguin* returned to New Zealand and the passenger/cargo service between Wellington and Nelson and Picton.

The little steamer's voyage into oblivion began quietly enough at 1820 hours on 12 February 1909 when she pulled away from the Picton jetty and headed up the sound for Wellington. By the time she entered Cook Strait proper – about two hours later – the weather was clear but threatening to deteriorate. Cook Strait, one of the roughest, windiest stretches of water on earth, is notorious for its fickleness. It can change from balmy and sunny to a raging southerly 'buster' within minutes. This is precisely what happened that fateful day. By the time that the ship was halfway across the narrow stretch of water, the weather was very thick and visibility minimal.

The *Penguin*'s master, Captain F. E. Naylor, set an outside course, intending to take her well clear of the rocky coast on the other side of the strait, and allowed for a strong southerly set. At 2145 he was still feeling his way towards the entrance to the harbour, expecting to pick up the Pencarrow light any moment, when the *Penguin* struck a rock with a grinding crash, sliding along the submerged object on her starboard side. In the words

The *Penguin* photographed at Wellington during her Cook Strait ferry service. Notice how much her superstructure was rebuilt during her 1892 refit; such alterations were common last century when shipowners held onto ships for longer than their modern counterparts' accountants will let them. *Wellington Maritime Museum & Gallery*

of seaman Charles Jackson, it sounded just like 'the rending of a gigantic piece of calico'.[1] As dawn would show, she had struck Tom's Rock, approximately abreast the outfall of the Karori Stream.

Tom's Rock is just one of several hazards on this rocky and unforgiving coastline. About 1.5 metres underwater most of the time, the rock is the outermost of the Terawhiti rocks and the most exposed. A vicious current of 3–6 knots sweeps past and anyone lucky enough to survive the initial impact has to contend both with this and the swirls that develop closer to the rocky shore. Several ships, including the barque *Grasmere* in 1895, had come to grief in the vicinity of Tom's Rock.

But back to 1909. Naylor swung out the boats as soon as soundings revealed that the chain locker and the forecabin were flooding. Soon the Nos 1 and 2 holds were filling and it was obvious that the old ship had reached the end of the line. Beaching was out of the question – the coastline was simply too exposed and rocky. Once the initial shock passed, the officers and men started putting women and children in the boats.

The first boat had hardly begun to enter the water, though, when it dropped bow-first into a heavy sea which swamped it, flinging the hapless occupants into the heaving seas. The men left aboard the *Penguin* gasped with horror at the sight, but most of the floundering passengers and crew made it back onto the deck. Soaked and scared, they reboarded the lifeboat with instructions to pull far out to let the flood tide take them around Terawhiti, but two boats sank before they could get very far.

Naylor was soon too caught up in his own personal struggle for survival to be of much assistance to others. Sensing that his

These photographs, taken on 13 February 1909, show the rocky and inhospitable nature of the western coastline where the lifeboats came ashore. Rocks are always the greatest hazard to shipwreck victims trying to scramble to safety. *Wellington Maritime Museum & Gallery*

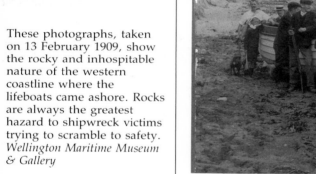

shattered command would not long provide much refuge, he had already stepped into the sea from his bridge, ready to accept what fate brought him. A wave drew him towards a piece of one of the wrecked lifeboats. Supported by these few fragments of timber, he was able to drift along with the current and observe how others were faring in their struggle for survival.

'I could see the rafts. They had a very rough time,' Naylor recalled, while fighting to retain his precarious hand-hold. 'They got into a swirling, treacherous sea, and were swung round and round. Several times those who were on them when they left the ship were washed off,' he remembered. 'I believe all on the rafts reached the shore,' he told a reporter.

The sea dumped Naylor on the beach about 0300 the following morning. Two rafts came ashore near him, with 11 and 12 survivors respectively. All had had a very trying time, one raftload being overturned completely three times. It was a bleak landfall. The night was pitch dark, the rain was falling

Nineteenth-century photographs of corpses are rare. These images attracted criticism at the time.
Wellington Maritime Museum & Gallery

heavily and the southerly was shrieking against the cliffs. Since it was too dark to risk going any further, Naylor crawled into the scrub and curled up, waiting for dawn. Other luckier survivors from the raft made it to the station of a settler named McMenamin, who soon had fires blazing and food and beverages on the table.

While the rafts had been heading shorewards, the occupants of the ship's boats had been fighting their own battles. For some it was a brief struggle. As we have seen, the first boat launched was smashed to pieces within minutes. The second fared little better. Partly stove-in, she first appeared to have made a successful escape. Shortly afterwards, however, a heavy sea sent her over on her side, drowning most of her occupants. The other boat, launched with great difficulty by Jackson and the second officer, also turned turtle within minutes. The crew made an attempt to launch the No. 3 lifeboat but by then the list of the ship was too great for it to be dislodged.

It was one of the night's saddest ironies, that the lifeboats, which probably looked safest to the passengers, provided the most illusory chances of survival. Only two people would reach shore alive on one and then it would be under the craft, not in it. When rescuers dragged a broken lifeboat out of the surf, they rolled it over to discover a youth named Ellis Matthews and Mrs Hannam, a passenger from Blenheim. Hannam, who lost her husband and four children in the disaster, was the only woman from the passenger list or crew to survive.

When the disaster struck, Mrs Hannam, along with the other women passengers, was called to board the lifeboat. Stewards were handing out blankets and although the weather was atrocious and the ship's position dangerous, Mrs Hannam was not flustered. Seconds later everything fell apart. As the crew struggled to lower the boat, the tackle collapsed, dropping it into the water, bow-first. Three of her children – Ralph (10), George (five) and Amelia (three) – were swept away in seconds. They cried out to her but she could do nothing to assist them.

For the rest of the night the boat drifted shorewards. Once she sighted a raft and called out but received no response. Then the rocks loomed up. The one seaman tried his best to keep clear of the rocks with his oar but to no avail. A big wave struck the boat, capsizing it and throwing everyone into the water.

'When the boat turned over, I clung to it again,' Hannam recalled.

> I could see my baby was still tied to the seat. There was a young boy named Matthews. I kept hold of him, for we were then underneath the boat. We both clung to the seats but could see nothing, for the boat covered us and our heads touched the bottom of it. The air in the boat kept us alive, because every time there was a big wave, it lifted the boat a little and let in the fresh air.

She calmly accepted the news that her baby, Ruby, who she had tied to the boat, was dead. 'Oh, let me untie it myself,' she told the men nervously offering assistance by untying the tiny corpse, 'I know how I fixed it up.'

So much for the lifeboats – what about the rafts that Naylor had observed? Once the boats had gone, the crew unlashed the rafts and pushed them over the side, shepherding the remaining male passengers aboard. By now the *Penguin*'s engines had stopped and, her bows well down, she was wallowing as each wave slammed into her. Jackson, being a strong and confident swimmer, was the first to leap towards a raft. 'I stuck to the painter,' he recalled,

The photograph bears the handwritten inscription:

WRECK of the S.S. PENGUIN
80 LIVES LOST 12·2·09·
SURVIVORS by the 1ST RAFT
AT SCENE OF LANDING
"TERAWHITI"
HOPKINS, BRIDGE
& PERKINS
(passengers)
FARREL, LUNN,
LUKE (ENGINEER)
THOMPSON (PURSER)
& McCORMICK
(crew)
"ZAK" PHOTO
Wellington.
3742A N.Z.

Survivors on the beach after their ordeal. These men, from the first liferaft, were: (front, left to right) Messrs Farrel, Lunn, Luke, Thompson and McCormick, all crew and (back, left to right), passengers Hopkins, Bridge and Perkins. *Zak photograph, Wellington Maritime Museum & Gallery*

and I looked up at the vessel. She was down by the nose with her stern high out of the water. Some of the men on the deck were afraid to jump but they soon recognised that the ship was fast settling down. One by one they commenced to leap over the side, and happily, all managed to reach the little craft which was being buffeted about in the waves. Altogether 12 people clambered aboard the raft, of which I took charge.

Their timing was impeccable. Just moments later the *Penguin*'s boilers burst as cold seawater met red-hot iron. The result was a tremendous explosion, which tore the ship apart and sent her to the bottom within minutes. Fortunately the wild waves had carried the occupants of both rafts far enough away to protect them from falling debris or from being sucked under by the vortex set up by the *Penguin*'s departure.

Jackson's passengers managed to pluck two oars from the water and used these to guide the drift of their pitching and tossing little craft. For three hours they drifted in the pitch dark, being overturned three times. Fortunately all were good swimmers and everyone managed to scramble back aboard. Then, at about 0300, the dim outline of the shore loomed up out of the haze and mist. With a final rush, the raft crashed up onto the rocks and everyone started to scramble ashore, cut and bruised, but thankful to be alive and safe on the shore.

Jackson's last glimpse was of Captain Naylor, who was floating nearby, on the battered fragment of a boat:

> He was accompanied by a passenger, apparently a young man, between 25 and 30. By some means, of which I am not aware, this poor fellow had one of his hands torn from the arm, and I myself saw the Captain taking out his handkerchief and binding it above the poor fellow's wrist. The captain managed to reach the shore, as we did, but his companion did not. His dead body is now lying on the beach.

It was just one of many bodies. For the next few days the police and volunteers scoured the coastline looking for survivors or bodies. They found none of the former but plenty of the latter. Eventually 61 corpses would be recovered, of which less than half would be identified. Today they lie in the nearby Karori Cemetery. Sightseers had a field day. Mud and the swift rain-swollen streams kept the better-attired at bay but many Wellingtonians made the rough journey out to gawp and gaze. Among the most visible was a photographer whom the press considered ghoulish in his exertions to record the corpses for posterity; since there was little in the way of wreckage visible, the bodies were all that could be photographed.

Perhaps inevitably, the court of inquiry slated Captain Naylor for his actions leading up to the disaster. Although it conceded that the presence of an exceptionally strong flood tide had contributed to the tragedy, it criticised him for not putting his vessel's head to sea soon enough after he had run a course of 18 miles. On a majority verdict, one of the nautical assessors dissenting, the court suspended his certificate for 12 months.

Notes
1. Information is drawn from the *Evening Post* of 13 February 1909 as well as the USS Co. files held at the Hocken Library.

Part 3

UNNATURAL CAUSES

The image that television would flash around the world; the *Rainbow Warrior* listing against Marsden Wharf, the banner above her wheelhouse still defiantly demanding a nuclear-free Pacific. *New Zealand Herald*

The Union Company's *Hawea* had many mishaps during her short but eventful career. This shows her ashore at Nelson on 30 March 1886. *Kingsford & Baigent, courtesy of Wellington Maritime Museum & Gallery*

Chapter 12

VILLAINY!

As insurance companies know only too well, there is a time-honoured, if far from honourable, practice of deliberately wrecking ships in order to claim the insurance money. The annals of British maritime history are replete with tales of 'coffin ships' – overloaded, poorly fitted out migrant ships sent to sea in the hope that they will come to grief – as well as simpler cases of deliberate wrecking. Last century the sea claimed so many ships that less scrupulous shipowners and speculators must have found it very tempting to abandon a ship or two halfway across the globe, knowing that the authorities, much less the insurers, would find it very hard to point the finger of blame. Nor is the practice over. Lloyd's of London, the venerable marine insurer, was plagued during the 1980s by a disturbing number of tankers sinking or being abandoned off the African coast.

The very nature of the crime means that documented cases of premeditated wrecking are rare in New Zealand maritime history. Suspicion abounds in several cases, one as recently as the 1960s, but suspicions are no substitute for hard evidence.

The earliest case may have been that of the brig *Wanderer*, which came ashore at Riverton, Southland, some time in early 1861. Evidence is sketchy. Ingram quotes an article on early Riverton which hints discreetly that: 'ships had a habit of coming to stay as when the brig *Wanderer* gently eased up on the beach and settled to rest. As the captain pointed out, she had had 24 years of service and was entitled to a pensioned old age.'[1]

Less cautious was Robert Fulton in his delightfully readable book *Medical Practice in Otago and Southland in the Early Days*. Writing about local general practitioner, Dr Monckton, Fulton records that:

> Dr Monckton found that vessels came to New Zealand for the express purpose of stopping there, and on one occasion the brig *Wanderer*, with a load of grain, came ashore in a perfectly calm sea only two miles from Riverton. When the tide receded the men stepped over the bows on to the beach, and camped under tents made of sails until the master had arranged for unloading and carting the cargo away. Dr Monckton had a look at her, and being a bit of "a practical man", and always inclined to mix with business

outside of his own, offered to get her off the beach and into the river for £25. Captain Howell, to whom he made the offer, laughed at him, saying that he knew it was quite practicable, and would cost half that; but as there was no Lloyds Agency in the neighbourhood to make objections on behalf of the underwriters, the wiser course was to let the brig rest her poor old bones where they were. She had been floating for 27 years, and if the doctor would be a wise man not to interfere in other people's business.[2]

Our next example, while not as melodramatically villainous, since it involved possible insurance fraud rather than outright wrecking, is nonetheless interesting. It concerns the loss of the Union Steam Ship Company's coaster *Hawea* at New Plymouth in 1888.

The *Hawea* was rather special to the Union Company, being one of the pair of new steamers with which it had started business in 1875. At 721 tons and powered by the new, highly efficient compound engine, the *Hawea* and her sister ship *Taupo* set new standards for the coastal routes. When Union's managing director, James Mills, and chairman, George McLean, puffed up the coast between Dunedin and Onehunga, they were feted at every port by a mesmerised press. 'Travellers, unless their business is very urgent, elect to wait a day or two in order to secure passage by them,' one paper observed.[3]

Bigger ships had followed in later years but the *Hawea* was still a valuable asset 13 years later when, late in the evening of 11 June 1888, she arrived off New Plymouth on a routine voyage from Onehunga. New Plymouth, like so many minor ports, was going through a troubled patch. Local squabbles had factionalised the harbour board and the breakwater had not made the progress hoped for. As a consequence, the place had an evil reputation among seafarers, who treated it with great caution. As it was pitch dark, Captain John Hansby dropped anchor and remained at anchor.

At 0630 hours the following morning, upon being signalled from shore, he began to approach the wharf. A strong north-wester was bouncing the ship about and the anchor slipped off its chain while being raised. Undaunted by this, Hansby continued to pick his way towards the breakwater wharf before reversing briefly to make room for the coaster *Gairloch* which was sailing. During the course of this manoeuvre, however, the *Hawea* struck heavily aft and started to take in water.

The ship settled by the stern and wound up with her bow poking high out of the water. Hansby gave the order to abandon ship and 11 passengers, their baggage and the mails were put in the first boat and rowed safely to the wharf. Loading the second boat was more eventful. The *Hawea* lurched over, almost on her beam ends, sweeping away chief officer William Waller. A whaleboat deftly picked him from the sea but Allegro, one of the two prize racehorses being unloaded, was not so fortunate and ended up being drowned in the surf.

By 0930 it was obvious that the *Hawea* was doomed. Water

pressure burst the engine room bulkhead and the steamer rested on an even keel. After seeing off the remainder of the 36 hands, Hansby and Waller abandoned the £35,000 vessel and stepped ashore. The Union Company's local agent, W. Newman, supervised the removal of the compasses and a few minor deck fittings before telegraphing Dunedin later that day: 'Weather now deteriorating, shall pay off all hands tomorrow'. The storm dashed any faint hopes that might have existed for salvaging the wreck which, at auction eight days later, fetched £120 and the fittings a further £90.

It was a pretty miserable return on a ship insured for £13,000 and the Union Company, a harsh taskmaster at the best of times, did not take long to exact vengeance on Hansby.

These photographs, believed to show the *Hawea*, show what a crucial part the breakwater played in making New Plymouth's exposed roadstead safe for shipping. *Taranaki Museum*

Although completely exonerated by the court of inquiry, which could not discover the cause of the disaster, Hansby was dismissed from the company's service. Broken, he wrote to the local newspaper, decrying the injustice of the decision, which in his view arose:

> solely through the fault of the "so-called" harbour, or instructions of their servants, and did I think them worth the powder and shot, might possibly resort to other means to vindicate myself. However, I will let a "sleeping dog lie" and do not intend by controversy to bring grist to the mill of the *Taranaki Herald*. Let them take any action they like to prove that I struck anything harder than water outside their "so-called" harbour and I will be quite prepared to fight the battle again.[4]

Hansby stamped off to find employment with an opposition company as master of the trans-Tasman trader *Jubilee*. He was struck by a tram and killed at Sydney a year later.

In fact, despite all the initial bluster and finger-pointing, no one really wanted to make much of an issue of the accident. The Union Company advised the hapless harbour board of its intention to claim £30,000, alleging that the board's staff acted negligently in signalling the *Hawea* to enter port and by failing to clear the channel of obstructions, but took the claim no further.

The reason was simple. It would have been too embarrassing to pursue the matter. The harbourmaster had been adamant that 5 metres of water should have lain where the *Hawea* was swinging and Newman was not inclined to dispute this. As he advised Union Company managing director James Mills in a confidential letter on 20 June 1888: 'I think it would be unwise to employ a diver to look for the supposed obstruction . . . as circumstances would indicate that it could not have been anything but the anchor which did the damage and so possibly open up the question of damages against ourselves.'

Although a rock had been located 76 metres astern of the wreck, Newman wrote that: 'I do not for a moment think that it contributed to the incident. . . . It would be policy no doubt to give the Harbour Board formal notice of action, which will obtain publicity and may prevent Keith [owner of the valuable racehorse Allegro] from pursuing his suit against us for the loss of Allegro . . .'[5]

And so it came about that the Union Company proceeded no further with its claim against the New Plymouth Harbour Board. The insurance companies paid out. The wreck sank into the sands of the harbour and eventual obscurity. Any last chance of rewriting the pages of history disappeared in the 1920s and 1930s when it was blasted apart during the course of dredging operations.

New Zealand's most infamous and best-recorded case of deliberately casting away a ship occurred at the mouth of the Waitaki River, just north of Oamaru, on the evening of 24 March 1901. The vessel concerned was an unusual one, the 230-ton schooner-yacht *Ariadne*. Built in a lavish manner at

The elegant schooner-yacht *Ariadne* ashore near the mouth of the Waitaki river, North Otago, 1901.
Alexander Turnbull Library

Gosport, England, in 1874 of oak, teak and pine, the *Ariadne* was the nineteenth-century equivalent of the private jet. Fast, stylish and elegant, she flew the flag of the Royal Thames Yacht Club and, when built, was described by her owner as the largest schooner-yacht sailing under the British flag.[6]

Luxuriously appointed, she had been the winner of the international yacht race and the German Emperor's Cup at Cowes. Owned by English gentleman T. C. Kerry, she had been cruising in the Pacific. Her voyage had already been marked by trouble. She had grounded on a reef off Thursday Island and had only been refloated with great difficulty. When she limped into Sydney in November 1900 Kerry paid off the master, Captain C. H. W. Willes, and the rest of the crew. Shortly afterwards he hired a new master, George Mumford, who had been recommended by former crewman A. Olsen, and made plans to sail the *Ariadne* across the Tasman to Dunedin.

The *Ariadne* had been beating her way down the coast on the final leg of an otherwise uneventful trans-Tasman voyage. At about 2000 hours in the evening of 24 March, however, less than 3 kilometres south of the Waitaki Mouth, the ship ploughed up on the shingle beach. Hitting at near high water, she ran so far up the beach that the 12-man crew was able to step ashore unharmed.

At first it was hoped that this might also be the saving of the ship, which was largely intact. The weather improved in the following days and initially it looked as though Port Chalmers businessman John Mill, who bought the wreck for £215 on 26 April, had got the bargain of the new century. His good fortune was matched only by that of the Kai Tahu from the Waitaki reserve who, in a nice example of local initiative, started charging townsfolk a toll for gawping at the schooner stuck in the shingle.

Unfortunately for both Pakeha and Maori entrepreneurs, heavy seas sprang up during the next few days and reduced the *Ariadne* to a complete wreck, scattering her high-quality debris for kilometres, to the delight of Oamaru citizens who souvenired items from the wreck. Mill went away happy, though. Before the sea scattered his prize far and wide, he managed to salvage the masts and enough lead ballast to make his little speculation highly profitable.

The court of inquiry, held at Oamaru under the jurisdiction of Major Keddell, SM, decreed that the master, George Mumford, was guilty of a grave error of judgement in not wearing (tacking) his ship 2 or 3 kilometres sooner than he did. It suspended his certificate for three months and fined him 15 guineas.

Case closed? For once, this was not so. The Oamaru water-front had been abuzz with rumours that the ship had been wrecked on purpose and word soon spread. Suspecting insurance fraud (the *Ariadne*, insured for £10,000 and valued at £5,000, had been bought by Kerry for £2,100), Captain S. Willis, Lloyd's agent at Christchurch, hired a detective and at the end of May went to Dunedin to interview Mumford.

At first the disgraced skipper refused to answer Willis's questions. At a second meeting, however, Mumford said that Kerry had offered him £400 for deliberately wrecking the ship, also promising him the additional incentive of the captaincy of a larger ship Kerry hoped to buy in England with the insurance money. This, too, he hoped to wreck for profit later. To Willis's delight, Mumford offered to put this confession in writing for £400.

Why would he do something so risky? Mumford professed to be angry with Kerry, now safely in Sydney, for not paying him the first instalment of his fee and seemed to want to get even, whatever the cost. In a bizarre letter to his former employer, Mumford repudiated their agreement (he claimed to have lost his copy of a written agreement he had received from Kerry) and threatened retaliation through Willis and the authorities. A few days later Mumford moved to Christchurch under the alias 'Captain G. Stevens', allegedly worried that Kerry might pursue him.

On 7 June Mumford presented Willis with the wrecking agreement which, he claimed, had – rather fortuitously – turned up in the lining of an old coat. Purportedly signed by Kerry, it read 'I, T. C. Kerry agree with George Mumford to pay him £12 wages as master of the *Ariadne*, and a further £400 if the vessel is totally wrecked'. Quite an unusual set of articles!

Although Willis at first found this document difficult to

On 2 April 1891 the New Plymouth coastline claimed another early Union Company steamer, the *Wanaka* (493 tons, 1877). This time the circumstances were less unusual. The ship was approaching the breakwater in thick fog and low visibility when she struck Puketapu Reef. All hands made it ashore safely but the *Wanaka* could not be refloated and later broke up. The master, James Meade, was censured for not slowing down and not heaving the lead under conditions of such poor visibility so close to land. *Wellington Maritime Museum & Gallery*

believe (Mumford's letter to Kerry had indicated that there had been no agreement), an investigation showed that the signature appeared to match that of Kerry on another document. Willis, who until then had merely been collecting evidence with a civil case in mind, paid Mumford and then approached the police who arrested Mumford on 8 October at Lyttelton where he had been working on the wharves. That same day Sydney police arrested Kerry and E. J. H. Freyke, Kerry's companion, whom Mumford had also implicated. All were charged and bailed on the very rare charge of deliberately casting away a vessel.

The affair then started to take on all the characteristics of bad penny dreadfuls. After Sydney barmaid Annie Downing told the Crown that she had overheard the men plotting to wreck the ship, Mumford met her at a Christchurch hotel and attempted to get her to retract her testimony. Alleging that he had spoken of wrecking the *Ariadne* while drunk, the increasingly irrational Mumford promised that Kerry would pay her well for her assistance.

By then he was, in the language of Edwardian melodrama, thoroughly undone. Two detectives had been listening to this highly incriminating conversation from behind a curtain and they dragged Mumford off to charge him with attempting to bribe a witness. This time there was no bail.

The trial opened before Mr Justice Denniston at Christchurch on 20 January 1902. All pleaded not guilty. The Crown outlined the case against the men, adding that Kerry had increased the suspicion of his involvement in unlawful activities by removing some valuable items from the ship just before she sailed from Sydney.

The third day of the trial was the turning point. That day the Crown produced scientific evidence to show that the document produced by Mumford had been traced over (in other words, it was a duplicate of one found in Kerry's possession) and that the incriminating words supposedly ordering Mumford to wreck the *Ariadne* had been added. Further damning evidence came from a waiter in a Christchurch hotel who said that he had seen Mumford writing intensely on a paper marked 'agreement'. At that point charges against Freyke were immediately dropped since this document was the only evidence against him.

Kerry also benefited from the exposure of this forgery and by the ploys which Willis had used in his endeavours to obtain evidence. When Kerry's counsel, Alfred Hanlon, asked why Willis had not suspected the agreement to be a forgery, since Mumford had first said that Kerry had not given him a written agreement, the case against the shipowner started to crumble.

The jury did not take long to decide. Mumford had by now completely discredited himself and was found guilty and sentenced to four years' hard labour. Kerry was found not guilty and returned to England with Freyke.

Notes
1. C. W. N. Ingram, *op. cit.*, p. 62.
2. Fulton, Robert Valpy, *Medical Practice in Otago and Southland in the Early Days*, Otago Daily Times and Witness Newspaper Co., Dunedin, 1921, p. 67.
3. Quoted in I. J. Farquhar, 'The Harbour Steam Company and the Origins of the Union Company', *New Zealand Marine News*, Vol. 26, No. 4, 1975.
4. A. B. Scanlan, *Harbour at the Sugar Loaves*, Taranaki Harbour Board, New Plymouth, 1975, p. 61.
5. M. Newman/James Mills, 20 June 1988, Mills Papers, USS Co. archives.
6. The Wreck of the *Ariadne* is described in the *Oamaru Mail* of 25 March 1901. Accounts of the trials are carried in the same paper of 1 November 1901 and the *North Otago Times* of 26 March, 12 April 1901 and 25 January 1902. For a very readable summation of the case, see R. Monigatti, *New Zealand Sensations*, A.H. & A.W. Reed, Wellington 1962, pp. 23–32.

Chapter 13

CASUALTIES OF WAR

Distance, often blamed for isolating New Zealand politically and culturally and for bumping up the cost of trade, has also shielded us from external attack. Although we have demonstrated a curious enthusiasm for joining other people's wars, distance has prevented the objects of our belligerence from invading or occupying us. The number of ships sunk in our waters through hostile action has been small.

The first marine casualties, which occurred at the beginning of the nineteenth century, were the result of Maori resistance to European invasion. Both sides had been exchanging occasional blows since Tasman's day and the situation was certainly not helped by the rough and ready way in which the masters of sealing and whaling vessels kidnapped Maori for service as pilots, deliberately or unintentionally flouted local customs and took goods and resources without paying. In a frontier society, justice was often swift and rough. In 1808 the crew of the schooner *Parramatta* paid dearly for wounding three Bay of Islands Maori and trying to make off without paying for a cargo. When the wind changed and blew the *Parramatta* back onto the rocks at nearby Cape Brett, all were massacred.

The first deliberate wrecking had taken place nearby two years earlier. The already troubled victim was the brig *Venus*. Mutineers had seized her at Port Dalrymple, Australia, in June 1806 and taken her to the Bay of Islands where local Maori had captured the brig, slaughtered all but one of her crew of 12 and stripped the hull of everything useable. In March 1816 Tokomaru Bay Maori boarded the American brig *Agnes*, murdered most of the crew and then plundered the ship when she drifted ashore. They eventually burned the empty wreck.

The incident that stays in many minds was the loss of the *Boyd*, best summed up by Wade Doak in his excellent book, *The Burning of the Boyd*, as a 'saga of culture clash'.[1] An English brig of 392 tons register, the *Boyd* had been dispatched by New South Wales entrepreneur Simeon Lord to Whangaroa to load the kauri spars that were making quite a name for themselves in the Royal Navy. The *Boyd* was the third ship Lord had sent to Whangaroa. Previous ships commanded by Captains Wilkinson and Ceroni had reported good timber and a friendly reception from the local tribes. Unfortunately, Ceroni's departure

Walter Wright's 1908 painting 'The Burning of the *Boyd*, Whangaroa Harbour, 1809'. *New Zealand Herald*

had been followed by a devastating epidemic which had carried off many Maori, including chief Kaitoke. The Maori would not welcome future visitors so openly.

The *Boyd* dropped anchor in December 1809. Her master, an insensitive brute named Captain John Thompson, had ill-treated chief George Tara during the voyage, flogging him and subjecting him to other indignities. Tara had been visiting Sydney and was returning with other Maori, all of whom were spoiling for vengeance by the time the *Boyd* reached New Zealand. Three days after her arrival they lured most of the crew away on a timber-cutting expedition; there they massacred Thompson and his men. Then they returned to the lightly manned ship after nightfall and killed all except four who had shown Tara kindness: cabin boy Thomas Davis, Anne Morley and her baby and the second mate. Both the child and the second mate later died. In all, about 700 were killed, most also being eaten.

Next day the Maori dragged the *Boyd* closer to the village and started stripping her of useful items such as nails and fittings. During the course of this, about two days later, someone made the mistake of striking a flint on an opened keg of gunpowder. The resulting explosion killed several, wrecked the *Boyd* and started a large fire which burned the ship right down to the waterline. Three weeks later when an expeditionary force descended upon Whangaroa, its leader, Alexander Berry, wrote that:

> We found the wreck in shoal water at the top of the harbour. Not far from the entrance. A most melancholy picture of wanton mischief. The natives had cut her cables and towed her up the harbour till she grounded, and then set her on fire, burning her to the water's edge. In her hold were the remains of her cargo; coals, salted seal skins and planks. Her guns, iron standards, etc were lying on top, having fallen in when her decks were consumed.

The Union Steam Ship Company's freighter *Wairuna*, the raider SMS *Wolf*'s first New Zealand victim. *Wellington Maritime Museum & Gallery*

Nearby on the beach were 'the mangled fragments and fresh bones of our countrymen, with tooth marks still upon them'.[2]

This was not the end of the killing. Berry incorrectly accused chief Te Pahi of the massacre and launched a punitive strike against his island pa, killing many innocent Maori, including Te Pahi himself.

Other ships lost as the direct result of Maori hostility were the whaling brig *Dragon* in 1833 and the French whaler *Jean Bart* at the Chatham Islands in 1838. The latter became a total loss, captured and burned at Ocean Bay after a violent fight initiated by the Maori response to the Frenchmen's punishment of Maori petty thieves. All aboard, believed to have numbered about 40 men, were killed. The Europeans later exacted revenge by burning the Maori village.

The next victims of warfare on the New Zealand coast came much later, during the First World War. Initially New Zealand saw little direct action. The Admiralty requisitioned much of its seagoing merchant fleet and many of these ships were lost in distant theatres of war, but no one menaced New Zealand directly – at least until 1917. That year the German auxiliary cruiser SMS *Wolf* arrived in our waters and began to make her presence felt.

The *Wolf* was a converted merchant ship. With a gross registered tonnage (GRT) of 6648 and capable of putting on 13 knots if really pressed, she carried a mixed armament of medium calibre guns (including two 5.9-inchers), 400-odd mines and a seaplane. Her first victims in New Zealand waters were the Union Steam Ship Company freighter *Wairuna* (3947 tons, 1904) and the American four-masted schooner *Winslow* (567 tons, 1899). Both fell victim to the raider off the Kermadecs. The *Wairuna*, two days out of Auckland and bound for San Francisco with a cargo of flax, hides and wool, sailed past the anchored raider but was brought to a halt by the raider's seaplane, which dropped a bomb in warning. Captured on 2 June 1917, the *Wairuna* was sent to the bottom two weeks later after the *Wolf* had transferred stores and prisoners. The *Winslow* made the

The 4700-ton freighter *Port Kembla*. Built in 1910, the ship fell victim to the SMS *Wolf*'s mines off Cape Farewell on 18 September 1917. *J. Dickie, Wellington Maritime Museum & Gallery*

mistake of blundering into these operations, was captured and sunk.

Next up was the 4700-ton Commonwealth & Dominion Line steamer *Port Kembla*. At 1300 hours on 18 September 1917, while off Cape Farewell, the steamer ran over a mine, came to a halt and started to sink. The blast smashed the compass, carried away her wireless aerials and scattered cargo on deck. Within half an hour the ship, which had been listing to starboard, was gone. No one was killed and the crew was picked up by the passing coastal collier *Regulus*, which took them to Nelson.

New Zealand's last local war victim was the Huddart Parker trans-Tasman liner *Wimmera* (3021 tons, 1904), another victim of the *Wolf*'s mines. On 26 June 1918 the ship, Sydney-bound from Auckland, was passing Cape Maria Van Diemen off the Northland coast in an area thought to be mined, when a terrific explosion lifted her stern out of the water. So severe was the blast that the ship was gone within 10 minutes. Of her total complement of 151 (76 passengers and 75 crew), 26, including Captain H. J. Kell, lost their lives.

The old principle that what worked well once will often work well a second time holds true in naval warfare. In 1934 German naval strategists, struggling to rebuild the Kriegsmarine from scratch, started planning a second generation of commerce raiders to supplement Hitler's small surface fleet. By 1939 Germany had a pool of fast freighters and banana boats ready for adaptation into fast raiders.[3]

The first of these unwelcome visitors was a former fast freighter, the *Orion*. Carrying six 5.9-inch guns, several lighter pieces, torpedoes and mines as well as a spotter aircraft, the *Orion* arrived off the Hauraki Gulf on the night of 13 June 1940 to lay a minefield across the approaches to New Zealand's busiest seaport, Auckland. For the next nerve-wracking 10 hours, always in sight of the mainland, and with the light

The Union Company's magnificent 13,000-ton trans-Pacific liner *Niagara* passing through the Narrows, Vancouver, 1926. *Wellington Maritime Museum & Gallery*

cruiser HMS *Achilles* and the armed merchant cruiser HMS *Hector* within striking range, Commander Kurt Weyher laid 228 mines in zig-zagging barrages, one across the eastern approach to the passage between Great Mercury Island and Cuvier Island and the other, more extensive one across the northern approaches to the Hauraki Gulf, running from the end of Moko Hinau Island, outside Maro Tiri Island in the Hen and Chicken Islands and finishing up well within sight of the Northland coast. All were conventional moored, contact mines. His job done, Weyher departed as speedily as possible, leaving his deadly cargo in wait for the unwary.

It took just five days for the mines to make themselves known. Early in the morning of 19 June 1940 the realities of war were brought home to New Zealand for the first time, when passengers aboard the Union Company Vancouver mail liner *Niagara* were blasted out of their slumbers by an explosion.

The *Niagara* was almost a household name in New Zealand. When built for the Union Company's Vancouver-Australian royal mail service in 1913, the 13,415-ton liner had turned many heads. Larger than anything on the busier Home trade, she was touted as 'the biggest and most luxurious liner that has ever come south of the line'. Her new oil-burning machinery was a first and even as late as 1940 she was still highly regarded by the company and the public alike.

The *Niagara* had had a narrow escape during the First World War, when she was spotted by the raider *Wolf*'s plane, but her luck ran out this time. Voyage 163 was to have taken her from Auckland to Vancouver via Fiji. Aboard were 136 passengers, 203 crew and a cargo that included half the New Zealand Army's small arms ammunition, urgently needed in a mother country under daily threat of invasion. There were also 590 bars of Bank of England South African gold. Valued at £2,500,000 (worth nearly NZ$120 million in present-day terms), this gold was destined for the United States to help for British arms purchases. Weyher's mines could not have found a better victim.

Looking aft from just behind the bridge as the *Niagara* puts on speed. *Comber Collection, Wellington Maritime Museum & Gallery*

At 0340 hours, in the fairway between Bream Head and Moko Hinau Island, a terrific explosion near the forward hold threw passengers from their bunks and brought the big liner to a complete halt. Within minutes Captain W. Martin knew that his beloved ship was doomed. While his radio operator broadcast distress messages and the crew started firing rockets, he gave the order to abandon ship. Fortunately the night was calm and clear, the ship's internal lights stayed on and the passengers were able to make it into the 18 boats without too much difficulty. No one had sustained any serious injury, the only fatality being Aussie, the ship's cat, who, not finding the lifeboat to his liking, scrambled back aboard the liner to go down with her. At 0532 hours the passengers and crew aboard the boats were able to watch the *Niagara*, which had been sinking by the bow, slip beneath the waves.

Help was at hand within about five hours, led by the RNZAF's high-speed rescue launch. Fear of mines kept the bigger ships such as the *Wanganella* and the *Achilles* at a respectful distance, but the coaster *Kapiti* from Whangarei and boats from the *Achilles* quickly picked up the passengers who were none the worse for wear despite their involuntary messing about in small boats. By evening they were back in Auckland harbour and minesweepers were tackling the first of the mines.

Salvaging the gold was a story in itself. The Bank of England hired United Salvage Proprietary Ltd of Melbourne which acquired the old coaster *Clansman* and set up operations from Whangarei in December 1940. By 2 February 1941 divers had located the wreck at a depth of 134 metres. This was deeper than anything previously worked on (the record was 120

metres, held by Italian salvors on a wreck off Ushant), but the huge amount at stake spurred on United's divers. Lying on her side at an angle of 70 degrees, the *Niagara* would have to be blasted apart so that access could be gained to her strongroom.

It was no easy job. The *Clansman* had to lie buoyed in the middle of a still largely unswept minefield (two mines would come to the surface during salvage operations) and was quite frequently buffeted by heavy seas which swept her entire length. Things were no calmer for the men working below in the diving bell. The *Clansman's* violent swinging had it bouncing up and down until United's men came up with a

Above left: Two *Niagara* crew members photographed aboard the *Wanganella* after the sinking. *T. W. Collins, Wellington Maritime Museum & Gallery*

Above right: *Niagara* survivors safely aboard the *Wanganella*. *T. W. Collins, Wellington Maritime Museum & Gallery*

Large ships had to keep clear of the scene of the sinking because of the danger from mines. Here the small coaster *Kapiti* approaches the liner *Wanganella* with a full deckload of passengers and crew. *T. W. Collins, Wellington Maritime Museum & Gallery*

solution by tensioning the winch to maintain position. It was a tough, lonely life made lonelier by the need to work under wartime secrecy. The divers broke into the strongroom on 13 October and brought up the first two bars of gold. By 7 December when salvage operations ceased, almost 95 percent of the gold had been recovered.

Of course, the remaining 35 bars have proved a lure to others. Using new technology, the British ship *Foremost 17* recovered 30 in 1953 over a three-month period. The others will probably remain with the wreck which, although knocked about by the salvage expeditions, is still largely intact.

The *Orion* had not, however, finished with New Zealand. Her second mine victim and, for New Zealand, the last loss in home waters through hostile action, was the minesweeper HMS *Puriri*. Pride of the Anchor Shipping & Foundry Company's small fleet, the *Puriri* had been a naval vessel for less than a month when she went down. On 14 May 1941, her officers and crew were still getting used to their recently converted ship and were working up with the other converted coasters of the 25th Minesweeping Flotilla when they were sent out to sweep the minefield in which the *Clansman* was still working.

The launch *Rawea* had buoyed a mine the previous day but the *Puriri*'s watchkeepers did not see it in time to take evasive action; the *Puriri* ran straight into trouble. A huge explosion rocked the ship, which sank within minutes. With her went her commanding officer, Lieutenant D. W. Blacklaws, petty officer B. A. Mattson, stewards G. E. R. Hobley and J. Richardson and able seaman L. Purkin. Another converted coaster, the *Gale*, picked up the remaining 26 survivors, five of whom were wounded.

The rest of the 25th continued their dangerous and unglamorous task and by the end of September had accounted for 106 of the 228 mines originally laid. Since it was assumed that most of the others had broken loose or sunk, the area could now more or less officially be declared mine-free.

Gunfire was no less destructive. After heading up into the Pacific for a while, the *Orion* returned to New Zealand waters a few months later. On the evening of 20 August 1940 the raider was cutting through the Tasman between Cape Egmont and Wellington when she sighted her next victim rolling in the heavy seas, the New Zealand Shipping Company's freighter *Turakina*. She was bound from Sydney to Wellington to top up with frozen meat for London.

One of a series of similar, solid-looking single-funnel coal-burners turned out for the NZS Co. and Federal in the early 1920s, the *Turakina* was no flyer. She was really just a huge floating freezer unit, and a poorly armed one at that, sporting nothing more impressive than a vintage 4.7-inch gun bolted to her poop, manned by a small contingent of naval gunners.

Her master, Captain J. B. Laird, was no quitter, though, and decided to fight it out in the hope that he could delay the raider long enough for Australian or New Zealand warships to catch

her. Ignoring the raider's requests to stop and to refrain from using her radio, the *Turakina* put on maximum speed, turned away from the *Orion* and started to radio that she was being shelled by an enemy raider.

She never stood a chance. The heavily armed *Orion* scored with her first salvos and very shortly reduced the *Turakina* to a blazing wreck. Down went the foremast, together with the lookout, and then the engines failed. Within 20 minutes the British freighter was sinking by the stern and half of her crew of 56 was killed or wounded. Shooting blind after the early loss of their rangefinder, her gunners had the satisfaction of straddling the German ship on a number of occasions, bending some hull plates and sending splinters whizzing along her decks. Even then Laird refused to give up, racing astern through the flames to urge his surviving gunners to 'have another shot at the __!'[4]

These shots kept Weyher at a distance and encouraged him to expend two of his precious torpedoes on the troublemaker. Both hit, one astern with little effect, the second amidships where it completed the work of destruction begun by the gunners. At 1822 hours the *Turakina*'s survivors abandoned their sinking command, leaving 35 of their number dead aboard her blazing decks. Despite the risk of detection, Weyher lingered long enough to pick up his gallant adversaries.

The *Orion* had travelled a long way to reach these happy hunting grounds, so it was perhaps unrealistic to expect that she would abandon them quickly. Avoiding Allied ships and aircraft, Weyher crossed the Tasman before rendezvousing with another raider, the *Komet*, and the supply ship *Kulmerland*. By the morning of 25 November they were back off the New Zealand coastline, searching intently for new victims, when smoke was seen on the horizon.

The New Zealand Shipping Company's freighter *Turakina* put up a gallant fight in the Tasman against the German raider KMS *Orion*. After the war some Oamaru friends of her master, Captain J. B. Laird, erected a memorial to this courageous mariner on their waterfront. *Comber Collection, Wellington Maritime Museum & Gallery*

Their victim was an unlucky little ship, the *Holmwood*. Built at Goole as far back as 1911 and better known to New Zealanders as the now-bankrupt Westland Shipping Company's *Tees*, the 546-ton coal-burner had been acquired a few months earlier by Wellington mariner Sydney Holm, renamed *Holmwood* and fitted out as the Chatham Islands supply vessel. Once a month she plodded her way slowly from Lyttelton with a few passengers and a mixed cargo of basic supplies.

On the morning of 25 November, she was on only her second trip back for Holm, with a dozen passengers and a cargo that included a horse and 1375 live sheep, when chief engineer Fred Abernethy sighted a ship bearing Japanese markings. Japan was then still neutral but Abernethy's suspicions increased when a second 'Japanese' ship appeared. At that point both hoisted the Kriegsmarine flag and ordered the *Holmwood* to stop.

Captain James Miller, the *Holmwood*'s master, had no choice. Unarmed and even slower than the *Turakina*, the *Holmwood* was not designed for heroics. Since atmospheric conditions made radio reception and transmission poor, he stopped engines and waited for a German boat to come alongside. The prize crew replaced the red ensign with the swastika, restarted the *Holmwood*'s engines and steamed her a safe distance from the Chathams where the 29 New Zealanders (12 passengers and 17 crew) were taken aboard the raiders. Fourteen shots finished off the little ship.

Two days later, the three Germans landed a much bigger prize, the New Zealand Shipping Company's motor liner *Rangitane*. One of three pioneering motor liners on the New Zealand–Britain run (the others were the *Rangitiki* and the *Rangitata*), the 16,737-ton, 17-knot *Rangitane* was one of the most prestigious ships serving New Zealand.

The Union Steam Ship Company freight *Komata*, victim of German raiders off Nauru. *Wellington Maritime Museum & Gallery*

She left Auckland the day the *Holmwood* came to grief, anchoring for the night in Rangitoto Channel. Aboard were 11 passengers, 200 crew and a full cargo of valuable primary produce. Her high speed enabled her to sail unescorted. At 0252 hours on the 27th, while the *Rangitane* was approximately 300 miles off East Cape, her master, Captain H. L. Upton, sighted suspicious vessels and ordered the radio operator to broadcast a warning. Upton's ship could have outrun either of the Germans but, worried about the safety of the passengers and the accuracy of the German gunnery, he ordered her to stop once he was satisfied that the radio message had gone through.

The *Orion* and the *Komet* continued shooting for some minutes, eventually killing five passengers and five crew and wounding several others, one of whom later died. When German boarding parties clambered aboard the biggest ship ever sunk by an armed raider, they found her ablaze on all decks; furthermore, they now had more than 300 prisoners to cope with. They opened her seacocks and fired several more salvos before heading away at speed for the Pacific where, at Nauru, they accounted for several more Allied ships, including the Union Company's new freighter *Komata*. The captured passengers and crew were left on Emirau Island later that year.

Ships have been lost through violence on two occasions (three if you include a small boat blown up in a drugs war in the 1980s) since the end of the Second World War. The first incident was little more than a bit of illegal neighbourhood beautification. On 2 June 1966 an explosion tore apart the engine room of the derelict 272-ton steam trawler *Hautapu* and sank her at her moorings in Shelly Bay, Wellington.

It was almost the last act in a long and undistinguished

The ship no one wanted. The old steam trawler *Hautapu* rests on the bottom at Shelly Bay, Wellington, in 1966 after someone detonated a bomb aboard her. Evening Post, *courtesy of Wellington Maritime Museum & Gallery*

career. The *Hautapu* had started life at Port Chalmers in 1943, one of a batch of obsolete steel minesweeping trawlers built for the Royal New Zealand Navy. Sold out of naval service, she had taken up the fishing duties for which her First World War-inspired plans had designed her. That career came to an abrupt halt on 2 November 1963 when she struck an unidentified object off the Kaikoura coast and ran ashore south of Cape Campbell.

There she lay for seven months until April 1964, when she was towed into Wellington Harbour for inspection. A survey revealed her to be beyond economic repair and so the old ship was declared a constructive total loss. Laid up at Shelly Bay, she lingered there for the next two years while the residents of plush Roseneath gnashed their teeth over her unsightly and unwelcome presence.

The Air Force had planned to use her as a target for its planes but was thwarted when the training ship arranged to tow her out to the firing range charged off on a rescue mission. Determined not to put up with the sight of her any longer someone – and their identity was never fully established – planted a bomb aboard her and sent her to the bottom. There she lay until 1972 while her owners, the harbour board, the Navy and the Air Force squabbled over the cost of removing her wreck. Eventually Navy divers, assisted by the port's floating crane, started cutting her up in 1972–73. By the end of 1973 she was just a memory.

The last, and undoubtedly the most sensational, attack in recent years was that of the French secret service on the Greenpeace protest ship *Rainbow Warrior* at Auckland on 10 July 1985. Shortly before midnight a loud explosion rocked the peace of Auckland Harbour. Another followed soon afterwards. It was all over in less than four minutes.[5]

The *Rainbow Warrior* had started life humbly enough in 1955 as the 418-ton British research trawler *Sir William Hardy*. For just over 20 years she sailed in and out of Aberdeen, catching fish and conducting experiments for the staff of the Torry Research Station. By 1977, however, the scientists needed a bigger ship and it seemed that the trawler's days were numbered. A classic British side trawler, she had many years of life left in her sturdy hull but no work to justify her existence; Britain's fisheries were in decline and those companies that were still investing in boats were changing over to the more efficient stern trawlers.

Then she was discovered by enthusiasts from the international environmental activists' group, Greenpeace. Canadian David McTaggart purchased her in 1977, patched her up, renamed her *Rainbow Warrior* (an anglicisation of the French name *Le Combattant de l'Arc-en-ciel*, not a reference to the colourful Cree legend so often quoted) and sent her out on the high seas campaigning against nuclear waste dumping and whaling.

Greenpeace worked the ship hard until 1983–84 when

Just hours after the explosions, the scene was a hive of activity. Here the Auckland police launch *Deodar* (since sunk in a harbour accident) attends to the stricken *Rainbow Warrior*. *New Zealand Herald*

engine problems and old age again seemed likely to send her to the scrapheap. By now Greenpeace was buying bigger and newer vessels and it took some arguing by dedicated supporters before she could be sent to Jacksonville, Florida, for a life-saving refit. There she was re-engined, fitted with tall masts and auxiliary sails and generally smartened up. Then she set sail for the Pacific to draw attention to the plight of indigenous people affected by American and French nuclear testing.

She had probably done her job too well by the time she motored up the Waitemata. The French Government, facing criticism on all sides for its colonial policies and its nuclear testing in the Pacific, had had enough of earlier protest voyages from New Zealand craft such as the *Fri*. It clearly did not relish the prospect of the *Rainbow Warrior* leading another protest flotilla from New Zealand to Moruroa. Unknown to anyone, a small group from the French secret service, the DGSE, almost certainly supported by the French Navy, began laying plans for bombing the vessel. In an act of unprecedented state-sponsored terrorism, teams of French agents infiltrated New Zealand, hired scuba gear and planted two limpet mines against the hull of the ship as she lay alongside Marsden Wharf.

The first explosion rocked the ship. Crew members and supporters, several asleep at the time, scrambled ashore, shocked and dazed. All made it off safely but one, Portuguese photographer Fernando Pereira, who went back for his camera equipment. A second explosion went off, trapping him in his cabin as the *Rainbow Warrior* sank rapidly. He drowned. Minutes later the vessel was listing to port, her stern in the mud of the Waitemata.

Initial doubts were dispelled when an underwater examination revealed that the ship's plating had been bent inwards by the force of the blast. Someone had placed a limpet mine

You can't sink a rainbow? In contradiction of the slogan, the stripped hulk makes its way under tow to the scuttling ground in December 1987. *New Zealand Herald*

against her hull. But who? The French were prime candidates and suspicions deepened as the police investigation, the biggest in New Zealand's history, turned up tales of strangers with foreign accents, Zodiac dinghies, diving gear and hired camper vans. Later two DGSE agents, Major Alain Mafart and Captain Dominique Prieur, were arrested trying to flee the country. The long court cases, international lobbying and power politics are outside the scope of this book; suffice it to say that the French Government did eventually have to compensate Greenpeace and the New Zealand Government.

The Navy refloated the *Warrior* which, now fit only for scrap, lay alongside the Western Viaduct for the next two and a half years. Fittingly, she ended her life as a fish reef. On 12 December 1987, escorted by scores of small craft, she was towed out to the Cavalli Islands for a dignified scuttling. There she remains, playing host to small fish and other marine life. Greenpeace used some of the compensation money paid out by the French Government to buy and convert a bigger, better *Rainbow Warrior*, which has since visited New Zealand.

Notes
1. Information on the *Boyd* incident is drawn from a variety of sources, the principal one being Wade Doak's *The Burning of the Boyd*, Auckland, 1984.
2. Wade Doak, *op. cit.*, p. 104.
3. For a good account of German raiders see Karl August Muggenthaler, *German Raiders of World War 2*, Robert Hale, London, 1978, and Paul Schmalenbach, *German Raiders: A History of Auxiliary Cruisers of the German Navy 1895–1945*, Patrick Stephens, Cambridge, 1977. Grant Howard, *The Navy in New Zealand: An Illustrated History*, A.H. & A.W. Reed, Wellington, 1981 contains a useful summary of both wars.
4. Karl August Muggenthaler, *op. cit.*, p. 77.
5. Information on the *Rainbow Warrior* is drawn from David Robie, *Eyes of Fire: The Last Voyage of the Rainbow Warrior*, Auckland, 1986, and Richard Shears and Isobelle Gridley, *The Rainbow Warrior Affair*, Sydney, 1985.

Part 4

RECENT WRECKS

Salvage attempts are underway as the salvors try to pump out the foreholds of the steamer *Star of Canada* off Gisborne in June 1912. Despite the best efforts of the harbour board and others the wreck, surrounded on all sides by rock, eventually sank. *Alexander Turnbull Library, courtesy of Wellington Maritime Museum & Gallery*

Chapter 14

HOME BOATS ON THE ROCKS

From the 1890s onwards there was a dramatic drop in the number of Home (Britain–New Zealand) trade ships coming to grief on our shores. There were several reasons. The ships had become larger and more powerful, the 1000-ton sailing ship of 1875 being replaced by a powerfully engined 5000–7000-ton steamer by 1900. Better harbour works and safer, better-lit coasts also played their part, as did more detailed charts and increased local knowledge by masters.

Even so, mistakes could still be made and the elements could still play their part in confounding the best intentions of mariners and naval architects. Between 1912 and 1939 several big, well-found ships – the *Star of Canada, Devon, Tyrone, Tongariro, Port Elliott, Wiltshire* and *Port Bowen* – went ashore in New Zealand waters. Most accidents happened at night and in bad weather. This chapter will look at the five ships lost along the east coast of the North Island during this period.

The hours either side of midnight can be dangerous ones for mariners. Late on the night of 23 June 1912 the 4623-ton, three-year-old steamer *Star of Canada* was lying at anchor in the Gisborne roadstead when the weather, already bad, swung round and turned into one of the wildest southerly squalls ever experienced locally.

At 2200 hours the *Star of Canada*'s master, Captain J. M. Hart, worried by the strength of the wind and the exposed nature of his position, decided to head out to sea. The anchor had held up until then but by 2315 the ship was dragging and heading for the beach at an alarming speed. Before a second anchor could be dropped or steam could be got up (the boilers had been closed down for cleaning), the *Star of Canada* had struck a rock and had started taking in water. Hart fired distress rockets at 2330 but the small local tug *Hipi* could do nothing in the face of the prevailing conditions and had to leave the ship to her fate. Hart and his crew dropped the other anchor and tried to keep their ship's bows to the oncoming seas but without success.

By the next morning the *Star of Canada* was resting on the seabed, with water in the three forward holds. She was almost broadside on to the waves and broken water fore and aft indicated the presence of rocks all around her. The *Star of Canada*, her bow buried in the water, resisted all salvage efforts and broke her back a fortnight later. Her deckhouse was lopped off and deposited on a section in Gisborne and some of the cargo was recovered, but the wreck itself eventually sank, its largely intact hull still providing interest to local divers. The subsequent magisterial inquiry exonerated Hart and his officers from all blame, finding that the accident was caused by the unpredictably sudden and furious nature of the gale.

A howling southerly was lashing Wellington, driving thick rain before it, on the night of 25 August 1913 when the 5489-ton Federal-Houlder-Shire liner *Devon* started picking her way carefully up the entrance. Heavy seas had been battering the ship for days and her acting master, A. H. Chaunce, who had taken over at Capetown when Captain Robertson went down with typhoid, was looking forward to the comfort of a snug berth at the capital's wharves.

It was not to be. At 2015 the *Devon* went ashore near the lower Pencarrow Head light and became a total wreck. Here, close to the entrance, the sea races through the narrows with greater velocity than out in the less sheltered expanse of Cook Strait. That night, Captain A. M. Edwin of the powerful new inter-island ferry *Wahine*, his ship's bows dipping well into the water once he passed Steeple Rock on the way out, reported poor visibility 'most violent bursts of wind, short, sharp and of great power, straight from the Antarctic, and bitterly cold'.[1] Although not the worst southerly he had encountered, it was pretty bad.

The *Devon* hit with a sharp, rending sound. Chaunce immediately stopped the engines and had the boilers blown in as reports came in of water entering the stokehold. Within minutes waves were breaking over the *Devon*'s decks aft,

The long list of victims claims by Pencarrow Heads, guarding the entrance to Wellington, includes the steamer *Devon*. *Wellington Maritime Museum & Gallery*

jolting the big ship up and down. Chaunce mustered the crew forward and started firing rockets. Fortunately help was already on its way. Ten minutes after she had hit the rocks the lighthouse keeper had informed Wellington that the ship was in trouble.

That was an understatement. It was too rough to launch lifeboats or for any ship to approach close enough to help the crew. The harbour ferry *Duchess* went out but could not help; the tug *Karaka* left the city at 0100 on the 26th, but was forced back as the storm continued to gain strength. While the *Devon's* seamen took what shelter they could on the crowded forecastle, the *Wahine* stood off the wreck site and the searchlights of Fort Dorset across the harbour lit up the scene. Although the seamen could plainly hear the shouts of people on shore, all attempts to fire a line across the water were defeated by the wind; after several fruitless attempts, they decided to wait for dawn.

By daybreak the wind was losing some of its strength and a small party of about 20 people, led by the harbourmaster, Captain J. Johnson, had assembled off the site of the wreck. As a press reporter in that party wrote somewhat floridly, the *Devon's* crew, shivering miserably in her forecastle, had been very lucky indeed.

> It was a piece of good fortune that the body of the vessel was gripped strongly by the rocks. If the steamer had swung around broadside after striking all lives might have been lost last night. Just about the bow rocks jut up like giant teeth, whetted for destruction, and flecked with the foam of ravening appetite. They would have pierced, cut, and crunched the labouring ship and how could men have lived in those wild waters in darkness?[2]

The men resumed their efforts to get a line ashore. Twice lifebuoys attached to ropes either slipped off or became hopelessly entangled in the rocks far out of reach of the shore party. A third time, however, one attached to a lifebelt was plucked out of the heaving seas by Captains Johnson and Hayward and by Messrs Edmonson, Peters and Knivig, whose task was not made easy by the treacherous backwash which several times threatened to take the rescuers out to sea:

> For some hours they proceeded, but the work was extremely difficult. Then one of the bulkheads was pressed into service and, making their way from rock to rock, some of the party at last got close to where the wires were entangled amongst the pinnacles. To get within reach, however, it was necessary to place a plank between two jagged outstanding rocks over which the sea was breaking perilously. This dangerous task was safely accomplished, however, the feat being breathlessly watched by those on ship and shore alike.[3]

Then began the long and laborious task of hauling the crew ashore one by one. First to reach dry land was the quartermaster, who made heavy going of the journey, being severely buffeted by the waves during the course of his hair-raising three-minute journey. Things got easier with each rescue,

By the time that this photograph was taken, a small steamer had drawn alongside the stricken ship to begin assessing salvage. Unfortunately, the *Devon*'s predicament was as bad as those rocks suggest and the ship eventually broke up. *Wellington Maritime Museum & Gallery*

because it meant another set of hands with which to pull on the ropes. The ship's mascot, a black and white cat, together with her litter of kittens, was not forgotten either. All made the journey across in the basket, the kittens with the quartermaster, arriving bedraggled and forlorn-looking but safe. Last ashore were Roberts, the chief engineer and Captain Chaunce, both weighing over 96 kilograms (15 stone)! Their feet touched ground to wild applause. An impromptu celebratory meal, hauled out from Muritai by packhorse, then followed; naturally, it included 'an ample supply of stimulants to warm the chilled and wet mariners'.[4]

The court of inquiry, in a majority decision, later suspended Chaunce's certificate for three months. It found that he had taken the *Devon* in too close to Pencarrow Head and too fast and had mistaken the lights. Chaunce appealed and a later Supreme Court decision overruled the magisterial inquiry, finding that Chaunce had mistaken the Falcon Shoal buoy for the red sector of Somes Island light, an error but not one that made him responsible for the accident. For the *Devon*, though, there was no second chance. Her port stern quarter, open to the full fury of the sea, soon disintegrated, scattering cargo and fittings along the shore.

The New Zealand Shipping Company's steamer *Tongariro* was about halfway through her voyage from Auckland to Wellington on the evening of 30 August 1916 when master Captain Harry Makepiece realised – far too late – that something was wrong. With a resounding crash, the big ship struck Bull Rock off Portland Island (between Gisborne and Napier) with her stern, swung around and came to a halt, listing badly to starboard and with her bow on the rock. From the beginning it was obvious that the ship was a write-off. She had been moving at a fair clip and had broken in two under the impact, shattering right across the No. 3 hold.

Even though the blow had been severe, everyone escaped serious injury. Many clad in just their night attire, the 96 officers and men made for the boats. The list made launching them a difficult task and five men were slightly injured when one of the port boats (the only ones useable) was smashed, throwing its occupants into the water. There was no panic and most of the crewmen – 75 altogether – were picked up three hours later by the NZS Co.'s lighter *Koutunui*, which was in the vicinity at the time, and transferred to the Huddart Parker liner *Westralia*.

News of the wreck came from settlers on Mahia Peninsula. By the time that the company's local manager reached the site, it was apparent that the ship and her cargo were doomed. The *Tongariro* was still afloat, her bow supported by Bull Rock, but water had invaded all her holds and the engine room. The decks were above water but seas were breaking over her bow and everyone expected her to slip off Bull Rock and sink in the deep water which lay under her stern.

Salvaging the cargo kept the Napier lighterage firm, Richardson & Co., in business for several weeks. Manager Kenneth McLeay took an oil winch out to the wreck and used this to unload into his fleet of small craft. One of the ship's holds was filled with whisky and brandy and this, naturally, was given priority. Richardsons' men got much of it away by smashing one case in each tier in order to free it, but when the *Tongariro* later broke in two it was a matter of 'whisky galore' as locals engaged in some very earnest beachcombing. Some outwitted Customs patrols by burying their windfalls on the beaches for recovery once the authorities had tired of the game!

The court of inquiry censured both the master and the chief officer, finding that the mishap was primarily caused by the latter failing to take ordinary precautions to verify his position when off Table Cape. Both had their certificates suspended. The *Tongariro*, a steel, twin-screw steamer of 8073 tons, had been built in 1901.

One of the more dramatic wrecks of the inter-war era occurred on remote Great Barrier Island on 31 May 1922 when the stately five-master Federal liner *Wiltshire* piled up on the rocks at remote Rosalie Bay, near the southern tip of the island. Just 10 years old, the *Wiltshire* was one of the biggest ships trading to the Dominion.

The ship had been punching her way through some of the dirtiest weather imaginable. Heavy weather and torrential rain had lashed her for the best part of half a day and visibility had fallen to less than a ship's length by the time she struck the rocks. There was a terrific crash, then four heavy bumps as the steel monster forced herself up and onto the rocks.

Captain G. B. Hayward summoned the 102 officers and men topside but quickly gave up any idea of launching the boats. Heavy seas were breaking over the *Wiltshire* and any attempt to launch a boat would be sheer folly – it would either be dashed against the side of the ship or thrown up onto the rocks at the foot of the towering cliffs in front of the bow. Unable to do anything, the men settled down to a nervous night in the saloon and prayed that the dawn would bring better weather.

It did not and the situation worsened at 1130 on the 1st when, with a deafening bang, the *Wiltshire* snapped in two just abaft

The *Wiltshire* also provided one of the more dramatic challenges to rescuers. Here we see her two junior radio operators coming ashore on a 'boatswain's chair' set up by a naval party from Auckland. *New Zealand Herald*

Opposite page: Imposing ships make for impressive wrecks. This photograph of the wreck, framed by some of rugged Rosalie Bay's trees, shows that the *Wiltshire*'s back is already broken and that the stern is under water. *New Zealand Herald*

the No. 4 hatch. Hayward, who was up on the bridge at the time, leaped down onto the deck, to be followed by his officers, who used a rope to join the rest of the crew in the forecastle. The *Wiltshire* was now a complete wreck. While the bow section remained firmly embedded on the rocks, the stern part, less firmly held and in deeper water, began to settle. The big question was – would the wreck remain intact long enough to enable the crew to escape?

Help was on the way, in the shape of the Union Company coaster *Katoa* and the coastal passenger vessel *Arahura*, but there was little that they could do. During the morning, while the *Arahura* stood by and provided radio contact with the rest of the world, the *Katoa* landed rescue parties equipped with storm gear and blankets. They met several groups of islanders who

T.S.S. WILTSHIRE

had been standing by impotently since the night before. As the *Herald* reporter recalled:

> Heartrending was the experience of watchers on the cliffs above the wreck prior to the line coming ashore. The watchers could hear cries from the ship but could do nothing. Hope was raised when one of the crew attempted to swim ashore with a line but this died down when the enormous seas running caused the effort to be abandoned, and the exhausted swimmer had to be hauled on board again.[5]

Rescuers had fired many rockets at the ship but the howling gale had carried away all lines. Attempts to float lines out had

The *Wiltshire* in her prime. Like her sister ship *Shropshire* (better known later as the New Zealand Shipping Company's *Rotorua*), she boasted five masts and a hinged funnel for Manchester Ship Canal passages. The masts and her sheer size gave her a most imposing appearance. *Wellington Maritime Museum & Gallery*

After the storm. A view of the wreck of the *Wiltshire* taken from sea. Note how cleanly the hull under the bridge snapped off.
Wellington Maritime Museum & Gallery

met with similar failure. Then, at 1345, the *Katoa* radioed Auckland that the *Wiltshire* had broken in half, that the stern had disappeared and that the bow was crowded with people.

Auckland was abuzz with rumour. News had reached there by radio at 2311 on the 31st and it had been all bad; the picture of the trapped crew huddling on the bow was uppermost in everyone's mind. The next day someone had even thought of using a seaplane to get a rope to the men – one of the first instances of the use of air-sea rescue techniques – but the attempt had to be abandoned.[6] Then a report came from Coromandel that a tug had arrived bearing the dreadful news that saving the crew was considered impossible.

Just an hour later, though, a report from Tryphena indicated that a line was now ashore and that four men had already made the hazardous journey ashore. 'Prospects of rescue now good,' it was decided.[7] A couple of hours later the *Katoa* broke the news that a line had been floated ashore and that the 99 men remaining on the wreck were well sheltered, well fed and waiting for daylight when a party from HMS *Philomel* planned to set up a breeches buoy to rescue them. With the seas moderating slightly and the forward part of the ship showing no sign of shifting, Hayward decided that it was better to wait for a safer means of getting ashore.

The hero of the hour was a seaman from the *Katoa* by the name of Kehoe. He scrambled down the dangerous cliff face and grabbed hold of a line attached to a hatchcover that had been floated ashore. He then made the slow and dangerous ascent. After what must have been an agonising delay, an endless line was fastened to a tree on the cliff and the first man was being hauled ashore metre by metre. Three companions followed before operations were halted for the night.

Next day's rain did not dampen the spirits of the *Philomel* party. With 10 men at a time hauling on the rope, the ship-wrecked sailors came ashore at the rate of two every six

The *Tyrone* (6664 tons, 1901), one of the Union Company's recently acquired 'Irish County' steamers, made landfall the hard way at 0400 hours on 27 September 1913 when she ran ashore off Wahine Point, Otago Heads to become a total loss. Her owners did not mind greatly. No lives were lost and the company pocketed a handsome insurance cheque. *Wellington Maritime Museum & Gallery*

minutes. By 2200 on the 2nd, two full days after the *Wiltshire* had first struck, all the ship's crew was ashore safe and sound.

Most of the mail bags found their way onto the shore but the vast bulk of the 10,000 tonnes of general cargo disappeared into the drink, along with the ship. The *Wiltshire*'s loss was felt especially keenly because she was one of the small number of ships recently chartered to open up a direct trade between New Zealand ports and Manchester. She was fitted with telescoping masts and funnel to make her suitable for the Manchester Canal.

The court of inquiry found Hayward guilty of two errors of navigation: in not exercising caution when unable to pick up Cuvier light when expected and in not acting immediately upon the danger signals given by the sounding taken about 20 minutes before the ship struck. He was ordered to pay the costs of the inquiry.

The hours before midnight claimed another victim just a few years later. The ship was the Commonwealth & Dominion Line's 7395-ton steamer *Port Elliott*, the place was Horoera Point, between Te Araroa and East Cape, and the date was 12 January 1924.

Better known to New Zealanders as the *Indrabarah*, the *Port Elliott* had already had one close escape, running aground on Rangitikei Beach in the Taranaki Bight in May 1913. Early newspaper reports gave her up for lost but the fact that she was embedded in sand, not rocks, kept the water out of her hull and her salvage chances alive. One salvage attempt after another failed and she gradually worked her way up the beach, closer to the waterline. Then, early in July, the combination of a very high tide, a wind from the right direction and some strong pulling from the Union Company tug *Terawhiti* freed her. This time, however, her luck would run out.

The night was pitch dark with thick fog hanging over the sea. The crew had no inkling of trouble until the big ship, steaming at near her maximum speed of 13 knots, crashed into the reef, slid over it and came to a complete halt. Her master, Captain A. J. Fishwick, ordered full speed astern but to no avail. The ship, pinned to the reef beneath her engine room, would be going nowhere. Water rushed into both her forehold and her engine room. By the early morning she was down by the bows.

News of the accident was supplied by an Auckland radio station which picked up an SOS message at 2352. Minutes later a Wellington station received one from the *Port Elliott* saying that she was ashore near East Cape. The Wellington station notified the sloops HMS *Laburnum* and *Veronica*, the government steamer *Tutanekai* and the Union Company coaster *Arahura* (which had tended to the *Tongariro* and *Wiltshire*) as well as Commonwealth & Dominion's *Port Victor*. All were on their way, assisted by smaller steamers from Napier and Tolaga Bay.

On shore, the inhabitants of the Horoera pa found themselves roused from their slumbers at about 0330 hours by the shrill cry of a ship's whistle. One local boy, Norman Bryant, set out on horse for Gisborne, unaware that the ship's radio was functioning. Others gathered around, convinced that the whistle was coming from one of Richardson & Co.'s small wool boats. By daybreak the mist was lifting sufficiently for the crowd to see the *Port Elliott*, apparently little damaged, her propellers half out of the water at half-tide. Soon everyone was in on the act. One man rushed into the East Cape lighthouse keeper's house shouting, 'A boat is sinking off the East Island; only her masts are left.'

The *Tutanekai* reached the scene of the accident at 0400 and stood by about a kilometre from the wreck. The *Port Elliott*'s crew, who had taken to the boats several hours before, sent some boats to the *Tutanekai* and some back to the ship, which was obviously in no danger of breaking up. A few hours later, however, a moderate sea started bending some hull plates.

With the arrival of the East Cape lighthouse keeper, shore-to-ship communication was at last possible; Smith, the keeper, started signalling by means of handkerchiefs tied to bits of sticks! In this way arrangements were made for the crew to land on the shore in the evening and go to the nearby meeting house, where things were being prepared for them. At the same time, the Napier shipping company Richardson & Co. began deploying its steam lighters to the wreck site in order to remove the ship's cargo. Not everyone was happy with this business-like efficiency. One Horoera Maori, surveying the orderly scene, was reported to have muttered, 'This wreck no

The *Port Elliott* remained relatively intact for long enough for salvors to remove much of her cargo and fittings. This photograph looks back to the bridge and the Richardson coaster *Awahou* standing off in the distance. *Wellington Maritime Museum & Gallery*

blurry good. Nothing washed ashore like the *Tongariro*. *Tongariro* wreck kapai.'[8]

The salvors did well out of the *Port Elliott*. Using the small steamers *Fanny* and *Ruru*, Richardsons offloaded a considerable amount of general cargo, cased benzine and 107 cased motor vehicles. Dried out and spruced up, they fetched reasonable prices at a Wellington auction. By 15 January the ship was settling deeper into the sand and only eight men remained aboard to stand guard. Now just the tip of the propeller was visible. Salvage operations continued until 28 March, by which time 1500 tons of cargo and 800 tons of fittings had been taken from the *Port Elliott*, which was then left to break up.

The magisterial inquiry found that the stranding had been caused by poor visibility, a set (current) inshore of which the master was unaware and the third officer mistaking a bush fire for the East Cape light. It returned all officers' certificates.

Notes
1. *Evening Post*, 26 August 1913.
2. *Ibid*.
3. *Ibid*.
4. *Ibid*., 27 August.
5. *Ibid*., 2 June 1922.
6. *Ibid*.
7. *Ibid*.
8. *Gisborne Times*, 14 December 1924.

Captain D. M. Todd.

One person often intimately involved in shipwrecks and other maritime dramas was the harbourmaster. Although the position has lost some of its status under the regimes of the new port companies, the harbourmaster was formerly a person of immense stature. It was his task to ensure the safe and efficient operation of shipping within his port limits and his word held good as far as shipping movements were concerned. All too often, though, it fell to him to try to clear up someone else's mess after a ship went ashore.

Wellington harbourmaster Captain David Martin Todd was one such man. Although he had originally dreamed of a life on the land as a farmer, Todd shipped out from Sydney aboard the barquentine *Alexa* when he was just 15. His head filled with adventurous tales of the sea, the youth spent 10 years crossing the Pacific on a variety of sailing craft and steamers.

It was a hard life with long periods away from home. Like many great maritime men, Todd suffered from seasickness throughout his life and leapt at the opportunity to come ashore as a pilot when a vacancy came up at Wellington. For the next 37 years he would be on call night and day, bringing in ships or answering telephone calls such as the one at 0400 hours one morning: 'Can you please tell me what time the tanker berthed at Point Howard is sailing because I have some of the boys from it at my house?'

Todd played a prominent role in rescuing three ships featured in this book, the *Wanganella*, and the *Taranaki* and the *Waipiata*. He was acting-harbourmaster at the time of the *Wanganella* stranding and remembered many people giving the badly damaged ship up as lost. Recalled from his Paraparaumu holiday, Todd worked on the ship until Australian salvor J. E. Johnstone arrived to take over. Todd later piloted the crippled liner during her nerve-wracking crawl up harbour to safety.

Captain Todd's greatest moment came three years later when the *Taranaki* and *Waipiata* collided at the entrance to the harbour. Worried that the *Waipiata* might sink if freed from the *Taranaki*'s bow, Todd piloted the two ships back into harbour. This action, carried out at night and with the *Waipiata* locked across the *Taranaki*'s bow, was recognised as an outstanding feat of navigation by marine insurers Lloyds of London, which subsequently presented him with an inscribed gold watch.

Captain Todd received the OBE in 1957 in recognition of his services to shipping. He travelled down to the Antarctic as a guest of Operation Deepfreeze in 1960 and retired as harbourmaster in 1964.

Chapter 15

BIG ONES THAT GOT AWAY

The twentieth century has had its share of challenging salvage jobs. One of the most unusual was performed on the whale factory ship *C.A. Larsen* in 1928. Foreign whalers had been absent from New Zealand shores for the best part of half a century when the Ross Sea Whaling Company of Norway started whaling in the Southern Ocean in 1923, using a base at Paterson Inlet, Stewart Island. (The politics and details are covered fully by J. P. C. Watt's book *Stewart Island's Kaipipi Shipyard and the Ross Sea Whalers*.)[1]

The new venture bore little resemblance to its predecessors. Gone were the frail wooden ships of last century, the oared longboats and the boozy, whoring seamen. In their place were fast, steam-powered whale chasers backed up by huge floating processing factories and well-trained, well-equipped crews. The *C.A. Larsen*, the subject of this sad story, was a former tanker, converted in 1926 with a large flensing deck and bow-mounted slipway capable of handling the largest whale carcasses. A huge brute of a ship (12,093 GRT), she was packed with the very latest technology – a massive floating factory.

On the morning of 21 February 1928 the two factory ships, *Sir James Clark Ross* and the *C.A. Larsen*, were picking their way up Paterson Inlet on Stewart Island towards Price's Inlet where the Norwegians had established their base in accordance with the wishes of the New Zealand Government. Each ship had had a good season and was brimful of whale oil. Neither carried a pilot, having crossed the difficult channel several times previously.

Hindsight would show that this was a mistake. Paterson Inlet, almost unmarked and unlit, is difficult for a large ship, especially one whose master is not fully familiar with its little quirks and eccentricities. Several tight turns have to be negotiated. The inlet, essentially a drowned valley, is open to westerlies and any ship running into trouble is a long way from help.

The smaller *Sir James Clark Ross*, taking advantage of the flood tide, led the way in and threaded her way up the channel, dropping anchor off the beach several hours later. Then it was the *Larsen*'s turn. Her master, Captain Oscar Nilsen, began his approach at 1600 hours on a falling tide. All went well until, when between The Neck and Bench Island, the big ship bashed heavily across submerged rocks just west of little

Whero Island, which lies between the two navigation points. Nilsen ordered full astern but the deeply laden monster held fast. Surplus crew (there were 166 aboard at the time) were transferred to the accompanying chasers and everyone waited nervously for the rising tide.

The *Larsen* floated off later that evening in a badly damaged condition. Down by the bows by about 1.5 metres, she presented a sorry sight. Fortunately, though, her unusual engines-aft design protected her power plant from serious damage. Nilsen, worried that she might founder, steered her into shallow water and beached her in a safe spot. Her foredeck awash, she settled for the night while the Norwegians began preparations for one of the most complicated salvage jobs ever undertaken in New Zealand waters.

By the evening of the following day the Southland Harbour Board tugs *Theresa Ward* and *Southland* had arrived with more pumps to stem the flow of water into the beached ship. The same harbour board's dredge had been chartered to begin searching for the anchor and cable sheared off during the collision. On 23 February another rescuer, the Otago Harbour Board tug *Dunedin*, steamed into Paterson Inlet with another pump and air compressors. With two tugs, a dredge and several steam chasers in attendance, the inlet was beginning to look crowded!

The immediate danger of sinking had disappeared, but the question of a more permanent solution remained. The island shipyard's facilities were too elementary to cope with the task and even Bluff, the closest port, had little to offer. The nearest port capable of doing the job was Port Chalmers, where there were two graving docks and several engineering companies; but that was a long way away and even the larger dock would have to be brought up to scratch before the Norwegians risked their big ship in the open sea.

Meanwhile the *Dunedin*'s pumps and divers worked day and night. An inspection had revealed extensive bottom damage – along 90 metres of her 161-metre length – with the bow area worst affected. Port Chalmers shipwright and salvage expert R. C. Miller estimated that it would take three weeks of hard work at Paterson Inlet to get the *Larsen* in shape for the dash across to Port Chalmers.

Speed was important. The wreck site lay open to the full force of the westerlies and it was in everyone's interests to get the ship secure before another storm bowled in and finished her off. Within days supplies of timber, canvas and cement were being freighted in from all over Southland and the salvors had hired every diver they could get their hands on. Working in freezing conditions, these men bolted timber and canvas patches over the *Larsen*'s worst gashes before moving inside to attack the holds and oil tanks with cement grouting. The fuel oil and foul-smelling whale oil sloshing about inside parts of the ship made the work very unpleasant.

Rough and ready it may have been, but it worked! Much of her oil and coal stores were removed and on 8 March the *C. A.*

The Norwegian whale factory ship *C.A. Larsen* at Wellington after completing extensive 'temporary' repairs at Port Chalmers. *Wellington Maritime Museum & Gallery*

Larsen was ready for refloating. With all pumps operating and air compressors creating pressure inside the ruptured tanks, the big vessel lifted her battered bow off the seabed. Shepherded by chasers and drawing 13.4 metres forward and 9.2 metres aft, the *Larsen* crawled painfully up the inlet to the more sheltered reaches of Big Glory Harbour.

There she licked her wounds and continued the task of lightening ship. Everything not considered essential was removed and stowed ashore or in the old hulk *Tarawera*. About 50,000 barrels of oil, nearly two-thirds of the amount aboard at the time of the grounding, was pumped aboard the new tanker *Spinanger*, then it was time to head for Port Chalmers. There the Otago Harbour Board had moved heaven and not a little earth to extend its larger dock by just over 8 metres to squeeze in the *Larsen*.

Escorted by the chaser *Karrakatta*, the *Larsen* cleared Big Glory on the afternoon of 12 April. With her various hired pumps working fulltime, the big ship reached Port Chalmers the following day. A large crowd watched her arrive and enter the dock on 17 April. With her rudder just 13 centimetres from the entrance, it was one of the tightest dockings ever carried out there.

The *C.A. Larsen* spent the next 18 days in the dock while local engineering firm Stevenson & Cook Engineering carried out £8,000 worth of repairs, sufficient to make her seaworthy for the long voyage back to Norway and permanent repairs. She cleared Port Chalmers on 20 May, put into Wellington for bunkering the following day, then left for Newcastle-upon-Tyne via Panama. She completed several other expeditions to New Zealand. Although sunk by the British in a raid against the battleship KMS *Tirpitz* in July 1944, she was salvaged and served until 1954 when she was broken up at Hamburg.

Wellington's notorious Barrett Reef almost claimed its largest victim on 19 January 1947 when the trans-Tasman liner *Wanganella* piled up on its jagged top and treated the capital's residents to a salvage job the like of which they had not seen for a long time.

Like so many other liners, including her erstwhile rival, the *Monowai*, the *Wanganella* had been absent from the run since May 1941, requisitioned by the Australian Government for the war effort as a hospital ship. Throughout 1946 her owners, Huddart Parker Ltd of Melbourne (in which the Union Company, unknown to anyone else, held a discreet 25 percent share), had been sprucing up its 1931-built twin-funnelled 9876-ton flagship ready for a triumphal restoration of peace-time travel. Her accommodation had been fully booked up for many months by holidaymakers and businesspeople and the ship left Sydney bedecked with coloured streamers. This was the start of a new era.

Less than half an hour before midnight on 19 January 1947, on her first post-war voyage, the *Wanganella*, under the command of Captain R. Darroch and with 400 Sydney passengers aboard, struck the edge of the reef, tearing open the forward section of her hull. Fortunately the sea was calm and the ship held onto the reef instead of sliding off and sinking. When the port tugs *Toia*, *Terawhiti* and *Kahanui* failed to budge her, the Eastbourne ferry *Cobar* came alongside the next morning and took off the passengers and most of the crew. Although many had been shaken out of their bunks by the impact, no one was seriously injured.

Luck was also on the *Wanganella*'s side this time. One good southerly might have finished her off but Wellington's weather remained unusually fine for the next 18 days that she lay on the reef. On 6 February a strong southerly swell and some good pulling from the tugs lifted her off the rocks. The tugs towed her stern-first to a wharf where she settled on the bottom. Shipwrights then started reducing her draught forward. She entered the Jubilee floating dock on 18 February.

There the ship's luck ran out again. Post-war New Zealand was an industrial battleground. Before much progress had been made, the shipwrights employed by local firm William Cable & Co. walked off the job, leaving her high and dry on the floating dock. Taken out and laid up at Clyde Quay Wharf to await supplies of steel for permanent repairs, the *Wanganella* was kept out of the dock until January of the following year. When she left Jubilee in November 1948, almost two years had passed since she struck the reef.

By then the court of inquiry's report was fast gathering dust. Held over three days in February 1947, it blamed Captain Darroch for mistaking the Barrett Reef floating buoy for the No. 1 leading light, 2½ nautical miles north of the reef. His certificate was suspended for three months.

Within another decade airline competition was strangling trans-Tasman shipping to death. In September 1961 Huddart Parker sold its shipping interests to fellow Australian company

Another Norwegian in trouble in southern waters; the 'Liberty' ship *Viggo Hansteen* aground off Tikoraki Point, near Moeraki, on 24 April 1952. Fortunately the weather was kind, enabling the ship to be refloated undamaged. *Otago Harbour Board*

McIlwraith McEacharn, which kept the old ship going until April 1962 when it passed her over to a Hong Kong company for a still-born liner service between the British colony and Australasia. A year later she was back in New Zealand waters at Deep Cove, Fiordland, as a hostel ship for workers on the Manapouri power project. Her engines silent, she carried out these humble duties until 1970 when she was towed to Hong Kong. Taiwanese breakers finished her off later that year.

The residents of Moeraki, North Otago, a port that had not seen a trading vessel for nearly 70 years, received a shock when they awoke on the morning of 24 April 1952 to see an ocean-going freighter ablaze with lights just metres from the shore off Tikoraki Point.[2]

The ship was a Norwegian-owned 'Liberty' ship, the *Viggo Hansteen*. Launched in Baltimore in 1943 as the *George M. Shriver*, but renamed in honour of a Norwegian patriot executed by the Germans in 1940, she was travelling from London to Dunedin. She had enjoyed only two days of fine weather during her long voyage halfway around the world.

Lacking radar and unfamiliar with local waters, the *Viggo Hansteen*'s crew mistook Moeraki's lighthouse for the one at Taiaroa Heads at the entrance to Otago Harbour. The lookouts stationed in the bow saw nothing and only took alarm when the ship ground her way across the rocks.

Fortunately the thick kelp beds cushioned the ship's impact and kept damage to a minimum. One hundred and forty metres offshore and in just 5 metres of water, the *Viggo Hansteen*'s position was more humiliating than life-threatening, especially since the sea was calm. From the start, a successful salvage seemed likely.

Later that day rescue arrived in the shape of the Otago Harbour Board's ancient steam tug *Dunedin* (345 tons), which had ministered to the *C.A. Larsen*. By 1520 hours she had the Norwegian ship off the rocks and following compliantly astern as both vessels made for Otago Harbour. A docking at Port Chalmers revealed no damage and the ship survived another 12 years until, as the *Alkimos*, she went ashore for good off the Australian coast.

On the afternoon of 13 July 1956 Captain C. M. Davies, the master of the coaster *Calm*, was praying for weather that could live up to the name of his charge. The 787-ton freighter, just six years old and the pride of the small Canterbury Steam Shipping Company's fleet, had cleared New Plymouth and was butting her way through a southerly gale bound for Dunedin.[3]

By the time he was off Opunake, Davies, a man with 38 years' seagoing experience to his credit, was worried. Mountainous seas had flung the powerful little ship off her course and were causing her to lose steerage way. Although she was in no immediate danger of foundering, the time had come for the *Calm* to seek shelter. Later that evening Davies turned her round and made for the protection of New Plymouth.

With the sea behind her, the ship rode much easier. Then, at 0118 hours on the 14th, in complete darkness and without any warning, the *Calm* crashed noisily onto the rocks off Waiweranui Point, Taranaki and started taking in water. An eerie darkness enveloped everything, including the Cape Egmont light, which had been visible on the way south but which did not reappear until much later, 6 miles to the south. Davies ordered the crew to ready the lifeboats but, believing it too dangerous to leave the vessel in the dark, withheld the order to abandon ship.

Daybreak revealed the beach just 100 metres away. By that stage of the tide the *Calm*'s bows were far enough out of the water to enable the crew to step ashore safely and raise the alarm at a nearby farm. Even the ship's cat, chaperoned shorewards by Paddy Leahy, reached the beach with dry paws!

By the time the company's marine superintendent, Captain W. D. Drake, reached Waiweranui Point later that afternoon, no one harboured any illusions about the magnitude of the task awaiting them. Drake found the *Calm* wedged fast on a reef of boulders jutting out from the point, about 65 metres from the shore. Heavy seas were pounding her starboard side and she was still taking in water. With a south-east gale blowing and heavy rain falling, things did not look good.

By Sunday morning the seas had calmed sufficiently for Drake's men to board the ship and inspect the damage. The port and starboard tanks were leaking oil and the double bottom freshwater tank was full of saltwater; it was obvious that the ship was badly damaged. The hold and the engine room, though, were dry.

Drake's men rigged up a flying fox and started lightening

Well wrapped up against the winter winds, company officials supervise the lightening of the ship's cargo. This photograph, taken at low tide, shows how far up the beach the *Calm* had gone and indicates why salvage would be so difficult. *Wellington Maritime Museum & Gallery*

ship. That afternoon they were joined by additional workers and a bulldozer. Much of the cargo and stores had been removed by the afternoon of the 17th when the Union Company's Wellington salvage tug *Taioma*, until then bottled up in her home port by the storm, arrived on the scene. She was joined by a small powered punt which quickly fouled the *Calm*'s lines and went ashore. In a matter of minutes the rescuers found themselves in need of rescue. Only quick thinking by the bulldozer crew averted tragedy and saved the lives of the two men working on the punt.

Weather conditions prevented work the next day and only the promise of a higher than normal tide the following day kept salvage hopes alive. By 1930 hours on the Thursday everything that could be moved off the ship had been taken ashore; the *Calm* was as light as she would ever become and was now bouncing about in the surf. With her engines going full astern and pulling on the wires, she eased her way off the rocks and out into the comparative safety of deep water.

Four hours later she was alongside New Plymouth's Newton King Wharf discharging her remaining cargo and undergoing a temporary patch-up. Permanent repairs, which set the Canterbury Company back a hefty £65,000 and took three months, were carried out at Port Chalmers. Canterbury later got back £40,000 from the Marine Department whose Cape Egmont lighthouse had gone out after a power failure just before midnight. Since the *Calm*, like all coasters, lacked radar and direction-finding equipment, this failure was held to be the primary cause of the stranding.

Once repaired, the trim little ship served her owners well – surviving a minor collision with a Port Chalmers fishing boat in May 1963 and a cargo fire off the South Canterbury coast in August 1966 – until 1971 when she was sold for trading around South-east Asia. She finally sank in the South China Sea on 3 July 1990 under the name *Angkor 2*.

How she looked from the shore. The *Calm*, the ship that often did not live up to her name, at Waiweranui Point. *Wellington Maritime Museum & Gallery*

That all the radar, satellite navigation equipment and technology in the world would still not prevent people from acting stupidly became apparent at 0304 hours on 21 May 1981 when the 10,000-ton bulk carrier *Pacific Charger* fetched up on the rocks at Baring Head just a few kilometres from the entrance to Wellington Harbour.[4]

Although a 'flag of convenience' ship (i.e. one flagged out by her owners onto a register which required cheaper crewing standards and numbers), the *Pacific Charger* was brand-new. With a GRT of 10,241 and a net of 7633, she had a length overall of 146 metres, a breadth of 22.9 metres and a depth of 12.6 metres. Although no beauty, she was of a well-proven, near-standard Japanese design for the flexible handling of log and container cargos.

Launched at the Sasebo Heavy Industries yard on 21 February 1981, the ship had been delivered to her owners, Ocean Chargers Ltd of Monrovia, Liberia, a wholly owned subsidiary of the Kansai Steamship Co. Ltd of Japan, on 24 April. Chartered back by Ocean Chargers' parent company, the bulker had been dispatched to New Zealand on her maiden voyage as part of an agreement with the British Crusader Swire Container Service. Confused? Others certainly were. These multi-level ownership arrangements, increasingly a part of the modern shipping scene, would give the court of inquiry plenty of detective work. At the time of the stranding the *Pacific Charger* was carrying 4000 tonnes of CKD cars and was under the command of Taiwanese-born Captain R. Y. Chiou.

The weather was as bad as Wellington's critics usually imagine it to be; a 70-knot south-easterly gale was shrieking through the strait and visibility was down to less than 2 kilometres. Alerted by radio, the pilot cutter *Tiakina* (which had been on her way out to meet the ship, anyway) and the tug *Kupe* arrived on the scene shortly afterwards but could do nothing since the freighter was a mere 55 metres from the shore and wedged fast. They could not get close enough to do anything and could offer little more than encouragement. Shore parties fared no better; washouts and slips on the road from Wainuiomata reduced them to crawling speed. Not until 1300 hours could the crew abandon ship by dinghy and rope ladder. Cold, wet and miserable, 23 of the 26 Burmese and Taiwanese seafarers were taken to a city hotel by army trucks, leaving the master, chief officer and chief engineer aboard to protect their owners' interests.

Despite being pounded by heavy seas, to which she was lying parallel, the *Pacific Charger* showed no signs of breaking up. Although no one had been able to survey the damage accurately, it was obvious that refloating the ship – if indeed that was possible – would be a lengthy and expensive undertaking. Kansai, therefore, called in outside help in the form of Singapore-based master salvor, Captain A. H. G. (Hugh) Murray. Murray's company, Selco Marine Salvage, signed a standard 'no cure, no pay' agreement with Kansai and issued sailing orders to its nearest salvage tug, the *Asiatic Triumph*, then at Papeete. A comparatively small tug with a bollard pull of just 28 tons, the *Asiatic Triumph* reached Wellington on the 29th.

By then Murray's teams had already accomplished a great deal. The Ministry of Works and Development bulldozed a road out from Eastbourne and and built a causeway out to the ship. This enabled road tankers to start the slow task of removing the *Pacific Charger*'s 800 tonnes of heavy fuel oil, which posed a potential threat to the environment. Most was still aboard when Murray later prised the ship off the beach.

By 2 June the weather had calmed sufficiently for an attempt to be made to refloat the ship. The Wellington Harbour Board tugs *Kupe* and *Toia*, the university launch *Tirohia* and the police launch *Lady Elizabeth II* added their considerable mechanical muscle to that of the *Asiatic Triumph*, but to no avail; by 1630, when the attempt was abandoned, the *Pacific Charger* was no further seaward.

Murray waited three days before trying again. On 5 June the two local tugs joined the *Asiatic Triumph* to take advantage of high water and a slight southerly swell which, it was hoped, might get her moving. This time the *Toia* and *Kupe* pulled together on one line and succeeded in moving her by 1935 hours. At last freed from the rocks, the *Pacific Charger* was taken in tow for a Wellington berth, making fast at King's Wharf in the early hours of the 6th.

There she lay, surrounded by a precautionary oil barrier. Selco divers patched up her crumpled hull and had her ready

for handing over to her owners by the 17th. Seven days later shore cranes were removing her oil-covered and water-damaged cargo at Glasgow Wharf. Even here, though, misfortune continued to dog the *Pacific Charger*. On 30 June a steel girder being lifted out of her No. 2 hold slipped from the sling and plunged through her bottom, allowing about 2000 tonnes of water to gush in before the fire brigade pumped it out. The next day a diver plugged the gap.

Kansai's chartered tug *Sumi Maru* arrived at Wellington on 13 July to tow the *Pacific Charger* back to Japan for permanent repairs. At first a writ of arrest prevented the ship from departing but by the end of the month legal objections had been overcome and she was on her way back to the shipyard for permanent repairs. There Sasebo renewed the complete bottom plating and the No. 4 hold tank plating, partly renewed other sections, stripped the engine for repair and withdrew the tailshaft. By the end of the year she was back in service as the *Cobalt Islands*, registered with another Monrovian single-ship company.

Of course, that was not the end of it. There remained the court of inquiry. Predictably, it was a lengthy affair, carried out through translators and featuring a number of serious charges and countercharges. The equally voluminous report did not hit the bookshelves until January 1982.

Reports of courts of inquiry do not usually make exciting reading but this one, for all its careful and legalistic wording,

On 21 May 1981 rescuers brave appalling winter conditions to retrieve the first line to be fired from the *Pacific Charger* to the shore. *Evening Post*

In this dramatic photograph a wave breaks over the bow of the *Pacific Charger* while salvage operations get underway. *Evening Post*

certainly launched a few headlines. Its bald answer to the Minister of Transport's question, 'What was the cause of the stranding?', provided plenty of good copy:

> The vessel was set in by the ebb tide in a south easterly direction, and was being navigated on an unsafe course. Also the inability of the master or second mate to plot the vessel's progress over the last 20 minutes. The incompetence of the master by his failure to study the tidal information or avail himself of the manuals dealing with that particular area or to even recognise the danger of the situation.

In placing much of the blame on the master and crew, the court did not hide behind verbosity or euphemisms. 'Despite all the international conventions as to safety at sea, it is useless to send a well found ship on a voyage if the officers and crew are incompetent.' Technology did not make human skills redundant. This was a new ship and none of the officers and crew had sailed together before. There were language problems with a Japanese-owned, Taiwanese-officered and Burmese-crewed ship operating in waters where English was the language of communication.

Few of the officers aboard the *Pacific Charger* stood up to close scrutiny. Chiou, on his first visit to New Zealand waters and relying on small-scale American charts, had considerable seagoing experience but 'no formal qualifications in the use of

This aerial photograph shows just how close the ship was to the Baring Head lighthouse. *Evening Post*

radar, although he relied upon it entirely and alone'. Soe Tint, the quartermaster on duty at the time of the stranding, 'could not be regarded as an experienced quartermaster and his failure to inform the master sooner than he did that he was having difficulty in keeping the ship on course clearly indicates this'. Second mate Kao Hing Ho, who was on duty at the time with Chiou, had never been to navigation school or done radar training. As the court noted, 'As 2nd mate on the *Pacific Charger* he was the navigation officer, but any skill or experience he had in that field was derived only from sea service, most of it in lower ranks'. Third mate Chung Chin Ming had not served at sea in any capacity for three years before joining the *Pacific Charger*. Only first mate Chang Yung Chung, who was not on duty at the time, could be considered fully competent in navigational skills.

The court found that, although weather conditions were bad – the second worst recorded after the 1968 *Wahine* storm – the master could have avoided danger by standing out to sea and waiting for conditions to clear. This would have been especially advisable since he was not familiar with Wellington.

Determined to get into sheltered water to pick up the pilot, and believing there to be shelter just past Baring Head, Chiou pressed on, reducing speed. This last action made the *Pacific Charger* more difficult to handle, since a big ship needs a certain amount of headway to retain full manoeuvrability. Ill-equipped, using inadequate manuals, off course, unaware of the effect that the set and drift of the tide of at least 1.5 knots was having on his ship, ignoring the echo-sounder which would have told him that he was entering shallow water and failing to take a visual compass bearing on the Baring Head light when it became visible, Chiou was now steering straight for land.

There was no excuse for this foolishness. Chiou had modern and reliable radar sets and the coastline around Baring Head is a very good radar target. His lack of radar training led him astray. Modern radar sets have a number of devices which enable skilled operators to make operational adjustments. The GAIN control varies the amplification of the receiver and thus the strength of the echoes as they appear on the screen. The STC control, better known as the anti-clutter sea control, varies the GAIN control over short distances; it can be used to remove returns from waves which might otherwise mask more solid objects behind them. The FTC control is the anti-clutter rain, hail or snow control. It can compensate for overuse of STC. Used intelligently by trained operators, these controls can remove confusing echoes from weather conditions. Twisted too far, however, the dials, and STC in particular, can remove everything – even land!

This is precisely what happened. Neither Chiou nor the mate had read the manuals for the set and used excessive GAIN and STC without even switching on FTC, which might have cut out the heavy rain and compensated for excessive use of the other controls. As the court reported:

> There had been no attempt on the voyage from Yokohama to Auckland to correct the charts from *Notices to Mariners*, and neither the master nor the 2nd mate had bothered to read about the New Zealand coast or harbours in the manuals on board, apart from the

Darkness was already falling on 5 June 1981 when the Wellington Harbour Board tugs *Toia* and *Kupe* started preparing to pull the *Pacific Charger* from the rocks. Four hours later she was free. *Evening Post*

brief reference in *Guide to Port Entry*, and no attempt had been made to consult New Zealand charts. If he had studied the appropriate NZ charts instead of relying on the small scale American charts he was using, he would have realised that the profile of Baring Head is virtually duplicated a short distance inland and he would have been alert to ensure that his observation of target related to the shore-line. His excessive use of the anti-clutter control obliterated the land inside his 2 mile variable ring and he had no idea where he was. However, he was so anxious to make his way into the harbour that he ignored the basic rule of seamanship to steer away from possible danger. He reduced speed, while looking for the pilot, to such an extent that in the weather conditions prevailing he had no steerage control, the ship just would not respond to the rudder . . .

No charges could be laid against Chiou or his officers because the court had no jurisdiction over non-British Commonwealth ships. It had to content itself with answering the minister's questions and repeating the warning against poorly manned and trained flag of convenience vessels. That its concerns were well placed became apparent just a few months later. Chiou returned to sea in command of another bulk carrier, the *Orient Treasury*, but he was reported lost at sea earlier that year.

Notes
1. For a comprehensive account of the Ross Sea whaling venture and the stranding of the *C.A. Larsen*, see J. P. C. Watt, *Stewart Island's Kaipipi Shipyard and the Ross Sea Whalers*, Hastings, 1989.
2. See Gavin McLean, *Moeraki: 150 Years of Net and Ploughshare*, Dunedin, 1986.
3. Information is drawn from the Canterbury Steam Shipping Company files held by the Wellington Maritime Museum and Gallery.
4. Information on the *Pacific Charger* is taken from contemporary newspapers as well as the 'Formal Investigation Pursuant to Section 325 Shipping and Seamen Act 1952, M.V. *Pacific Charger*, Shipping Casualty 21 May 1981, Report of Court and Annex Thereto', Wellington, January 1982.

These photographs of the small trader *Neptune* show the hazards of small river ports such as Blenheim. The top photograph of her ashore on the Wairau bar in February 1897 was the last; she became a total loss. The bottom photograph, taken earlier, shows her inside the river. *Marlborough Historical Society, courtesy of A. J. Sprosen/Wellington Maritime Museum & Gallery*

Chapter 16

UNLUCKY SHIPS

Some ships seem to trail trouble in their wake. The merest flick through a few fleet lists shows that for each vessel with an uneventful career, there was one which appeared to have every kind of accident imaginable. The state of the coastline during the early days of European settlement made such disasters inevitable.

The following Press Association piece from the *Evening Post* of 21 October 1895 may be brief, but the tale of woe outlined in these few lines should remind us that tragedy was often part of the mariner's everyday work; dramatic, total wrecks accounted for only a minority of the lives lost at sea last century.

AN UNLUCKY VOYAGE
EXTRAORDINARY SUCCESSION OF DISASTERS
MELBOURNE, THIS DAY

The ship *Lindisfarne* had a terrible experience on her last voyage Home.

After striking a rock and putting back for repairs, she lost a seaman overboard when three days out.

The vessel then encountered a fearful hurricane and was partially dismasted.

The chief officer had his spine fractured by a falling spar, and succumbed to the injuries.

The second officer was also severely injured and was confined to bed.

Several seamen were incapacitated by frostbite and the crew being consequently short-handed, the great difficulty was experienced in working the vessel.

In this chapter, though, we will follow the misadventures of three twentieth-century coasters, each of which managed to clock up more than her fair share of trouble. The first pair traded to Blenheim for much of their adventurous lives. One is gone now but the other, a 'lucky unlucky' craft, survived a variety of maritime accidents and is still clinging precariously to existence on the Picton foreshore. The last in this floating rogues' gallery, a veritable floating disaster, went down off Banks Peninsula almost 30 years ago.

The first ships with overly adventurous careers were two that became well known in the Blenheim–Wellington trade for many years – the steamer *Wairau* and the hold scow *Echo*. The *Wairau* is gone now, her derelict hulk burned by an arsonist, but not so the *Echo*, which survived just about every maritime calamity imaginable. She may still be seen on the Picton waterfront, in a dubious state of 'preservation'.

The *Wairau*, or 'the Jonah Ship' as sailors (always a superstitious lot) called her, began life as the schooner *Ronga* for Kerr and Brownlee of Lyttelton. A product of the famous Totara North yard of T. M. Lane, she was a pretty little craft of 92 tons. Completed in 1900, she partnered the same firm's schooner *Falcon* in the timber trade between Lyttelton and Pelorus Sound. Faithfully built of selected timber, mostly kauri, and heavily sparred for her size, she was designed for speed. Unfortunately, her tender lines and those heavy spars would also prove her undoing.

The timber run was a one-way trade. The *Ronga* normally left Lyttelton in ballast which was dumped overboard when she came up the sound to begin loading. This was an extremely dangerous operation – given what the gusts in the sounds could do to an empty ship under sail – and suspicions about her seaworthiness were roused when she capsized in Pelorus Sound in September 1901 during a squall.

A strong nor'-easter was blowing at the time and second mate J. C. Ipsen protested when Captain Ned Petersen gave his customary order to jettison the ballast.[1] Petersen was a Swede with a reputation for 'hard driving', but the *Ronga* simply was not the right type of craft for this treatment. Off Four Fathom Bay, just 12 miles from the sawmill at Havelock, a strong gust sent the *Ronga* over onto her beam ends. Luckily, there was time for everyone to make it into the lifeboat and most did not even get their feet wet.

In those pre-radio days coasters often released pigeons at the entrance to the sound to warn of their arrival. When the *Ronga* failed to follow her feathered heralds, search parties were sent out. They found the ship lying on her side at Four Fathom Bay. The crew had spent the night in a nearby hayloft and had already started to strip gear from the basically undamaged ship.

When the *Ronga* did the same thing in Pelorus Sound almost exactly a year later, tongues really started to wag. She was off the jetty when, 'without warning,' a former crewman recalled, 'we were hit. The *Ronga* turned over and the next instant we were floundering in the water.'[2] Everyone made it to shore and the government lighthouse tender *Tutanekai* was on hand to help right her and pump her out. The Marine Department inquiry ordered her masts to be cut down as it considered her 'overhatted' – too heavily sparred.

Thereafter her owners had trouble attracting crews. Peterson had another close shave in Pelorus Sound at the end of 1905. The men's fears were not unfounded; on 21 April 1906 the ship capsized for the third time, this time with fatal consequences. The *Ronga* had followed the barque *Annie Hill* out of Lyttelton that morning. Petersen had been in a great hurry to

The *Moa* (127 tons, built 1907) was a typical New Zealand scow. Note the low freeboard and the timber cargo stacked on her deck; most scows carried their cargos on the deck and, unlike the *Echo*, did not have conventional hatches and holds. The *Moa*, immortalised when she was captured by von Luckner during the First World War, stranded and became a total loss at Big Wanganui on the West Coast of the South Island in March 1935. *Wellington Maritime Museum & Gallery*

leave Lyttelton to take advantage of the wind and had not taken the precaution of properly trimming the 30 tonnes of coal left in her hold. Because he had no shifting boards to contain it, this coal would prove the undoing of the *Ronga* once things got rough.

And get rough they did. Petersen passed the breakwater at 1100 hours under full sail. Later that afternoon a terrific gale sprang up and the steamers *Talune* and *Pateena*, themselves battling the elements, reported seeing the upturned hulk of a derelict schooner 15 miles off Cape Campbell. Several days later the steamer *Gertie* intercepted the wreck off Kapiti Island and towed it into port. Fishermen from Paraparaumu righted the hull, baled it out and identified it as the *Ronga*. No clues were found as to the fate of the six men aboard.

Moored at Wellington's rotten row, the ill-fated ship was later purchased and refitted as a steamer by William Cable & Co. In 1908 she recommissioned as a steamer of 143 tons under the new name *Wairau* (after the river leading to the sea from Blenheim). A change of name did not immediately revive her fortunes and she remained a 'hoodoo ship' for a while yet. On 25 February 1910 the *Wairau* was wrecked at Wanganui in a gale; no one was killed. Another round of extensive repairs followed. She had been back in service for just a few weeks on 16 May 1911 when she collided with the steamer *Himitangi* in the Manawatu River and sank. No lives were lost but it was back to the shipyard for more costly repairs.

Thereafter life was quieter. Under the Eckford flag, the *Wairau* settled down into more or less regular running, partnering the scow *Echo* and suffering no more than the usual run of minor strandings and machinery breakdowns. A pre-war trade downturn took her out of service in the mid-1930s but in 1942 the old ship returned to service after the Americans requisitioned the *Echo*. Converted to diesel after the war, the *Wairau* continued to cross Cook Strait until 1951 when she was withdrawn and hulked. Taken to Motueka, she was burned there in 1976 while lying derelict.

Although they have their counterparts in several parts of the world, most notably around San Francisco, scows were the only major trading vessel built especially for New Zealand conditions. Flat-bottomed for beaching at undeveloped 'ports' and for trading far up barely navigable rivers, they were ideally suited to pioneering conditions, especially in the north. The first appeared in 1873, when the *Lake Erie* was built at Omaha, north of Auckland. Several hundred more would follow her until the 1920s, when steam and the oil engine finally won out.

And the scows were tough! Although most eventually succumbed to the power of the sea or the inevitable decay of old age, many bounced back time after time from accidents that would have meant the end of the road for the finer-boned schooners and ketches. Writing in his book *Phantom Fleet*, scowman Ted Ashby had this to say about his beloved craft: 'The short time I was in the *Rimu* she stranded twice, but so versatile were the scows that though strained and twisted out of shape they would soon be patched up and back to work. In my time the *Ngahau* rolled over three times, the *Lena* twice, the second time drowning three people, the *Vesper* once, drowning all hands and the *Glenae* once.'[3] Designed for beaching, they were almost indestructible and easy to salvage, often being refloated full of empty oil drums and towed back to the shipyard for refitting.

The scow that tested the theory of the design most was also one of the largest ever built. She was the 126-ton hold scow *Echo*, whose exploits were immortalised (albeit somewhat inaccurately) in the early 1960s film *The Wackiest Ship in the Army*. She began life at the Kaipara yard of W. Brown & Sons in 1905 to a slightly unusual design, incorporating an oil engine. This was installed mainly to assist berthing; for the rest of the time she relied upon the cheaper power of the wind. Retained initially by the builder, she was passed over to the Karamea Steamship Co. later that year and ran in its employ until 1916 when she passed into the hands of Napier-based shipping company, Richardson & Co. Richardsons held her until 1920 when she was sold to a Blenheim shipowner, Charles Eckford.

The *Echo* would remain part of the Eckford family for the next adventurous 45 years. The Eckfords had been involved in the Cook Strait trade since 1880 when Thomas Eckford started the ball rolling with the steamer *Mohaka*. By 1920 son Charles Eckford was looking for a small, shallow-draught ship to run between Blenheim and Wellington. Until the 1960s Blenheim merchants had an alternative route to Picton, using the Wairau River. This enabled them to unload their produce and stores right in the centre of town and to cut out trans-shipment. Although the meandering river and the shallow, treacherous bar were difficult and expensive to work, the direct service was very popular with farmers supplying the tables of the capital.

The Wairau bar racked up the biggest tally of incidents for the *Echo*. Fortunately most were minor. The bar varied with the

The scow *Echo* shown as originally rigged. *Cliff Hawkins, courtesy of Wellington Maritime Museum & Gallery*

The *Echo* at Wellington later in her career, showing her cut-down rig and built-up steering position. *Wellington Maritime Museum & Gallery*

state of the weather but usually gave her between 1.8 and 2 metres of water. Since she usually drew 1.7 metres forward and 1.8 metres aft loaded, she had very little margin for error. In practice she often hit the bar with her stern, relying on her momentum and the following sea to carry her across it. Needless to say, this cost a fortune in bent propellers and crankshafts down through the years.

There were times when the *Echo* did not make it, sticking fast to the bar or else stranding on the nearby beach. Then there was nothing for it but to lighten ship and pray that the weather

The *Echo* ashore on the Wairau bar on one of her many strandings. The launch *Gannet* (left) was not so fortunate, becoming a total wreck. *Wellington Maritime Museum & Gallery*

A famous photograph of the *Echo* after her encounter with the rocks off Pencarrow Head in November 1932; amazingly, she returned to service. *Wellington Maritime Museum & Gallery*

held. Fortunately it usually did. During her worst stranding, she spent a whole fortnight on the bar, bringing Blenheim's direct trade to a complete halt.

On 17 October 1960, the *Evening Post* reported one of her more noteworthy clashes with the bar:

> A sojourn on the beach until about the end of this week seems to be ahead of the scow *Echo*, which grounded on the Wairau Bar while outward bound from Blenheim to Wellington on Friday.
>
> Her stern grounded on the landward side of the river channel, which runs almost parallel with the beach, with a boulder bank on the seaward side.
>
> It was unfortunate that the mishap came at a time of weakening tides and that a heavy westerly swell set in which pushed the *Echo* about 20 ft [6 metres] up the beach, for this combination of conditions put her in a position where nothing can be done to move her until the tides improve.

Today the scow was broadside on to the beach with her bow pointing south-eastwards up the river channel and her starboard side high and dry. A track was cut through the shoulder of the beach with a bulldozer to enable motor-trucks to be taken alongside to receive the cargo which was being unloaded – the bulldozer standing by to assist them up the beach when full.

Three days later she was on the move again. With her cargo gone, the lightened ship was moved 35 metres towards the river channel by two good pulls on a 'deadman' positioned across the channel. By the following day she was off and heading for Blenheim Wharf to reload the cargo before sailing for Wellington. She repeated the performance in May 1961, grounding heavily and sticking fast for a week.

Strandings were relatively mundane events, since once inside the bar she was safe from the destructive force of the waves. To put some more spice into her life, the *Echo* added collisions to her repertoire; she hit five other vessels while running in and out of Wellington. Two were Eastbourne ferries, the *Muritai* (30 April 1932) and *Cobar* (9 December 1932). Other victims were the coaster *Gael* (17 January 1935), the launch *Bon* (27 May 1946) and the tug *Toia* (2 January 1931).

Dismastings were also not uncommon. Early in the 1920s the *Echo* lost her foremast while beating up Wellington Harbour. A few years later, it was the turn of her mainmast. She was on the way to Blenheim with a full cargo at 0720 hours on 31 October 1926, on her last port tack midway between Ward Island and Somes Island and facing a hard northerly gale when both engines packed it in. This threw a sudden weight onto her canvas. The mainmast snapped almost a metre above the level of the aft deckhouse and fell over the starboard side, narrowly missing the five men working topsides at the time. Captain Radford stopped the engine and the crew, with the aid of the *Echo*'s petrol winch, fished the broken mast out of the water. The tug *Toia* towed the scow safely back to Queen's Wharf.

The *Echo*'s worst moment came on 26 November 1932 (a bad year for her) when she stranded on Pencarrow Head at the entrance to Wellington Harbour. A heavy squall, which had struck just as Captain W. Jarman was entering the harbour, had obscured all the harbour lights. Blind, she struck rocks just before midnight and, badly holed, was abandoned by her crew who made for Scorching Bay. While they did so, the *Echo* made away in the opposite direction. Next day she was found semi-submerged off Somes Island. It took the harbour board's floating crane *Hikitia* to right the wrecked hulk.

Other accidents included two fires, machinery breakdowns, numerous strandings and weather damage. Until the 1950s very few years went by without at least one incident. Requisitioned by the Americans for war service in the Pacific supplying coastwatcher stations, the old *Echo*, sporting a couple of Oerlikon light cannon, nosed around in some very dangerous waters. Japanese reconnaissance aircraft flew over her on several occasions but none attacked, despite the presence of the Stars and Stripes at her stern. While up in the

South Pacific she carried out a variety of other duties, which included rescuing the crews of downed American aircraft and carrying Allied troops to suppress a rebellion by Melanesians opposed to colonial rule.

By 1965 old age and competition from the new Cook Strait rail ferry service were catching up with the *Echo*. On 20 August she left Wellington for Blenheim on her final cargo-carrying trip. True to form, she managed to ground just inside the Wairau River mouth soon after midnight at high tide. She was met by a launch crowded with well-wishers determined to escort her up the river for the last time. Just moments after they set foot on her deck, however, the old scow touched bottom, stranding the would-be partygoers, who then decided to toast her from her position on the mudbank. Townsfolk, awaiting her arrival at the wharf, were kept up with the play by a notice chalked on a crate outside the wharf shed: '*Echo* on the mudflats, due to arrive in Blenheim approximately 4.00 pm today.'

After a brief period 'in lay-up', the *Echo* was bought by J. Gisby of Stewart Island for use as a mother ship off the Chatham Islands. After returning to Lyttelton, the *Echo* passed into the hands of R. Mason of Picton who retained her until the following July when the Echo Preservation Society bought her, minus her engines.

The society returned the old scow to Blenheim for restoration as a public relations office and maritime museum. Sadly, the society's means did not match its ambitions and the much-vaunted restoration programme failed to get much beyond the planning stage. By July 1968 when the *Marlborough Express* highlighted the *Echo*'s plight, vandals had prised off everything that moved and Eckford family member Captain T. S. Eckford was insisting that sinking at sea would have been a more dignified end for her. Stripped of her fittings and looking very sorry for herself, the *Echo* eventually filled with water during a flood and sank in the Opawa River. The volunteer fire brigade became a regular visitor with its pumps and appliances.

That should have been the end but some enthusiasts in the nearby Marlborough Cruising Club decided that the *Echo* deserved a better fate. They pumped her dry and in June 1972, with the help of several jet boats, towed her down river, over the Wairau bar for the last time and along the coast to her final resting place. Placed on the Picton foreshore and given a very basic 'restoration', the *Echo* still does duty as a clubhouse, tourist attraction and relic of earlier, more adventurous times, although her future is once again clouding.

The second 'hoodoo ship' was the *Turihaua*, pride – and, for that matter, sole example – of the Gisborne Sheepfarmers' Frozen Meat & Mercantile Company Ltd's fleet. Built at Bergen in 1948 as the *Anne* and renamed *Sunny Girl* two years later, this attractive, 509-ton steel motor vessel came onto the New Zealand register in mid-1951 when the Gisborne company went shopping in Europe for a replacement for its ageing motor vessel *Margaret W*.[4]

The unlucky *Turihaua* as she first appeared on the New Zealand coast. *Wellington Maritime Museum & Gallery*

Through the good offices of the ever-present Union Company (which found itself dragged into this deal in order to protect the interests of its Napier subsidiary, Richardson & Co.), the *Sunny Girl* was purchased for £84,000, spruced up at Henry Robb's shipyard and sent out to New Zealand. Her mixed cargo of newsprint, steel, prefabricated houses, boilers and tinned foods reflected the small scale of the contemporary New Zealand manufacturing sector. She reached Auckland on 24 February 1952.

Four days later at Gisborne, a proud Gisborne company renamed its *Sunny Girl Turihaua*, after a local placename. Comments from a seaman after her loss 11 years later suggested that there might have been something in her name. The *Taranaki Herald* said that the Maori name Turihaua's interpretation '"is crippled or battered by the wind and water" and this ship has lived up to her name'.

The *Turihaua* spent most of the rest of 1952 being refitted for New Zealand requirements. The most noticeable alterations were the addition of heavy belting along the hull and additional derricks. Gisborne Sheepfarmers had high hopes for its new flagship.

Just six days short of Christmas, however, the *Turihaua* struck trouble – literally and metaphorically. Auckland-bound, while rounding Tuahine Point in a heavy swell, the little coaster hit a submerged object and started taking in water. Things became serious when the water started to threaten the engine room. Her master turned around and just made the safety of Gisborne Harbour before all power was lost.

There the local fire brigade pumped out the water and a collision mat was fitted in preparation for more permanent repairs at Auckland. These kept the *Turihaua* out of service until June 1953. The hull was patched and the machinery and electrics in the engine room were inspected. At the same time, the foremast was relocated amidships and an extra pair of derricks were added in an only partially successful attempt to improve her turnaround time and earning potential.

On 20 November 1953 the little ship was again in trouble when she struck the bottom while swinging off Tokomaru Bay Wharf. Her master failed to report the incident, which was only discovered the following year during a routine docking. A formal court of inquiry censured the master but did little else. The *Turihaua's* October 1954 docking revealed further minor hull damage, the result of an unreported incident on 20 May that year.

This marked the end of the road for the upstart Gisborne company, which had been contesting the run with Richardsons since the days of the Depression. By August 1955 Union had transferred the mortgage for the vessel to Richardsons. On 1 September the long-established Napier company placed her on charter to Union for its Auckland–Wellington service.

Any hope that the change of colours might have improved the vessel's fortunes were dashed just 16 days later when the *Turihaua* ran aground on the western side of Great Mercury Island while on a voyage from Auckland to Gisborne. The accident, which happened just minutes before midnight, resulted in the ship being pinned to a reef, bow up. The master radioed Auckland of his plight and then made an unsuccessful attempt to get off the reef using the vessel's engines. By 0200 hours in the morning, flooding was increasing and the tide was falling, causing the *Turihaua* to bump. Things were serious.

Another attempt with the engines, however, freed the ship before damage got any worse. By 0500 hours the *Turihaua* was reversing slowly into deeper water to await the arrival of another Richardson coaster, the *Kuaka*, which would escort her to Auckland. By 4 o'clock on the 17th, the unlucky ship, escorted by the *Kuaka* and the tug HMNZS *Manawanui*, had made the safety of Auckland Harbour.

Once again the *Turihaua's* owners went through the dreary procedures of repairs and courts of inquiry. The court admonished both the master and the second officer. Repairs, completed by 4 January 1956, cost £19,500. The *Turihaua* was fast becoming an insurer's nightmare.

Possibly hoping that the old adage 'out of sight, out of mind' held true, Richardsons shuffled the *Turihaua* down to Nelson for a one-year bareboat charter to another Union Company subsidiary, the Anchor Shipping & Foundry Company Ltd.

On 8 May 1956, while sailing from Nelson to Wellington, the little ship with the big nose for trouble ploughed into Walker's Rock in Cook Strait. Walker's Rock is an evil place, where vicious tides and swift currents have pushed several vessels into trouble, and the master of the *Turihaua* must have felt relieved to have got off so lightly on this occasion. A survey of the damage at Wellington revealed some bumps and dents but no leaks or torn plates and she re-entered service early the following month.

With the exception of a minor stranding at Nelson on 25 October, the rest of the *Turihaua's* time under the Anchor flag was uneventful. She returned to the Richardson fleet in January 1957 and the following month was once again char-

tered to 'big brother' Union Company. Due to take up a fort-
nightly run between Auckland and Wellington via the East
Cape ports, from 8 February, she was leaving the capital for
Auckland on the 7th when her engines failed while off Steeple
Rock. Fortunately the pilot boat *Arahina* was close by to tow her
in to port.

That year, 1957, brought one annoying incident after
another. On 14 February the steering gear again failed.
Fourteen days later a main engine broke down off Gisborne; it
was restarted before any serious trouble developed. On 15
March one of the generators failed. On 11 May the starboard
main engine broke down at Portland, obliging the *Turihaua* to
limp to Auckland on just one engine. The Marine Department
had to give her permission to sail on this one engine for the
next three weeks, but restricted her to trading between
Auckland and Gisborne. On 14 June another failure in her
steering gear sent her crashing into Gisborne's old Kaiti Wharf,
splintering some stringers in the latter. On 7 October she had to
be assisted into the same port by the pilot boat after an engine
broke down.

By now Richardsons had decided that enough was enough.
The Napier company had felt aggrieved by Union's power
politics with the Gisborne Sheepfarmers Company which had
involved it with the *Turihaua* in the first place and felt that the
£80,000 that Union had valued her at did not represent
anything like her true worth. On 23 December 1957 the agreement was cancelled and the *Turihaua* was laid up at Auckland,
her inefficient and unreliable engines (made worse by New
Zealand engineers' inability to maintain them) effectively
ruling her out of further service within the Union Company
fold. She spent the next two years on the sale block, her price,
reputation and low speed deterring most buyers.

This early photograph
shows the *Turihaua* after
major modifications to her
cargo-handling gear.
Although they meant
greater efficiency, they
brought no better luck.
*Wellington Maritime Museum
& Gallery*

The *Turihaua* under the name *Holmbank*, just before her final accident off Banks Peninsula. *J. F. Holm Collection, Wellington Maritime Museum & Gallery*

Even tied up at a wharf, though, she twice managed to land herself in trouble. The first scrape took place on 9 May 1959 when the freighter *Indian Reefer* grazed her stern while shifting berths. A few bent stanchions and guard rails were the extent of the damage that time. More serious was some flooding which took place on 15 March 1960 when engineers, removing the old engine, accidentally flooded the hold bilges, causing a list.

The re-engining marked a final attempt by Union and Richardsons to get something back on their original investment. For a hefty £48,000 (split between the two companies), the twin A/S/ Bergens Mek Verk engines were ripped out and replaced by a more familiar Crossley V-8. Trials took place in July 1961 and after one breakdown, little more than the usual teething problems, the *Turihaua* re-entered service.

But her return to service coincided with the start of the long downturn in the conventional coastal trade and she was soon placed on another long-term bareboat charter, this time to the Union Company's Wellington affiliate, the Holm Shipping Company. The charter commenced on 12 January 1962. Several months later, Richardsons at last extracted itself from involvement with the ship when Holm acquired her for £55,000 and renamed her *Holmbank*. Under new colours and sporting a new name, the ship began running between Onehunga and South Island ports.

This, however, did nothing to improve her luck. She ran at a loss during her first year and ran aground in her second. This time it was for keeps. On the evening of 20 September 1963, while on a voyage from Timaru to Wellington with over 400 tonnes of general cargo, the *Holmbank* struck a rock close inshore of Peraki Bay, on Banks Peninsula. Earlier the master, Captain Walter Home, had set a course calculated to take her 1.75 miles clear of Akaroa light. Visibility was moderate but weather reports of low visibility in the area of the light meant that the crew remained unconcerned when the light did not appear as expected. Without the knowledge of anyone aboard, a strong current had been pushing the ship off course, towards the land. The grounding, which happened at 2022 at high tide, was immediately recognised as serious.

By the morning of the 21st the coastal tanker *Tanea* and the trans-Tasman freighter *Waimea* were standing by while a tug was summoned from Lyttelton. Fortunately the sea was calm and the wind slight; the master was able to get part of the crew of 16 off in perfect safety. By the time that the tug *Lyttelton II* reached the scene it had become obvious that nothing could be done. The *Holmbank*'s hull was two-thirds full of water and any attempt to tow her off would have resulted in her sinking immediately.

Although an engineering firm was asked to prepare materials for a salvage job, all such thoughts vanished that morning when a loud cracking sound revealed that her back had broken. Recovery was now impossible. By midnight a rising swell was completing the job. About dawn on the 22nd she finally split in two and slid off the reef, the bow sinking first, to be followed soon afterwards by the stern. The wreck remains there today, still partially intact.

The court of inquiry found that the wreck had been caused by an unanticipated set coupled with the fact that weather reports of low visibility at Akaroa seemed to explain why the crew could not see the shore when the vessel was within range.

And so ended the story of the unluckiest ship on the coast.

Notes
1. Unattributed press clipping in the Wellington Maritime Museum and Gallery collection.
2. *Ibid.*
3. Ted Ashby, *Phantom Fleet*, Auckland, 1975, pp. 54–55.
4. Most of the account of the *Turihaua*'s career is based on Union Company files now held in the Wellington Maritime Museum and Gallery collection.
5. S. V. Lampard, 'A Thousand Curses on the *Turihaua*!', *New Zealand Marine News*, Vol. 40, No. 4, pp. 24–33.

The Holm Shipping Company's attractive little coaster *Holmglen* which sank with all lives after leaving Oamaru on 24 November 1959. The radar antenna above her wheelhouse shows that she was a well-equipped vessel for her days. *Cliff Hawkins, courtesy of Wellington Maritime Museum & Gallery*

Chapter 17

COASTERS AND CATASTROPHES

By the middle of this century it was rare for a commercial trading ship to go down in the open sea. Radio, aircraft and, in the post-war era, radar kept a watch on the sealanes and took away much of the uncertainty. Yet such disasters did happen from time to time. In the course of just a decade three relatively modern motor vessels, the *Holmglen, Maranui* and *Kaitawa*, went down off the New Zealand coast, all with heavy loss of life.

The 485-ton *Holmglen* provided the biggest surprise. No ship is unsinkable, but this little one, less than five years old and fitted out for the worst that her planned role of supply ship to sub-Antarctic islands could throw at her, should not have foundered when she did. The 'strongest vessel on the New Zealand coast', as her owners, the Holm Shipping Company, fondly called her, sailed from the Port of Oamaru late in the afternoon of 24 November 1959, bound for Wellington and Wanganui. That day the seas were moderate and, although she was carrying 30 tonnes of deck cargo, the *Holmglen* was well above her marks. As the Oamaru harbourmaster, Captain J. E. Hancox, would later testify, she was in every respect in first-class condition.

Six hours later everything changed when the operator of the Taiaroa Head radio station near Dunedin picked up the message 'Heeling hard to port . . . accommodation awash . . . crew attempting to launch boat', followed by an ominous silence. The signalman, R. Malthus, repeatedly called '*Holmglen* – are you receiving me?', but got no answer and requested the Awarua marine radio station to summon assistance. By then seas were heavy, it was raining and it was becoming apparent that the trim little ship must have run into serious trouble.

Within hours a large fleet of ships was converging on the South Canterbury coastline, battling heavy seas and deteriorating weather conditions all the way. At least one would-be rescuer, the Northern Steam Ship Company's coaster *Tawanui*, found herself unable to hold her course to take part in the search. The freighters *Cape Ortegal, Korowai* and *Holmburn*, the survey launches HMNZS *Tarapunga* and HMNZS *Takapu* and more than 20 Oamaru and Timaru fishing boats joined in the search for wreckage or survivors.

Ironically, the sad duty of locating the wreck by echosounder fell to another member of the small Holm fleet, the

Holmburn. Diverted to the position where a spreading patch of oil and wreckage had been sighted, the *Holmburn* located the wreck in about 55 metres of water. Radioing the Timaru harbourmaster the melancholy news 'Coming across more wreckage all the time. Weather is freshening all the time', the *Holmburn* marked the spot with a red anchor buoy and left the area. Two Timaru fishing boats, the *Nella* and the *Craigewan*, picked up two of the three bodies that would be recovered. Shortly afterwards, worsening conditions forced the Timaru harbourmaster to order the remaining vessels back to port.

The *Holmglen* had been carrying a crew of 15, all of whom lost their lives. The dead men were Captain E. J. Regnaud (master), K. D. Billinghurst (chief officer), H. L. Barker (second officer), R. A. McFoster (chief engineer), A. J. Wolgast (second engineer), W. H. Harding (third engineer), S. McKenzie, J. Cleary, D. Whorlow, H. Wetherby and A. Pemberton (able seamen), G. J. Boyce (ordinary seaman), J. Anson (cook), A. S. McClellan (steward) and J. McEwan (wiper).

A stunned John Holm confessed to the press that 'it is a complete mystery. *Holmglen* was the strongest built and the best equipped ship in New Zealand. Of all the ships in New Zealand likely to come to this end I should have picked the *Holmglen* as the least likely.'[1] During the next few days, the rest of the Holm fleet would drop wreaths over the site of the wreck while the company waited for the verdict of the court of inquiry.

The inquiry brought its share of horror stories. A former chief officer related how, on one occasion, the *Holmglen*'s accommodation had been awash while running before a storm off Campbell Island. On another occasion, the ship had lost way and developed a port list in Cook Strait. He criticised the practice of carrying heavy deckloads aboard small coasters.

Yet, despite this, the court could not come up with any firm cause for the catastrophe. Naval divers giving evidence said that the wreck was intact apart from a crushed guard rail. The ship lay upright in the mud; the rudder lay hard to port and undamaged and there was no sign of damage to the hull. As its report, released in April 1960 stated, 'the cause (of the sinking) arose with great rapidity and the vessel foundered with great rapidity.'[2] The sinking was not the result of engine explosion, opening of plates, collision or wreck. Although the report made no firm statement, the waterfront wisdom was that the *Holmglen*, which had always been a somewhat 'cranky' ship, had lost way, been overwhelmed by a sudden gust of wind which had passed over Oamaru earlier that evening and had foundered when her cargo shifted.

The court made 17 recommendations to the Minister of Marine. Principally, it recommended that the design of ships of the *Holmglen* type and the apparent vulnerability of small, low freeboard ships should be examined. It also recommended making it compulsory for small ships to carry inflatable liferafts and for the Marine Department to exercise caution in the issuing of deck cargo licences.

The next major loss was of the Union Company collier *Kaitawa*. Once again, a well-found ship went down with all hands. In terms of lives lost – 29 – it was the worst New Zealand maritime disaster in more than half a century.

The 2485-ton *Kaitawa* was 17 years old. One of a generally similar bunch of 'AC' coasters, she had first taken to the water at Henry Robb's yard at Leith, Scotland, in 1949, at the start of the Union Company's great post-war renewal programme. Like most of the company's workhorses of the day, she would not have won any prizes for looks or sophistication. She was just a big, cheap cargo carrier, slow but sturdily built and ideal for the cargo trade between the West Coast ports and the rest of New Zealand.

She was on her old route, with another cargo of coal (2957 tonnes to be precise) for the Portland cement works, when everything started to go wrong. No sooner had Westport's moles dropped astern than Captain G. R. Sherlock had to turn around and drop anchor off the bar while the second officer, R. P. Oakton, who was ill, was landed and replaced by M. G. Collins. The *Kaitawa* resumed her broken voyage the next morning at 1313 hours. Oakton, who had collapsed while the ship was off Karamea, would soon have cause to celebrate his rushed and undignified trip to Buller Hospital.

As the *Kaitawa* motored up the western coast of the North

The *Kaitawa*, photographed on trials in Scottish waters in 1949. *Wellington Maritime Museum & Gallery*

Island the weather worsened steadily, causing Sherlock to revise his estimated time of arrival several times. His ship, not known as one of 'the slow greens' for nothing, was crawling as she battled her way northwards in the teeth of a howling gale. At 2000 on the 23rd, when the British freighter *Cape Horn* passed her about 5 miles west of the northern tip of the Pandora Bank, about 12 miles from Cape Reinga, the weather was atrocious, with a heavy sea, thick rain and a wind gusting up to 35 knots. Still, she was moving.

The British thought nothing more of her but then, 59 minutes later, Auckland radio picked up a PAN (an emergency signal denoting danger but not imminent danger) from the collier. Another minute later it heard the more serious and urgent Mayday message from the ship, indicating a rapid change in her fortunes. It read: 'Mayday from *Kaitawa* ZMVC. Position . . . (word missing) . . . 10 miles Cape Reinga. Bearing zero three five (words missing) . . . require immediate assistance.' This position (almost certainly not accurate) would have placed the ship about a mile west of Pandora Bank, a shallow patch just south-west of Cape Reinga.

And that was all. No one heard or saw anything more of the ship. At no stage did the collier show up on the *Cape Horn*'s radar. Search and rescue swung into action within a short time. The *Cape Horn*, about 15 miles to the south, swung around at 2118 and retraced her course. At 2350 she spotted a red flare somewhere between 5 and 10 miles to the west, very near the Pandora Bank. Her radar, badly cluttered by weather conditions, failed to pick up anything and lookouts fared no better.

Next morning was the first day of an extensive six-day search. The Air Force sent up Sunderlands and Dakotas, the Navy dispatched the training ship *Inverell* and the Northland Harbour Board sent its ocean-going tug *Parahaki*, but all to no avail. Indeed, the rescue ships soon found themselves struggling to make any headway at all; the *Parahaki*, normally capable of 15 knots, had her work cut out trying for just 10. In all, 14 ships, eight aircraft and several hundred shore-based searchers would take part in the hunt.

By mid-afternoon a Sunderland had located an oil slick a mile north of Pandora Bank and the first pieces of wreckage were being picked up from off the beaches. Search parties found the 11 kilometres of coastline south of Cape Maria Van Diemen littered with pieces of timber and broken fittings. A. Martin, wife of an assistant lighthouse keeper, told the *New Zealand Herald* that 'Pulped would be a better way to describe some bits . . . the wreckage ranges from little pieces the size of a pencil to bits seven or eight feet long.'[3] One party, which included Cape Reinga schoolmaster, J. P. Hyndman, also picked up 13 life-jackets; all were in good order, bearing station tickets and regulation whistles. Later two lifeboats were found in Twilight Bay. Another party, accompanied by a *Herald* reporter, found part of a lifebuoy with *Kaitawa* stencilled on it. Despite extensive searching by Sunderland flying boats, though, no trace was found of lifeboats or intact liferafts.

An underwater photograph of the wreck of the *Kaitawa* showing a close-up of the damage to the bottom of her hull. *RNZN*

In the absence of any evidence, it was assumed that the ship had foundered so quickly that most of the crew had not had time to abandon their ship. At least one person inflated the wrecked liferaft and discharged the emergency flare but he could not have survived for long. Only one body was recovered, on the 30th, that of motorman John Wright.

On 8 June the oceanographic research ship HMNZS *Tui*, using sophisticated underwater camera gear, located the *Kaitawa*. She was at a point 246° 20', less than 5 nautical miles from Cape Reinga light. She lay at a depth of about 50 metres, upside down. Her superstructure had vanished completely, either torn off while she was drifting capsized or crushed into the hull when she hit the bottom.

Later that month divers from HMNZS *Inverell*, under the command of Lieutenant Neil Merrick, after examining the *Kaitawa*'s sister ship *Kaitangata* at Auckland, dived on the wreck site. They discovered a hole, about 3 metres by 2 metres, in the *Kaitawa*'s hull in the approximate vicinity of her No. 3 hold. They also found that the hatchcovers on the Nos 1 and 2 cargo holds had gone. There was no sign of coal in the wreck or nearby, which indicated that the ship might have drifted some distance after striking trouble. Also visible were two depressions, running more than 320 metres along the bottom of the ship's hull, and slight damage to the two propellers.

This damage seemed to indicate that the cause of the disaster had been the *Kaitawa*'s striking the Pandora Bank, a relatively poorly charted shallow patch of water about 5 miles long and 3 miles wide. Although the bank was known to mariners, the *Kaitawa* had the disadvantage of navigating without radar or echo-sounder. In the view of several mariners such as Captain H. Gordon, harbourmaster at Greymouth, Sherlock probably did not know that he had entered the danger zone until it was too late.

There was about 6.5 metres of water over the bank at the time. Although the *Kaitawa* drew just 5.8 metres, the 6-metre swell would have had her striking the seabed at just over 9 metres. After hitting once or twice, it was surmised that she would almost certainly have broached to and become beam-on to the seas, lurching forward and causing her coal cargo to shift. From that point, the end must have been very quick. Any on their feet would have been thrown onto the decks. Those below in their cabins would have been trapped and unable to do anything. It would have been impossible to put on a life-jacket as the ship capsized and continued to roll like a log, breaking off her masts and superstructure before sinking in deeper water. Even if anyone had made it off the ship, they almost certainly would not have survived in the terrible seas.

The court of inquiry heard this and other theories but was forced to conclude that, in the absence of reliable evidence from any survivors, no cause could be stated with certainty. It did, however, favour the theory presented by nautical surveyor Captain E. Milroy.

Milroy speculated that as the *Kaitawa* wallowed in the trough of the sea, a wave burst in the port forecastle door leading to the crew's accommodation. As the water rushed in, the ship started listing sufficiently for Sherlock to change his PAN message (less urgent than 'Mayday') to Mayday. The more she listed, the worse the storm damage became. Wave after wave struck her, splintering the bridgework and other parts of the superstructure. At that point the crewmen, who were possibly mustering in preparation to abandon ship, were probably swept overboard.

From then the *Kaitawa* was out of control, drifting towards the Pandora Bank, her engine failing at some point along the way. Almost certainly abandoned, she would have drifted past the *Cape Horn* (the red parachute flare probably came from the liferaft) and onto the bank where, down by the port bow and low in the water, she would have struck the seabed, causing the long indentation later found by the divers. At that point she probably capsized, losing her hatchcovers, cargo and possibly some of her superstructure. Still floating upside down, she drifted again until she lost her residual buoyancy and plunged down to the seabed sometime before dawn.

The Union Company collier *Kaitawa*. Typical of the company's ships of the period, she spent much of her life carrying coal from the West Coast ports to the rest of New Zealand. *Wellington Maritime Museum & Gallery*

The inquest, presided over in November by the Auckland coroner, A. D. Copeland, found that all 29 crew died from drowning. Although there had been demands for further investigations, divers reported that conditions for diving on the wreck site were extremely difficult. A surge on the seabed and jagged pieces of metal protruding from the hull made it dangerous to enter. Merrick ruled out the use of explosives on the grounds of the risk of explosion from the build-up of gases or in attracting sharks.[4]

The men lost were Captain G. R. Sherlock, chief officer R. C. C. McEwen, second officer M. G. Collins, radio officer P. D. Mowat, chief engineer O. P. Horrobin, second engineer G. Emmerson, third engineer J. W. Fox, fourth engineer R. Williams, electrician W. Underwood, boatswain R. I. Hill, able seamen B. Oliver, A. Meekin, T. F. Walker, G. G. Casey, J. Wilson and V. Clarkson, ordinary seamen K. Sheldon and C. Pulekula, deck boy I. A. Hayward, crew orderly T. W. Byrne, motormen J. E. Wright, J. McLean, J. McLeary and C. Fletcher, chief steward J. Pickles, assistant stewards G. Jones and J. O'Connell, chief cook B. W. E. Smith and assistant cook D. Collett.

The last major loss was that of the Northern Steam Ship Company's motor vessel *Maranui* (739 tons) in 1968. The *Maranui*, the first coaster built for Northern in 25 years, was a handsome little Dutch-built coaster, dating from 1953. Built in sturdy style by Jac. Bodewes, the *Maranui* had served Northern's general cargo routes from Auckland and Tauranga to South Island east coast ports for over a decade. In 1967, however, the impact of competition from the Cook Strait rail ferries prompted the company to divert her to the South Island-

Launching the Northern Company's new coaster *Maranui* at Hoogezand, the Netherlands in March 1953. The trim little *Maranui* was one of a series of modern motor vessels built in Dutch shipyards by Northern during the decade as it restructured its shipping operations away from intra-provincial services to longer-distance trading between northern North Island ports and South Island East Coast ports such as Bluff, Dunedin, Oamaru, Timaru and Lyttelton. *Wellington Maritime Museum & Gallery*

North Island bulk grain trade, along with the *Bay Fisher* and the *Poranui*. From then on she became a familiar sight at Lyttelton, Oamaru and Timaru, loading wheat for the northern markets.

The *Maranui* cleared Lyttelton at 1830 hours on 10 June, bound for Auckland with a cargo of approximately 900 tonnes of bulk wheat. All went well until she crossed the entrance to Cook Strait the next day and strong winds and heavy seas started to shift her cargo. With a list of about 5°, she continued up the coast.

By the 13th she was in the normally placid Bay of Plenty. Just between the Mercury Islands and the Coromandel Peninsula, however, worsening seas increased her list. At 1125 it was 10°; by early afternoon the wind had reached storm proportions and by 1535 the little ship was obliged to hove to, with the list reaching a disturbing 35°. Water had been finding its way below, through vent pipes above the scuppers and through a warped and damaged door under the forecastle door on the port side. A broken hinge-pin thwarted all efforts to shut it; heavy seas poured over the forecastle head, flooding the port side of the well deck as the list increased. Her stability was soon affected as water sloshed about her double bottom, and the cargo, unrestrained by shifting boards, moved further.

At 1703 the ship started issuing Mayday calls. Two ships responded, the survey ship HMNZS *Lachlan*, sheltering off Great Mercury Island, and the Swedish freighter *Mirrabooka*. Although the naval vessel did her best, strong head winds and extremely boisterous seas (up to 12 metres high) forced her to hove to with weather damage. Later she limped north to the Devonport Dockyard for repairs. Only the *Mirrabooka*, then a few miles away, could reach the ship. At 1742 she established visual contact with the coaster.

Thirty-three minutes later Captain David Bruce ordered his crew to abandon ship. Although Bruce had swung out the ship's two lifeboats, the conditions prevailing made them useless; he opted instead for the inflatable liferaft, which went over the side with great reluctance. Once in the water, the 15 men found that their troubles were only beginning. The raft had filled with water at the moment it hit the water and waves swept in and out of the craft, which was to all intents and purposes uncontrollable. For the next two hours it drifted around out of sight of the nearby *Mirrabooka*, which did not sight the liferaft until 2019.

Captain Thorsten Wahlstedt then manoeuvred his big ship within reach. It was not easy. Four times he tried and four times he failed. The fifth attempt was successful but by then only six men – chief officer R. C. Ingham, second officer C. J. Taylor, able seamen E. Hampson and G. B. Monk, ordinary seaman F. McHardy and cook J. E. Cameron – were able to make the hazardous ascent up the ropes and nets strung along the Swede's side. One man was dashed against the *Mirrabooka*'s high side (things were not helped by her being so lightly laden) and then swept away; two or three others were seen to be carried away before the raft, still containing four men, dis-

appeared from view astern. It was next seen on 16 June at the base of a cliff on Great Mercury Island.

No more survivors were found and only one body was ever recovered, by the crew of HMNZS *Kahawai*. Those lost were the master, David Bruce, chief engineer M. C. O'Flaherty, second engineer R. G. Watson, third engineer J. Walton, boatswains S. C. Henry, R. E. Orr and L. S. St Bruno, able seamen, wiper J. H. McPherson and steward J. C. Roberts.

The court of inquiry found that the ship had sunk after her cargo shifted. As a result the *Poranui* and *Bay Fisher* were taken out of service and fitted with shifting boards.

Notes
1. *Oamaru Mail*, 25 November 1959.
2. *Ibid.*
3. *Dominion*, 26 May 1966.
4. *Ibid.*, 24 November 1966.

The *Maranui* sailing up Otago harbour while on the East Coast general cargo run. *D. Wright, Comber Collection, courtesy of Wellington Maritime Museum & Gallery*

Sleek, modern and
magnificent, the new
Wahine flies through her
paces during her trials in
Scottish waters in 1966.
*Wellington Maritime Museum
& Gallery*

Chapter 18

PASSENGERS IN PERIL – WAHINE AND MIKHAIL LERMONTOV

We have become so accustomed to the lure of airline travel that it is sometimes easy to forget that, even today, sea transport still moves hundreds of thousands of people around New Zealand each year. The Interislander service links the two islands, Auckland and Wellington's harbour ferry services, long neglected, are enjoying a revival, tourist catamarans and launches are increasing in numbers throughout the rest of the country and cruise liners are paying New Zealand more attention each year.

Sea travel seems so planned, so safe. Large steel-hulled ships, with mind-bogglingly sophisticated satellite navigation equipment and hourly weather forecasts over the facsimile should have removed all danger. Yet, as the wrecks of the inter-island ferry *Wahine* in 1968 and the Soviet liner *Mikhail Lermontov* in 1986 showed, even the largest and best-maintained ships are immune neither to the forces of nature nor to rash human actions.

'Sleek New *Wahine* is World's Biggest Roll-On, Roll-Off Ship,' proclaimed the headlines in June 1966 as the Union Company's latest and largest Lyttelton–Wellington ferry sailed up Wellington Harbour to test the new linkspan at the refitted Interisland Wharf. For more than 70 years the company's swift 'steamer expresses' had criss-crossed the boisterous seas of Cook Strait virtually without incident and so punctually that some Wellingtonians boasted they set their watches by the ships. Everyone who saw her that day predicted that the *Wahine* would have an equally long and quiet career.

She certainly looked the part. At 8944 GRT, she was one of the world's largest roll-on, roll-off passenger ferries. And she had style! The sharply raked bow, the raked masts, the fully enclosed wheelhouse and the prominent funnel managed to blend the best of the old and the new aesthetics. The *Wahine*'s powerful turbo-electric engines gave her a speedy 21 knots, with several more in reserve if needed. The very latest radar and echo-sounders made her safer than any other ship on the coast.

But the *Wahine* was a 'bad luck ship'. Her difficulties had started in the shipyard, where labour disputes had spun out her building time by almost a year. Mechanical 'teething

After striking Barrett Reef in the morning of 10 April 1968, completely powerless, the *Wahine* drifts up harbour, slowly filling with water. Here passengers and crew peer out at Steeple Rock, dimly visible in the murk. *Wellington Maritime Museum & Gallery*

problems' and a potentially fatal accident with the gangway at Lyttelton marred her first year. Then, in April 1968, came the disaster that left such an indelible mark on most New Zealanders' memories of the 1960s.

It all began in the faraway Coral Sea on 5–6 April when tropical Cyclone Giselle sprang to life. In the next few days, the storm swept down into the Tasman Sea, gathering intensity. It passed over the North Island during 9 April, its winds peaking at more than 100 knots off the Wairarapa coast. Wellington, traditionally maligned as one of New Zealand's windiest cities, reeled under the impact; rain and hurricane-force winds battered the city, ripping off roofs, sinking small craft and testing the city's emergency services.

These were the appalling conditions into which the *Wahine* sailed on the morning of 10 April. The Union Company's ferries had punched their way through some violent storms before and at first the *Wahine*'s veteran master, Captain Gordon Robertson, was not unusually concerned. The meteorologists said that the storm was abating; with her radar and powerful engines, the *Wahine* should have been able to get her 610 passengers and 123 crew safely into harbour.

But the weather experts got it wrong; the storm swung south further than predicted. The *Wahine* was nosing into harbour early in the morning when, in deteriorating visibility, her radar

failed at the critical moment, just as she entered the narrow and rocky entrance to the harbour. Several strong gusts of wind then caused her to sheer off course. Next, a massive sea struck her on the port side, sending Robertson and his chief officer flying the length of the wheelhouse. For 30 minutes they struggled to regain control and head the ship out to the safety of Cook Strait, but to no avail. At 6.40 the *Wahine*'s luck ran out when lookouts called out 'Rocks ahead!', then 'Rocks astern!'

The *Wahine* struck Outer Rock, the southernmost part of Barrett Reef, tearing open her bottom and wrecking her engines. Robertson closed all watertight doors and dropped anchors but there was now little that anyone could do to save the helpless ship as she drifted up harbour completely out of control. The only ship that could have done much for her that day was the Union Company's tug *Tapuhi* (232 tons, 1945). Underpowered and rather long in the tooth, this war-surplus relic attached a towline to the stricken ferry about 1120 but lost the tow just 20 minutes later. In danger herself, the *Tapuhi* wheezed for shelter while crewmen planned a way of towing the ferry into Worser Bay. Meanwhile, the *Wahine* drifted closer to the shore and total destruction.

By about noon the *Wahine* had drifted close to Steeple Rock, off Seatoun, where the last hours of the drama would be acted out. For passengers the first real warning of danger had come at 0610 when the ship graunched her way across the reef. Reassured that they were in no danger, they mustered on B deck 20 minutes later. For the rest of the morning they sat around in their lifejackets, anxious but still hopeful that all would be well. The ship had started listing to starboard about 1010 but an extemporised lunch off Seatoun had offered some temporary reassurance.

At 1000 hours the *Wahine* began to list badly and wallow. Ten minutes later the order to abandon ship, the first given aboard a large New Zealand passenger ship in over 30 years, sent passengers and crew scurrying. These water-damaged photographs show conditions topside as people start to abandon the vessel. *Wellington Maritime Museum & Gallery*

An hour later, though, at 1300, the *Wahine* started to list badly and wallow. The order to abandon her, the first given aboard a large New Zealand passenger ship in over 30 years, came barely 10 minutes later. Suddenly shocked and dazed, passengers found themselves climbing into lifeboats or scrambling over rope ladders down the side of the ship and into the surging waters. Leaving a ship, even one as obviously doomed as the *Wahine*, can be a terrifying experience, especially if you are elderly, as many of the ferry's passengers were. There was considerable confusion about which was the starboard side. The ship's list increased dramatically, throwing many off their feet and making it impossible to launch the port lifeboats. Some passengers jumped into the sea, others simply fell.

Those who made it into the starboard boats were the lucky ones. Even so, with the wind shrieking past and the rain pelting down, they went through hell before finally hitting the beach. Less fortunate were those who ended up in the frigid water. Some swam to Seatoun but for most of those swept towards the rocky, inhospitable coastline on the eastern side of the harbour, small craft offered the only real hope of survival. These eastern shores, beautifully bleak on even a sunny winter day, are less hospitable than those on the western side of the harbour. Virtually unpopulated, rugged and rocky, they accounted for most of the *Wahine* casualties, as exhausted swimmers were dashed against rocks.

Rescuers were at hand, although they were greatly restricted by the sea conditions. Just before 1400 the New Zealand Railways ferry *Aramoana* arrived on the scene. Although she gave a big psychological boost to those in the water, her great size kept her at a distance, launching boats and doing her best to form a breakwater. Most of the real rescue work fell to the smaller craft such as the scow *The Portland*, the RNZNVR launch *Manga* and private craft. All had to work hard because the winds and waves were still strong and the water chillingly cold. The first lifeboat was launched at 1330 amid great confusion; by mid-afternoon the first survivors were coming ashore at Seatoun and volunteers were being rounded up to bring blankets, clothing, food and tea. People from all over the city turned up to help.

By the middle of the afternoon, the Wellington Railway Station, the marshalling station for the frozen, drenched and battered survivors not injured badly enough to be hospitalised, resembled a battlefield. Early newspaper reports spoke of the possibility of 140 dead or missing; the final death toll was a still mind-numbing 51. Most of those who died were elderly, meeting their end on the rocky eastern shore where most of the bodies were recovered.

New Zealand was stunned. NZBC camera crews recorded the shipwreck in a way never before possible and tributes flooded in from all over the country. For years afterwards the television images of the graceful, doomed ship sliding over onto her side would be a stock shot for the supposedly swinging '60s.

Although the big ships could not get close enough to render much practical assistance, small craft began rescue work at once. Here we see survivors coming ashore at Seatoun in one of the ship's boats (*top*) and the surf club rescue boat (*middle*).

Less fortunate were those carried across to the rocky, isolated eastern shores of the harbour. (*lower*). The majority of lives were lost on this bleak coastline. Evening Post, *courtesy of Wellington Maritime Museum & Gallery*

The inevitable court of inquiry was a more civilised affair than that for the Erebus tragedy a decade later. It cleared the senior officers, the Union Company and the Wellington Harbour Board of all major charges of wrongdoing. It found that the main cause of the *Wahine*'s loss was that the ship, struck by one of the worst storms in New Zealand history, sheered off course in zero visibility, went out of control and struck Barrett Reef, sustaining serious underwater damage. The immediate cause of capsize was free surface water on the vehicle deck.

The court also stated that loss of life would have been much greater had the ship been abandoned off the entrance. While criticising Robertson for not warning shore authorities of the damage sustained by his ship, the court praised his seafaring skills once he found himself in trouble. It also said that it could not criticise his decision to enter harbour; the storm had changed direction and character, so much so that the assessment given the ship at 0500 was no longer valid an hour later when she was entering the harbour. It also made a number of recommendations about ship design (although it could not fault the *Wahine*'s basic design – she was a superbly built and well-equipped craft) and recommended that the harbour board provide a fleet of modern salvage tugs – the 'big reds' that now dominate port activities.

It was all over. Relatives buried their dead, the harbour board ordered its tugs, shipping companies sharpened up

As if to taunt, the weather became fine just a couple of days later. Here we see how close the *Wahine* was to Seatoun when she capsized. *Wellington Maritime Museum & Gallery* shipboard safety procedures and the Union Company ordered a replacement ship. That vessel, the *Rangatira*, was the last to make the Lyttelton–Wellington run. Spiralling fuel and crew costs and competition from air travel soon spelt the end of the service. Union sold the *Maori* without replacing her and handed over the charter of the *Rangatira* to the Government. By 1976, the magnificent ship was sailing back to Europe to face an uncertain future. Ironically, she had outlasted the *Wahine* by less than a decade.

The *Wahine* was not left to rest in peace. The Wellington Harbour Board insisted on her removal; optimistic salvors talked of refloating the ship intact by pumping her full of polyurethane foam, but later storms soon broke her up too badly for this to happen. And those storms almost broke the salvors, United Salvage Proprietary Ltd. Its chartered coaster, *Holmpark* (588 tons, 1953), assisted by the port floating crane, would be a familiar sight to Wellingtonians for many years as the company and its successors struggled to carry out the terms of an increasingly burdensome contract.

Today little remains to mark the dramatic events off Seatoun 23 years ago. There are a propeller and a plaque at Seatoun and the Wellington Maritime Museum and Gallery boasts a large scale model of the ship in her death throes, complete with lifeboats and struggling swimmers. In 1990 Lambton Harbour Management Ltd erected one of her masts, gifted to the museum by a prominent entrepreneur, in a place of honour in the newly refurbished Frank Kitts Park.

The Soviet cruise ship *Mikhail Lermontov* showing the satellite navigation equipment and the white hull that distinguished her from her sister ships. *New Zealand Herald*

Souvenirs of the most recent passenger ship loss may also be seen around Wellington, although less conspicuously displayed. They are lifeboats from the Soviet liner *Mikhail Lermontov*, which became New Zealand's biggest shipwreck in February 1986 when she foundered in Port Gore in the Marlborough Sounds after striking rocks.

The stylish, white-hulled *Mikhail Lermontov* was no stranger to New Zealand waters. The last of the five *Ivan Franko* class (the others are the *Ivan Franko, Aleksandr Pushkin, Tara Shevenko* and *Shota Rustaveli*) built at Wismar in East Germany between 1963 and 1972, the *Mikhail Lermontov* (which dated from 1972) had made many voyages to New Zealand cruising for the hard Western currency that her owners coveted. She was big. Some 19,872 GRT and 176 metres long, when built she could accommodate 750 one-class passengers and a crew of 300. Twin 21,000 shp (shaft horsepower) Sulzer diesels pushed her along at 20 knots. Just four years before her final voyage, Hapag-Lloyd's Bremerhaven shipyard had rebuilt her accommodation areas to take 550 passengers in greater comfort and had transformed her into the Soviet Union's prestige liner. In her new guise she measured 20,352 tons.

In February 1986 she was in the middle of a four and a half month cruising season for travel firm CTC Lines of Sydney. Nine 11-day cruises were planned, together with a 41-day Asian voyage. She had visited Auckland and Tauranga before arriving at Wellington on the morning of 15 February. After giving her passengers a day exploring the sights of the capital, the ship pulled away from the Overseas Passenger Terminal about midnight, bound for Picton. There she would spend the morning and part of the evening before starting the return journey to Sydney via the scenic highlight of the tour, Milford Sound.

The ship left Picton at 1510. Marlborough Harbour Board harbourmaster Captain Don Jamison (who also held a pilot's

The *Mikhail Lermontov* alongside Wellington's overseas passenger terminal on 15 February 1986, just a day before she foundered. *Evening Post*

licence for Milford Sound) was on the bridge, pointing out places of historic interest as he took the big vessel through Ship Cove on her run up Queen Charlotte Sound out to the open sea. At 1635 the master, Captain Vladislav Vorobyov, retired to his cabin, leaving instructions to be called back to the bridge when the *Mikhail Lermontov* reached Ship Cove. He was notified at 1700 but he did not reappear, effectively leaving Jamison in charge.

As the ship neared the head of the sound, she was steering a course of 040°T, which should have taken her well clear of trouble. When the passage between Cape Jackson and its offshore lighthouse opened up, Jamison ordered the helmsman to 'port 10°'. On hearing this, second mate Sergey Gusev warned chief navigator Sergey Stephanischlev that Jamison's course was taking the ship into danger. Stephanischlev queried Jamison but was told that the pilot was merely taking the ship closer to Cape Jackson in order to give passengers a better look. When the clearly worried Stephanischlev again questioned the wisdom of Jamison's move at 1734, he was informed that the pilot intended to take the ship through the passage. Stephanischlev neither sent for the master nor overruled Jamison's order.

By now it was probably too late, anyway. The *Mikhail Lermontov* swung from 040° through north to approximately 300° and headed through the narrow passage, slightly nearer to the shore than to the light tower. At 1737, while steaming at a fairly fast 15 knots, the *Mikhail Lermontov* grounded on her starboard side, just forward of amidships. She kept moving but rapidly developed a list to starboard as water rushed in. Vorobyov returned to the bridge and, instantly realising the gravity of the situation, turned his ship into Port Gore, intending to beach her before she sank in open water.

He almost made it. The ship's designers had allowed for the flooding of two watertight compartments but four were already awash and the ship's generating room was damaged. By the time Vorobyov beached in Port Gore an hour later, his ship had lost almost all power and was down by the bows. She drifted onto a sandbank and waited for help to turn up. Luck was not with her. The incoming tide started to push her off the sandbank (for some reason, Vorobyov had not dropped the anchor) and out into deeper water in the bay where she sank at 2050.

Ships converged on the scene quickly, the leader being the LPG tanker *Tarihiko* which had been sheltering off D'Urville Island. Other rescuers were the coastal cement carriers *Golden Bay* and *Milburn Carrier*, the naval patrol boats HMNZS *Taupo* and HMNZS *Wakakura* and the rail ferry *Arahura*. Also dispatched from Wellington were the tugs *Kupe* and *Toia* (both of which were turned back), and the police launch *Lady Elizabeth II*.

Heavy rain and moderate seas did not make the night-time rescue an easy one. Nevertheless, the rescue flotilla picked up all the passengers and crew, except for a Soviet engineer

believed to have drowned when the *Lermontov* sank, and transferred them to the *Arahura* and *Tarihiko*, which brought them across to Wellington the following morning. Considering the remoteness of the accident, the weather conditions and the age of many of the passengers, it could have been much worse. Only 11 passengers suffered minor injuries. By that evening most of the mainly Australian tourists were on their way out of Wellington Airport, bound for home.

Then the real trouble started. The Marine Section of the Ministry of Transport held a preliminary inquiry under Captain Steve Ponsford. It found that Jamison, who was operating the ship just outside the limits of the Marlborough Harbour Board pilotage area but who nevertheless knew the area like the back of his hand, had taken the big ship through a narrow channel

Above: This dramatic photograph and the two following it were taken by passing fisherman M. H. Harris. Here we see the *Lermontov* beginning to founder late on the night of 16 February. *M. H. Harris*

Below: The *Lermontov* seen from astern as passengers abandon her. Note that she is well down by the starboard bow. *M. H. Harris*

All that remained of a once-proud ship. Although only one person died in the sinking, the huge, completely intact wreck continues to draw divers to their deaths; by 1990 three people had died while diving on the *Lermontov*. M. H. Harris

which he knew to have insufficient draught for her.

Why he did so, we will never know. At that point Minister of Transport Richard Prebble announced that, since the cause of the accident had been established (it was really just stating the obvious), no formal inquiry would be held. Despite vociferous criticism from several quarters, not the least from angry passengers who felt that they ought to know what had happened and why, as well as from the Christchurch branch of the Company of Master Mariners who felt that unanswered questions might blacken the reputation of New Zealand pilots, Prebble refused to budge. Nothing would see the light of day. A Ministry of Transport decision to release the full transcript of the preliminary hearing was then blocked by Jamison, who took legal action to prevent its publication.

The Soviets, more open than Prebble, held their own inquiry. This put the blame on Jamison's decision to take the ship through a dangerous channel which had insufficient depth of water to take a vessel of the *Mikhail Lermontov*'s size. It censured Captain Vorobyov (who was transferred to a shore job), Stephanischlev (who, because he was on the bridge at all times, was sentenced to four years' imprisonment) and Gusev (who had his certificate suspended for two years).

Salvage was considered uneconomic and since the wreck lies in about 30 metres of water far away from normal shipping channels, it was left in peace. Between March and August 1986 teams working from the salvage catamaran *Little Mermaid* recovered the oil from her tanks (about 1300 tonnes) and secured the wreck site.

Notes
Information on the *Wahine* is based on material held by the Wellington Maritime Museum and Gallery collection. For the *Mikhail Lermontov*, I have had to rely on newspaper and magazine articles.

GLOSSARY

barque: sailing vessel of three or more masts, carrying square sail on all but the mizen mast.

barquentine: sailing vessel of three or more masts, fully square-rigged on the foremast and fore-and-aft rigged on the remainder.

brig: two-masted sailing vessel, carrying sail on both masts.

brigantine: two-masted sailing vessel, carrying sail on just the foremast.

bowsprit: the spar projecting from the bow of a sailing ship.

coamings: the built-up surrounds to a ship's hatches.

cutter: small, single-masted sailing vessel; can also refer to a large, open boat carried by a ship.

fore-and-aft rig: sails set along the central bow-to-stern line of a ship; fore-and-aft was typically carried on schooners, ketches and cutters.

forecastle: the built-up structure at the bow of a ship, traditionally the accommodation area of the crew.

intercolonial: dated term for what is now referred to as the trans-Tasman trade.

jury rig: improvised rig erected after storm or battle damage to masts and/or sails.

keelson: strengthening timber attached to the keel of a ship.

ketch: two-masted, fore-and-aft rigged sailing vessel, similar to a schooner but with a mizen mast shorter than the foremast.

lose way: to slow down.

mainmast: the tallest mast in a ship, next behind the foremast.

mizen: the last mast in a ship.

port (direction): left.

poop: a short deck nearest the stern.

prize crew: crew put aboard a captured vessel to ensure its compliance with orders.

quarterdeck: the deck raised above the maindeck and running towards the stern.

schooner: sailing vessel of two or more fore-and-aft rigged masts; topsail schooners carried some square sails on the foremast.

scow: small, flat-bottomed sailing vessel, usually of two masts and fore-and-aft rigged.

ship: sailing vessel of three or more masts, carrying square sails on all masts.

shrouds: rigging supporting the mast, part of the standing rigging.

standing rigging: the fixed ropes that support a ship's main spars, masts, bowsprit and jib-boom.

starboard (direction): right.

start (a plank or plate): spring a leak after collision or grounding.

stay: part of the standing rigging of a sailing ship.

tack: to turn a sailing ship by moving its bow towards, then past, the source of the wind.

touch: strike the seabed or other submerged object.

wear (ship): come about by turning into the wind.

FURTHER READING

This list is not exhaustive, merely providing a guide to the best titles made available in New Zealand recently. For earlier books, or ones not widely released here, refer to the reading lists in these publications or consult your nearest reference librarian.

GENERAL BOOKS ABOUT SHIPWRECKS

Fowles, John, *Shipwreck*, Jonathan Cape, London, 1984. Later reissued by Penguin, this elegantly written book features the superlative photography of the Gibsons.

Throckmorton, Peter (ed.), *History From the Sea: Shipwrecks and Archaeology*, R. D. Press, Sydney, 1987. Encyclopaedic coverage from antiquity to the *Titanic*.

BOOKS ABOUT NEW ZEALAND SHIPWRECKS

Bradstock, Mike, 'Shipwrecks: the Problem of Marine Archaeology', in Michael Trotter and Beverley McCulloch (eds), *Unearthing New Zealand*, GP Books, Wellington, 1989.

Church, Ian, *The Wreck of the Hydrabad*, Dunmore Press, Palmerston North, 1980.

Doak, Wade, *The Elingamite and its Treasure*, Hodder & Stoughton, Auckland, 1969.

Eunson, R. K., *The Wreck of the General Grant*, A.H. & A.W. Reed, Wellington, 1974.

Fairburn, Thayer, *The Wreck of HMS Orpheus*, Whakatane Historical Society, Whakatane, 1987.

Glennie, John and Phare, Jane, *The Spirit of the Rose-Noelle*, Viking, Auckland, 1990.

Ingram, C. W. N., *New Zealand Shipwrecks*, 7th edn, Beckett Books Ltd, Auckland, 1990.

King, Michael, *Death of the Rainbow Warrior*, Penguin, Auckland, 1986.

Locker-Lampson, Steve and Francis, Ian, *Eight Minutes Past Midnight: The Wreck of the S.S. Wairarapa*, Rowfant Books, Wellington, 1981.

——————, *New Zealand's Shipwreck Gallery*, Rowfant Books, Wellington, 1983.

——————, *The Wreck Book*, Millwood Press, Wellington, 1979.

McIntosh, Joan, *The Wreck of the Tararua*, A.H. & A.W. Reed, Wellington, 1970.

Robie, David, *Eyes of Fire: The Last Voyage of the Rainbow Warrior*, Lindon Publishing, Auckland, 1986.

Shears, Richard and Gridley, Isobelle, *The Rainbow Warrior Affair*, Unwin Paperbacks, Sydney, 1985.

Wilkinson, Douglas, *Shipwrecks: Selected New Zealand Maritime Accidents*, Southern Press, Wellington and Dunedin, 1974.

BOOKS ABOUT NEW ZEALAND SHIPPING

Bott, Alan, *The Sailing Ships of the New Zealand Shipping Company 1873–1900*, Batsford, London, 1973.

Brett, Sir Henry, *White Wings*, Brett Printing Co., Auckland, 1924 and 1928. Later reissued in facsimile reprint by Capper Press, Christchurch.

Grady, Don, *Sealers and Whalers in New Zealand Waters*, Reed Methuen, Auckland, 1984.

——————, *The Perano Whalers of Cook Strait*, A.H. & A.W. Reed, Wellington, 1982.

Johnson, David, *New Zealand's Maritime Heritage*, Collins/David Bateman, Auckland, 1987.

Kirk, A. A., *Anchor Ships and Anchor Men*, A.H. & A.W. Reed, Wellington, 1966.

——————, *Express Steamers of Cook Strait*, A.H. & A.W. Reed, Wellington, 1968.

——————, *Fair Winds and Rough Seas*, A.H. & A.W. Reed, Wellington, 1975.

McLean, Gavin, *Canterbury Coasters*, New Zealand Ship & Marine Society, Wellington, 1987.

——————, *Richardsons of Napier*, New Zealand Ship & Marine Society, Wellington, 1989.

——————, *The Southern Octopus*, New Zealand Ship & Marine Society, Wellington, 1990.

Morton, Harry, *The Whale's Wake*, University of Otago Press, Dunedin, 1982.

Ross, John O'C., *Pride in Their Ports*, Dunmore Press, Palmerston North, 1977.

Tod, Frank, *Whaling in Southern Waters*, the author, Dunedin, 1982.

Watt, J. P. C., *Stewart Island's Kaipipi Shipyard and the Ross Sea Whalers*, the author, Havelock North, 1989.

Whyte, Phillip, *Gisborne's Battle for a Harbour*, Gisborne Harbour Board, Gisborne, 1985.

MAGAZINES AND JOURNALS

Bearings, Auckland 1990 – the journal of the Auckland Maritime Museum.

New Zealand Marine News, Wellington, 1949 – the journal of the New Zealand Ship & Marine Society (PO Box 5104, Wellington). Published quarterly, *Marine News* contains much useful information on shipping, seaports and shipwrecks. Recent articles updating Ingram's *New Zealand Shipwrecks* have appeared in Vol. 35, No. 4 and Vol. 37, No. 4

INDEX

All that remained . . . a launch tows some of the *Mikhail Lermontov*'s boats back to port. *New Zealand Herald*

.Other Grantham House Illustrated Histories

NEW ZEALAND TRAGEDIES
Tangiwai and other Railway Accidents
Geoff Conly and Graham Stewart

Notable railway accidents since 1880. The miraculous escapes and the tragedies – of human failings and the force of the elements against man-made structures. The complete story of Tangiwai – Christmas Eve 1953 – when 151 people lost their lives through forces and circumstances beyond man's control.

PORTRAIT OF THE ROYAL NEW ZEALAND NAVY
A Fiftieth Anniversary Celebration
Grant Howard. Paintings by Colin Wynn

Fifty colour plates of the naval ships which have served New Zealand. The book traces the part played by the Navy since the arrival of Lieutenant James Cook, RN, in HMS *Endeavour* in 1769. Black and white photographs of human interest complete the story.

PORTRAIT OF AN AIR FORCE
The Royal New Zealand Air Force
Geoffrey Bentley and Maurice Conly

A celebration of RNZAF aircraft, squadrons and personnel – a timely tribute to our Air Force. 28 full-colour oil paintings, 73 charcoal drawings and over 200 photographs.

SILVER WINGS
The Story of New Zealand Women Aviators
Shirley Laine

An overdue recognition of the role of women in New Zealand aviation. Shirley Laine, a pilot herself, supports her story from the pioneer era to the present with a remarkable collection of photographs of women flyers, parachutists, skydivers, gliders and aircraft.

WHEN TRAMS WERE TRUMPS IN NEW ZEALAND
Graham Stewart

Suburban travel before the motorcar. New Zealanders rode them to school, to work, to sports and many to fame. A pictorial parade of these classic vehicles through the changing facades of streets in our cities, spanning more than 100 years.